Object-Oriented Programming in COMMON LISP

A Programmer's Guide to CLOS

> > > > > >

Sonya E. Keene
Symbolics, Inc.

Contributions by Dan Gerson

Foreword by David A. Moon

ADDISON-WESLEY PUBLISHING COMPANY

Reading, Massachusetts • Menlo Park, California • New York
Don Mills, Ontario • Wokingham, England • Amsterdam • Bonn
Sydney • Singapore • Tokyo • Madrid • San Juan

Library of Congress Cataloging-in-Publication Data

Keene, Sonya E.

  Object-Oriented Programming in COMMON LISP:
A Programmer's Guide to CLOS, Sonya E. Keene.
    p. cm.
  Bibliography:
  Includes index.
  ISBN 0-201-17589-4
  1. COMMON LISP (Computer program language)
2. Object-oriented programming (Computer science)
I. Title.
QA76.73.C28K44 1988   88-14607
005.13'3--dc19   CIP

Reprinted with corrections December, 1988

Text written and produced on Symbolics 3600-family computers by
Sonya E. Keene of Symbolics, Inc.

Reproduced by Addison-Wesley from camera-ready copy supplied and ap-
proved by Symbolics, Inc.

CDEFGHIJ-HA-89

Foreword

Object-oriented programming in LISP has a long history. Researchers have been experimenting with object-oriented extensions to LISP for at least fifteen years. The ideas of SMALLTALK have been imported into LISP several times. In addition, many people have used LISP to experiment with entirely original ideas for how to organize object-oriented programs.

By 1986, a "tower of Babel" situation had developed. Several object-oriented extensions to LISP were available, some in quite wide use. Each of these dialects was different from all the others, sometimes in important ways, sometimes just accidentally. The flowering of experimentation and novel ideas was certainly a good thing, but it led to practical problems. Academics had trouble communicating because they used divergent dialects and could not read each other's programs. Software developers interested in deploying their applications on a wide variety of platforms were inhibited, because each system had a different language for object-oriented programming. New implementors had a difficult time choosing which object-oriented language to implement. In short, the LISP community was being balkanized.

At the ACM LISP and Functional Programming conference in the summer of 1986, many LISP users and implementors insisted that it was time to standardize. The sense of the community was that experimentation ought to continue, but that people needed something practical that they could use until the experimenters came up with the ultimate object-oriented language, if such a thing could exist.

There had been earlier calls for standardization, with little result, but by 1986 the convergence of aesthetic, academic, and economic interests in favor of a standard was unstoppable. An ad hoc standardization group formed at the conference. Soon afterwards, the X3J13 committee for formal standardization of COMMON LISP was formed and the group became part of it. The initial idea was to adopt one of the existing dialects as the standard, but examination of the differences among dialects revealed some interesting facts: Many programmers were passionately committed to the particular dialect that they used and were unwilling to switch unless the standard offered comparable features. Although no existing dialect contained all the right features, several of the dialects had an underlying unity, once one saw past the superficial syntactic differences, and were aiming towards the same ideas from different directions. At this point, the group decided to develop a new dialect that would combine the best features of the most popular existing dialects, while discarding features that were ill-defined or insufficiently useful. This dialect would be called CLOS, the COMMON LISP Object System.

The two years since then have been a long, strange trip, as we designed, experimented, argued, redesigned, negotiated, documented, and evolved our understanding of what object-oriented programming ought to be. It's unlikely that anyone would have volunteered had they known how much time the project would take. Still, most people would agree that the result is a much better language than any we started with. Not every worthwhile feature of the original dialects survives in the final standard, but CLOS is powerful, consistent, precisely—albeit informally—defined, and efficiently implementable.

As a member of the CLOS group almost from the beginning, Sonya acquired a deep understanding that served her in good stead while writing this book. However, this is not really a book about CLOS. An early decision she had to make was whether to write a reference work on CLOS, or instead to teach the arcane art of object-oriented programming, using CLOS as the language with which to exercise that art. She chose the more courageous path, writing an introduction to an art rather than a catalog of language features. I think this choice resulted in a book that will be valuable to more people for a longer time. It was surely a more challenging book to write, but also a more engaging book to read.

The nature of object-oriented programming is such that it is most beneficial for large programs that are written by multiple authors and are expected to last a long time. The ease of implementing a small, simple program does not much depend on what programming methodology is employed, and one who has dealt only with small programs may not see any point to the object-oriented discipline. However, anyone who has been through the design, development, documentation, testing, and maintenance of a large software system in a non-object-oriented fashion, and then has experienced the same process in an object-oriented system, will understand why there is so much interest in object-oriented programming. It isn't magic, but it is a good technique for organizing large software systems and making them comprehensible.

As an introduction to the art of object-oriented programming, this book does not pretend to cover every nook and cranny of that art, nor describe every feature of the CLOS language. However, a programmer who grasps everything in this book has gained a journeyman's understanding of the art of object-oriented programming. The next step is to apply this knowledge to the construction of "real world" object-oriented programs, starting with small programs the size of the examples in this book and building up to programs of substantial size. Through experience, one eventually masters the art and then can easily learn the more esoteric features of CLOS or another object-oriented language.

If you are interested in learning the art of object-oriented programming, this book should help you become a better software engineer, no matter whether you are in the programming, documentation, testing, or management branches of the profession. If you already practice object-oriented programming in another language, this book will help you learn both a philosophy of how programs should be organized and the particular language features of CLOS.

Cambridge, Massachusetts   David A. Moon

Preface

The COMMON LISP Object System (CLOS) comprises a set of tools for developing object-oriented programs in COMMON LISP. An object-oriented program is usually designed and constructed in a modular fashion. The object-oriented style of programming makes it practical to organize large programs; it helps you decompose complex problems into functional modules.

CLOS has been adopted as part of COMMON LISP by the X3J13 committee, which is working on creating the ANSI Standard COMMON LISP. This book corresponds to the June 1988 version of the "Common Lisp Object System Specification," and does not reflect any revisions of the specification made after that date.

Roadmap of this Programmer's Guide

This book is intended for CLOS users. Because CLOS is a set of tools for software development that stands on the foundation of COMMON LISP, its users are software developers who are familiar with COMMON LISP. People who have written medium-sized LISP programs should be able to understand all the code in the examples in this book.

On the other hand, this book teaches object-oriented techniques for software design and development; these techniques may be of interest to people outside the COMMON LISP community who want to apply these ideas to other programming languages. People who are unfamiliar with LISP should be able to understand the major ideas in this book, but should not expect to understand all the LISP code in the examples.

The purpose of this book is to help you take the best advantage of the power CLOS offers. Use it as a practical guide to get started writing object-oriented programs as quickly as possible.

This book *is*:   A tutorial
                       A user's manual
                       A programmer's guide

This book *is not*:   A language specification
                       An implementor's guide
                       A theoretical discourse

The style of this book is like a spiral. It starts by describing the central concepts of CLOS and the basic techniques that are essential to writing CLOS programs. Once you understand how the elements of CLOS work together, you will be able to write object-oriented programs using only a handful of macros and functions.

The spiral then unwinds by adding techniques and features to the central model. You will find some of these immediately valuable for a particular application; you will probably mark others as "something to remember for the future." It is a rare application that requires all the features CLOS offers.

This book is driven entirely by programming examples that demonstrate the power of CLOS. We introduce the central concepts of CLOS by proceeding step by step through the development of a straightforward object-oriented program that implements locks for concurrency control. We demonstrate additional techniques by showing other sample programs, including a remote evaluation program and a software-installation program. Finally, we present an extended example that suggests how COMMON LISP streams could be implemented using CLOS. These examples illustrate modularity and good design principles, as well as most of the CLOS features.

A few of the examples can be typed into a CLOS implementation and executed. You cannot execute the longer examples (locking, remote evaluation, and streams), however, without undertaking some extra work. The locking example assumes an environment in which there are multiple processes that can contend for a resource at any given time. Remote evaluation depends on a model in which two computers are connected by a network. Streams need to access devices such as disks with device-specific primitives. COMMON LISP does not include processes, net-

works, or device-specific primitives in its definition, although any COM-
MON LISP implementation is free to implement such primitives. Originally, our goal was to define examples that used only portable COMMON
LISP functions, but this goal conflicted with a more important one: to
demonstrate how to solve large, real-world problems with object-
oriented programming. Thus, we chose more sophisticated examples
rather than smaller examples that would work in any COMMON LISP implementation. When we use functions that are not part of COMMON LISP,
we document exactly what the functions do. You can define these functions yourself if you wish to execute the examples, which is what we did
when testing them.

Along the way, the book presents information in summaries; since
the summaries repeat information given elsewhere in the book, you can
skip or skim them during the first reading, and use them for reference
later on.

About this Book

I wrote this book using CONCORDIA, the Symbolics workbench for writers. CONCORDIA assumed the burden of many of the mechanical tasks associated with writing and revising, and enabled me to concentrate on
the content and organization of the book.

CONCORDIA itself is an object-oriented program. (Currently, it is written in New Flavors, but it could be converted to CLOS.) The writer
composes a document as a collection of "records," objects that can include a title, simple textual contents, "generic markup instructions,"
graphic pictures, indexing commands, cross-references to other records,
and other attributes. A document as a whole is defined by a single top-
level record that includes links to all the records to be treated as chapters. Each chapter record includes links to the records to be treated as
its sections, and so on. The writer can reorganize any portion of the
book by simply adding, deleting, or changing the order of the links to
other records. When different documents cover the same material, there
is no need to copy the text: the writer can include links from multiple
documents to the single record that contains the material. This flexible
sharing of records minimizes the need to maintain duplicate versions of
text.

Records are stored in a documentation database, which can be accessed in hypertext fashion with another tool called DOCUMENT EXAMIN-
ER. Readers can explore any topic of interest with this tool, by providing
words that serve as keywords for DOCUMENT EXAMINER's search of the
documentation database. Although each record can be accessed individ-

ually, the organization of the document is not lost for the online readers; they can view the relationships among the records to see how the document as a whole is arranged.

CONCORDIA supports the book-design phase with the PAGE PREVIEWER tool, which shows pages on the screen formatted as they would appear on paper, thus making it easy to experiment with different designs. The book designer controls the appearance of the book by giving instructions on how the generic markup in the online manuscript should be treated. A generic markup instruction includes directives as simple as "these lines should appear in an itemized list" or "this is a figure." The book designer specifies how itemized lists appear on paper, as well as designating variables such as the fonts and margins for the text, the style of figures and tables, the appearance of chapter headings, and the format of the index. The final step is to transfer the online manuscript to paper, resulting in camera-ready copy.

Thus, CONCORDIA offers three interfaces for dealing with records: one for the writer, another for the readers, and yet another for the book designer and producer. The object-oriented design of the program makes it convenient to use one set of objects (the documentation records) in different ways for different purposes. The objects are shared freely among the three tools.

CONCORDIA is one real-world example of a program that takes good advantage of the object-oriented style and offers an invaluable service to its users. I am grateful to Rick Bryan, Dennis Doughty, and Janet Walker for inventing this remarkable program, and to Kelly Bradford, V. Ellen Golden, Bob Mathews, Mark Widzinski, and Bill York for their contributions in developing and enhancing CONCORDIA. The Symbolics Graphics Editor is a related tool (also object-oriented, of course), and I am grateful to Mike McMahon for making it possible to draw pictures so easily and to integrate them into this book.

Acknowledgments

First, I want to thank the other members of the CLOS working group, who gave time, thought, and energy in creating this language standard and integrating the power of object-oriented programming into COMMON LISP. These people are: Daniel G. Bobrow, Linda G. DeMichiel, Patrick Dussud, Richard P. Gabriel, James Kempf, Gregor Kiczales, and David A. Moon. Many other people contributed ideas and assistance to the working group, including Kenneth Kahn, Larry Masinter, Mark Stefik, Daniel L. Weinreb, and Jon L. White. I would also like to thank Robert Mathis and Guy L. Steele Jr., the conveners of the X3J13 committee, for creating an environment in which technical work is supported and encouraged.

This book depends on information covered in the "Common Lisp Object System Specification," which is the complete definition of the behavior of CLOS, and should be considered the primary source of information on CLOS. The authors of the "Common Lisp Object System Specification" (Daniel G. Bobrow, Linda G. DeMichiel, Richard P. Gabriel, Sonya E. Keene, Gregor Kiczales, and David A. Moon) have kindly given me their permission to adapt that information in this book. I am responsible for the form, style, and content of this book, and for any errors in it.

My first step in writing this book was to find or develop good example programs. Most object-oriented programs are sizable—a window system is one example. For this book, however, I wanted straightforward examples that would illustrate CLOS without distracting readers by the implementation details of a window system or some other complicated application. Dan Gerson showed me a locking program that was part of a larger application; it was simple, yet took good advantage of multiple inheritance. We adapted it for this book. Dan became interested in the book and developed the remote-evaluation and stream examples. I am very grateful to Dan for these examples and for his insights into object-oriented programming.

Jonathan Ostrowsky and Tom Parmenter supported this book when it was nothing more than an idea. When I broached the idea to Tom, I convinced him that I could write this book, and several weeks later he convinced me that I could write it. Jonathan and Tom paved the way for me to write this book by giving me the time and resources to do it. Kate Johnson shaped my book by editing early drafts, showing me the places where it didn't make sense, and even finding bugs in the example programs. Bob Mathews was my first technical reviewer, and he stayed with me until the book was finished. His kind and careful reviews made this a better book. These people generously gave their support not only to the book itself, but also to its author.

I received valuable technical reviews from Daniel Bobrow, Patrick Dussud, Richard Gabriel, James Kempf, Gregor Kizcales, and Guy L. Steele Jr. Several people at Symbolics gave me advice on object-oriented programming, answered LISP questions, and reviewed my book for technical correctness. These people include John Dunning, Neal Feinberg, Neil Mayle, Kent Pitman, David Plummer, Steve Robbins, Steve Rowley, Janet Walker, and Daniel Weinreb. Tom Diaz, Brad Goldstein, Ilene Lang, Christine Skatell, and David Stryker encouraged me in this project and in other endeavors.

The book design was done by Symbolics Press using the CONCORDIA document-preparation system. Sheryl Avruch, V. Ellen Golden, and Thom Whitaker designed the book. Rick Bryan and Dennis Doughty spent many late nights implementing special design features for the book, and Rick customized the fonts.

Sheryl Avruch of Symbolics Press gave me the benefit of her experience in publishing; she advised me on the process and coordinated the copublishing arrangement with Addison-Wesley. At Addison-Wesley, I enjoyed working with my editor, Peter Gordon, who recently celebrated ten years with Addison-Wesley, and with his able assistant, Helen Goldstein, and with Bette Aaronson, who transformed the camera-ready copy into a real book.

David Moon believed in this book from the beginning. He answered innumerable questions, reviewed drafts several times over, and helped me understand the value of these programming techniques. I particularly appreciate his style of giving help—he pointed me in the right direction and encouraged me to get there myself. David evokes the best in people, and working with him is a great pleasure.

As I wrote this book, I found many doors open to me. Friends, colleagues, and strangers (many of whom turned into friends) offered me not only the concrete kind of help that goes directly into the book, but also advice, encouragement, and spirited conversations about bookwriting and object-oriented programming. I had imagined that I could express in these acknowledgments my delight in receiving this bounty of support, but that was a naive hope; I find it impossible to express. All the people already mentioned—along with Suzanne, Wayne, Nancy, and Evelyn Keene, Althea and Richard Lewis, and Valerie and Mun Moy—have contributed to my joy in writing this book.

My husband shared my enthusiasm over this book for the entire year of writing. I dedicate this book to him, John Moy.

Contents

List of Figures

1

Introduction to the CLOS Model

Many computer programs create "objects" and manipulate them. Sometimes these objects represent real-world things. A traffic-simulation program needs to represent vehicles, pedestrians, intersections, and traffic lights. In other cases, programs manipulate objects that represent abstractions, such as the buffers, windows, and processes that are manipulated in operating-systems engineering.

The COMMON LISP Object System (CLOS) supports the style of programming called object-oriented programming, which makes it easy to create and manipulate objects. CLOS encourages the software developer to create a working model that describes the various classes of objects in terms of their structure and behavior. Often, the working model includes classes that are related to one another; they are similar but not identical. For example, window systems usually need to support different kinds of windows for different purposes. One kind of window might have a border; another might have a label; another might have both a border and a label. The design of a window system would likely include several classes of windows.

CLOS makes it easy to represent relationships among classes, and it supports a flexible means of inheriting (sharing) structure and behavior. Inheritance allows the design and implementation of an application program to be highly modular, and obviates the need for maintaining several bodies of nearly identical code.

1

CLOS promotes modularity in another important context, by separating the implementation of a program from the interface. The clients of a CLOS program (which are other LISP programs) depend on only the interface, which is a high-level description of operations that can be performed on a set of objects. Clients use these operations to create and manipulate objects; they do not depend on knowledge of the underlying implementation. This separation frees the programmer to change or extend the implementation without interfering with clients of the program.

CLOS makes it easier to design, develop, maintain, and extend a complex program. The benefits of the object-oriented style are most striking for large, complex programs, but medium-sized programs can also realize benefits from this style.

Any CLOS program could be written using the traditional style of LISP programming. An important advantage of using CLOS lies in the automatic control of the interaction among the objects. Here, we summarize some of the benefits of using CLOS:

- *The program more closely resembles the world it is modeling.* An object-oriented program is designed at a higher level of abstraction than a traditional LISP program. The programmer is encouraged to focus on the abstract properties of objects, rather than being distracted by the way the objects are implemented. An object-oriented design allows for objects with meaningful names, behavior, and interaction.

- *Client programs benefit from a well-defined interface.* Client programs can use a CLOS program through a well-defined interface; clients are shielded from the internal details (implementation) of the CLOS program. This means that clients continue to work even if modifications are made to the underlying implementation. Even more important, if the implementation is extended (to support additional classes, for example), all clients immediately and automatically take advantage of the extensions.

- *The programmer benefits from a modular implementation.* CLOS enables the programmer to define an organization of classes that models the relationships among the various kinds of objects. The programmer can define classes that serve as building blocks; each individual aspect of structure and behavior is abstracted and defined separately. The programmer then creates new classes that inherit the desired combination of building blocks.

- *A CLOS program is conveniently extensible.* Until now we have pictured the CLOS program as being a complete program, in and of itself. Some CLOS programs, however, **are** written with the goal of being extended and customized by the users. Such a program offers a set of classes with documented structure and behavior; these classes are intended to be used as building blocks. Users can create new classes that inherit from those building blocks and add customized behavior.

. *CLOS defines conventions that are shared across the COMMON LISP community.* The benefits already mentioned are offered by other languages that support the object-oriented paradigm. CLOS, however, has the additional advantage of being a language standard. CLOS defines a standard set of conventions that will be supported by a wide variety of COMMON LISP implementations. Thus, CLOS programs will be portable across different implementations.

CLOS itself does not enforce modularity or make it impossible to organize programs poorly. Instead, it provides tools that can help you design modular and extensible programs. The goal of this book is to help you learn how to exploit these tools to good advantage.

2

Elements of CLOS Programs

The elements of CLOS programs are classes, instances, generic functions, and methods. None of these elements can be considered in isolation, because each one's purpose is to interact with the others in useful and predictable ways. We begin by presenting the most important aspects of these elements and examining the relationships among them. We then describe how CLOS is integrated with COMMON LISP, focusing on the common ground between classes and types.

2.1 CLASSES AND INSTANCES

The first step in writing a CLOS program is to define a new type of data structure called a *class*. A class is a COMMON LISP type. Each individual object of that type is an *instance* of the class. Each instance of a given class has the same structure, behavior, and type as do the other instances of the class.

We might define a class named month, which would have instances representing January, February, March, and so on. Or we could define a class named window to represent windows that appear on the screen of a display terminal. When we need to create a new window, we make another instance of that class. Figure 2.1 shows a class with three instances.

5

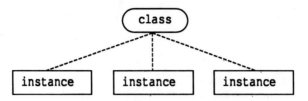

Figure 2.1 Instances of a class.

We can query an instance for its type with the usual COMMON LISP type functions. Although all instances are recognizably of the same type, each one has a separate identity. This is compatible with the COMMON LISP model, in which two objects can have the same type and the same structure (such as two arrays with the same contents), yet be two different objects, each with its own identity.

2.2 SLOTS

We have said that all instances of a class have the same structure. That structure is in the form of *slots*. A slot has a name and a value. A slot's name describes the characteristic it is modeling, and the value describes the slot's state at a given time. This state information can be read and written by *accessors*.

CLOS offers two kinds of slots: *local slots* and *shared slots*. For local slots, each instance holds its own value for the slot. For shared slots, the instances share a single value for the slot. Since local slots are used more frequently, we concentrate on them here; we discuss shared slots in "Local and Shared Slots," page 66.

The class named window might have local slots named x-position, y-position, width, and height. This state information describes, for any given window, that window's size and its position. Figure 2.2 shows the names and values of the slots of two instances of the window class.

instance of window		instance of window	
x-position	15	x-position	99
y-position	0	y-position	123
width	1300	width	50
height	1300	height	25

Figure 2.2 State information stored in local slots.

Notice that two instances of the same class have the same set of named slots. In other words, they have the same structure. Each instance, however, maintains its own values for its local slots; that is, each instance has its own state.

2.3 SUPERCLASSES

CLOS enables you to build a class from other classes; the component classes are called the new class's *superclasses*. The new class inherits both structure (slots) and behavior from its superclasses.

This style of programming is well suited to the task of modeling several kinds of objects that are related to one another. For example, we might want to have different kinds of windows. In addition to plain windows, we might need windows with labels and windows with borders.[1] The new kinds of windows are similar to the existing `window` class, but they have extra features. Figure 2.3 shows two new classes, `window-with-label` and `window-with-border`, which are built on the existing class, `window`.

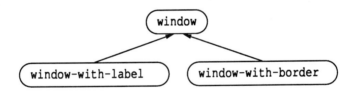

Figure 2.3 Two new classes built on the `window` class.

To build a class from components, you include a list of classes in the definition of the class. These are called the *direct superclasses* of the new class. In Fig. 2.3, each arrow points from a class to a direct superclass of the class. In fact, a class is built not only from its direct superclasses, but from each of their direct superclasses, and so on. The *superclasses* of a class are all its component classes. The term *subclass* is the inverse of *superclass*. Here we apply this terminology to the window classes:

---

[1]The example of windows, windows with labels, and windows with borders, is adapted from the paper "Flavors: A non-hierarchical approach to object-oriented programming," Symbolics, Inc., 1982, with permission from the author, Howard I. Cannon.

window is a *direct superclass* of window-with-border.
window is a *direct superclass* of window-with-label.

window-with-border is a *direct subclass* of window.
window-with-label is a *direct subclass* of window.

Figure 2.4 shows an instance of window-with-label and an instance of window-with-border. The class window-with-label inherits the four slots of its superclass window and also has a slot named label. Similarly, the class window-with-border inherits the slots of window and also has a slot named border-width. Thus, the basic structure of a window is defined only once (by the class window) and is inherited by many kinds of windows.

instance of window-with-label		instance of window-with-border	
x-position	15	x-position	90
y-position	0	y-position	0
width	250	width	400
height	250	height	100
label	ToolKit	border-width	5

Figure 2.4 Slots inherited from superclasses.

The order in which slots are stored in memory is implementation dependent, and is not normally visible to the programmer.

2.4 GENERIC FUNCTIONS

Programs and users operate on instances by using *generic functions*. To the caller, a generic function appears exactly like an ordinary LISP function; the function-calling syntax is identical. When you call a function, you do not need to know whether the function is defined as an ordinary function or as a generic function.

Conceptually, a generic function performs a high-level operation, such as "refresh a window." For different kinds of windows, this operation might require different work; whereas a plain window is simply cleared, a window with a border must be cleared and then have its border redrawn. The high-level goal "refresh a window" must be implemented differently for different kinds of windows. In other words, each kind of window needs an implementation that is appropriate to it.

When we compare the workings of ordinary functions and generic functions, we find semantic differences. An ordinary LISP function definition specifies both the interface and the implementation of the operation it performs. As shown in Fig. 2.5, when an ordinary LISP function is called, the LISP system locates and executes the single body of code that implements that function.

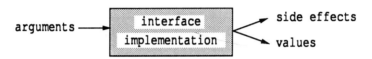

Figure 2.5 Ordinary LISP function.

A generic function specifies only the interface. The implementation of a generic function does not exist in one place; it is distributed across a set of *methods*. Whereas the implementation of an ordinary function does not vary from call to call, the implementation of a generic function does vary, depending on the classes of its arguments.

Consider the task of refreshing the three kinds of windows. We can define a generic function called refresh, which can be used to refresh any kind of window. The interface is the same, regardless of the class of window. However, each of the three classes of window requires a slightly different implementation of refresh. Instances of window are simply cleared; the region of the screen covered by the window is made empty. For an instance of window-with-border, the window is cleared and the border is redrawn. Similarly, for an instance of window-with-label, the window is cleared and the label is redrawn. Figure 2.6 shows that a generic function can have several separate implementations.

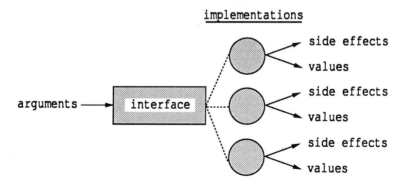

Figure 2.6 Generic function.

When `refresh` is called, CLOS determines the class of the argument and chooses the appropriate implementation for that class. Each implementation might consist of one method or several methods. The procedure for determining which methods to call and then calling them is called *generic dispatch*. It happens automatically whenever a generic function is called.

In the `refresh` example, the generic dispatch uses only one argument (the window) to choose the implementation. In "Multi-Methods," page 75, we shall show that the CLOS generic dispatch can use more than one argument to choose the implementation.

2.5 METHODS

Methods are the underlying implementation of generic functions. Like ordinary LISP functions, methods take arguments, perform computation, perhaps create side effects such as producing output, and return values. Unlike ordinary LISP functions, methods are not called directly; they are called only by the generic dispatch procedure.

A programmer attaches a method to the generic function the method implements, and to one or more classes by stating in the method's lambda-list the classes of arguments the method handles. The method is called only if the arguments to the generic function are of the appropriate classes.

For example, Fig. 2.7 shows that the `refresh` generic function might have three methods attached to it, one for the class `window`, one for `window-with-label`, and one for `window-with-border`.

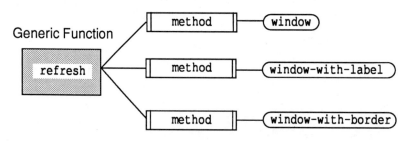

Figure 2.7 Methods for `refresh`.

We have said that all instances of a class have the same behavior. Methods implement the behavior of instances. A class inherits methods from its superclasses. For example, the classes `window-with-border` and `window-with-label` inherit methods from the class `window`.

There is not necessarily a one-to-one correspondence between an implementation for a set of arguments and a single method. When a generic function is called, the arguments may select an implementation consisting of more than one method.

2.6 METHOD ROLES

CLOS makes it possible to split up the work of a generic function (for some given arguments) into several methods. This capability stems from the facts that methods are inherited, and that methods can have different *roles*. The role of a method states what part it plays in the implementation of the generic function.

A *primary method* performs the bulk of the work of a generic function. Sometimes, one primary method does all the work of the generic function for a particular set of arguments. In other cases, the primary method can be assisted by auxiliary methods, such as *before-methods* and *after-methods*. Before-methods are called before the primary method; they can do set-up work in advance of the other methods. After-methods are called after the primary method; they can do clean-up work or any other computation. (CLOS also supports *around-methods*, which we discuss in "Around-Methods," page 102.)

The primary method returns the values of the generic function. Before-methods and after-methods are intended for side effects only; they are not called for value.

Given that classes inherit methods, this scheme allows for a division of labor among a class and its superclasses. For example, one class might provide the primary method that performs the bulk of the work, while other classes provide auxiliary methods that do additional work.

The implementation of refresh can take good advantage of this model. All three kinds of windows must be cleared. Thus, we can define a primary method for window that performs the clearing. For instances of window, this method is sufficient.

That primary method for refresh is inherited by the classes window-with-border and window-with-label. This is desirable, because windows of both classes need to be cleared before anything else is done. An instance of window-with-border must then have its border redrawn; this can be done with an after-method attached to the class window-with-border. Thus, the window-with-border class provides an auxiliary method to perform its specialized behavior, but it inherits the primary method from its superclass. Similarly, we need to define an after-method attached to the class window-with-label to redraw the label.

Figure 2.8 shows that each method contains LISP code to perform some task, and that each method has a role. The implementation of refresh is distributed among three different methods. The primary method attached to the window class does the shared part of the work, and that method is inherited by the two classes built on window. When an instance of window is refreshed, CLOS calls only one method—the primary method attached to the window class.

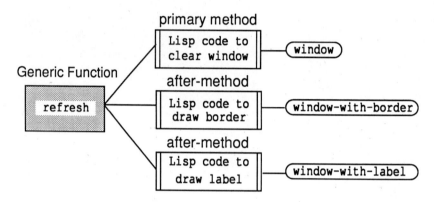

Figure 2.8 Roles of the refresh methods.

Figure 2.9 shows an inside view of the implementation chosen when the argument to refresh is an instance of window-with-label.

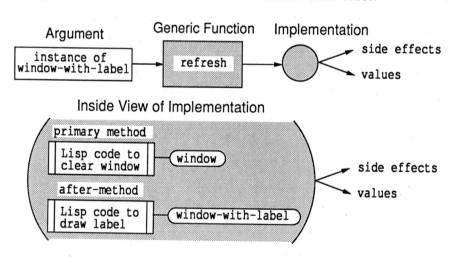

Figure 2.9 Sample generic dispatch of refresh.

In Fig. 2.9, CLOS chooses an implementation consisting of two methods: the primary method attached to the `window` class, and the after-method attached to the `window-with-label` class.

2.7 THE CONTROLLER OF INHERITANCE

Inheritance is the sharing of characteristics and behavior among a set of classes. Slots are one example of inherited characteristics. Class definitions can specify other characteristics, such as default values for slots; these are inherited as well. Behavior is represented by methods, which are inherited. A class inherits from all its superclasses.

When you put together a program from a set of classes, it is essential that the inheritance occur in an orderly and predictable way. For example, consider what happens if two superclasses offer competing characteristics, such as methods for the same generic function. How is such a conflict handled?

This concept has an analogy in human genetics: A baby might have a gene for brown eyes and a gene for blue eyes. The baby's eye color is determined by the dominance of the brown-eye gene over the blue-eye gene. When two classes offer competing traits, CLOS resolves the conflict by checking which class has *precedence* over the other class.

When you design an organization of classes, you are specifying the precedence relationships among the classes. CLOS computes a *class precedence list* based on your organization. The class precedence list governs how methods, slots, and other characteristics are inherited.

Each class has a class precedence list, which includes the class itself and all its superclasses. The classes in a class precedence list are ordered from *most specific* to *least specific*. When one class is more specific than another in this list, it has precedence (or dominance) over the other class. Thus, if the two classes offer competing traits, the more specific class takes precedence over the less specific class. The class precedence list is discussed in detail later on, in "The Class Precedence List," page 118.

2.8 SUMMARY OF THE CLOS MODEL

Real-world objects are modeled by LISP objects, which are called *instances*. You manipulate these objects using *generic functions*. When generic functions are called, the generic dispatch automatically arranges for the appropriate implementation to be invoked, based on the classes of the arguments.

The structure of an instance is dictated by its *class*. Each instance maintains a set of named *slots*, in which it stores state information. All instances of a given class have the same structure and the same behavior. The implementation of a generic function on an instance consists of one or more *methods*, which are selected according to the class.

You can build classes on other classes in order to inherit structure and behavior; this is the key aspect of modular design. A class inherits both slots and methods from its superclasses.

2.9 HOW CLOS EXTENDS COMMON LISP

CLOS is a compatible extension to COMMON LISP. This section draws parallels between COMMON LISP types and CLOS classes, compares defstruct structures and classes, and focuses on the new power that CLOS offers.

We begin by discussing the similarities between types and classes. In COMMON LISP, every LISP object has a type. In CLOS, every LISP object has a class as well as a type. CLOS is based on the existing COMMON LISP type system; it does not invent a whole new type system.

A class is a COMMON LISP type, which means you can use a class as the second argument to typep. Recall that typep tests whether an object is of a given type, where "of a given type" includes the type itself or less specific types. Since CLOS class names are type specifiers, the form (typep *instance class-name*) returns t if *class-name* names the class or a superclass of *instance*.

COMMON LISP enables you to select an operation based on the type of an object by using typecase. CLOS provides automatic support for selecting an operation based on the class of an object. You write methods that are attached to classes; when the generic function is called, CLOS automatically chooses the appropriate methods, based on the classes of the arguments.

The COMMON LISP defstruct facility enables you to define a new data type with internal structure that is customized for your program. This new data type can inherit from a type previously defined using defstruct. Similarly, the CLOS defclass facility enables you to define a new class with internal structure that is customized for your program. The new class can inherit from existing classes.

The similarities between types and classes raise one important question. Why are classes needed at all? The following comparison, although not exhaustive, points out the most important advantages of CLOS classes.

- *CLOS supports automatic association between code and a type of object.* The COMMON LISP `typecase` mechanism offers a way to associate a body of code with a type of object. However, this association is localized; it is necessary to use `typecase` explicitly in every place where the operation depends on the type of object. To upgrade a program to support additional types of objects, you would need to edit each `typecase` form to create the link between the new types and the operations appropriate to those types.

  CLOS helps you abstract the operations appropriate to different types. Callers can use operations on objects without being aware of how those operations are implemented for different types of objects.

  CLOS enables you to define methods, which are intrinsically linked to a class of object. The process of choosing the operation appropriate to the type of object (the generic dispatch) is entirely automatic. CLOS provides a convenient way to link code permanently to the type of an object, and removes the burden of maintaining links within `typecase` forms.

- *CLOS provides multiple inheritance.* With `defstruct`, you can build a new type from one component type by using the `:include` option. In contrast, `defclass` allows you to build a new class from any number of component classes. The CLOS multiple inheritance offers a great deal more flexibility and power than does the single inheritance of `defstruct`.

- *CLOS offers flexible inheritance of behavior.* CLOS supports the inheritance of structure in much the same way that COMMON LISP `defstruct` does. Although both `defstruct` structures and classes inherit slots from their components, the CLOS mechanisms for inheriting behavior are much more powerful than the limited mechanisms of COMMON LISP `defstruct`.

  A COMMON LISP `defstruct` structure can use any accessors for reading or writing slots provided by its component; this is the extent of inheritance of behavior. In contrast, CLOS supports a much more transparent and flexible means of inheriting behavior: Classes inherit methods from their superclasses. A class can override inherited behavior by providing a primary method that shadows the inherited method. A class can modify inherited behavior by adding a before-method or after-method to customize the work done by the inherited primary method. In addition, CLOS offers several advanced techniques that give you further control over the inheritance of behavior.

3

Developing a Simple CLOS Program: Locks

This chapter demonstrates the power of programming with CLOS by following the development of a sample application program. We begin by defining classes and setting up the organization that reflects how the classes are related to one another. Then we define the interface that specifies how clients can create and manipulate objects of these classes. Finally, we define the implementation; this is the LISP code underlying the interface. The interface is a set of generic functions, and the implementation consists of methods for those generic functions. The interface states what operations you can perform on these objects, and the implementation states how the operations work internally.

In this chapter, we take different points of view on the program: we design and develop it as a programmer does; we use it as a client does; and finally we analyze how its pieces interact, as CLOS itself does.

3.1 OVERVIEW OF LOCKING

The goal of this sample application is to implement locks—objects that are used to control concurrent access to some shared resource. For example, in a meeting it is desirable for only one person to be speaking at any given time. The expression "Mr. Smith has the floor" makes it clear that the "floor" (a shared resource) is protected against simultaneous use by other people. Throughout this example, we use the term "seize" to describe the act of securing or obtaining a lock, and "release" to mean giving up a lock.

Locks are meaningful only in an environment where more than one process can contend for a resource at a given time. Here, processes are defined as multiple independent threads of control within a single LISP environment. Locks are used to ensure that a shared resource is accessed in a consistent fashion. Before accessing the resource, a process should seize the lock associated with it. When finished, the process should release the lock.

We recognize that processes are not part of COMMON LISP, and that this sample program would not be meaningful in a COMMON LISP implementation that does not have multiple processes. However, our goal is not to develop a program that works in all environments; rather, we want to show a simple example of the object-oriented style. So, even if locks would not be useful in your COMMON LISP environment, please read on.

We call a lock "busy" if it has been seized but not yet released, and "free" if it is available to be seized. When a lock is busy, the process that seized it is called its "owner."

We shall implement locks as LISP objects. The interface to locks must include the following operations:

Create   Create a new lock.

Seize   Seize a lock. When successful, the lock object is the
                    returned value.

Release   Release a lock, if it is owned by the same process
                    that is now trying to release it.

There are many possible kinds of locks, and we want our locking program to be extensible, since we plan to support more complex types of locks later. For example, we might eventually need a lock that can avoid deadlock situations. (Deadlock happens when one person picks up the butter dish and reaches for the butter knife at the same time that another person has picked up the butter knife and reaches for the butter dish. Neither person can obtain butter until the other has finished.)

We start by defining two elementary kinds of lock, which we can later use as building blocks for other kinds of locks.

Simple lock   This kind of lock has a name. The lock is either
                    busy or free. If the lock is busy, it keeps track of
                    its owner, which is a process.

Null lock   This kind of lock also has a name, but it does not
                         keep track of whether it is busy or free. In effect, a
                         null lock is always free. A null lock supports the
                         normal locking operations without actually protect-
                         ing itself from being seized by other owners. This
                         kind of lock allows programs to deal consistently
                         with resources that sometimes need to be protected
                         against simultaneous access and sometimes do not.
                         The program goes through all the motions of seiz-
                         ing and releasing the lock, and the kind of lock
                         (whether null or another kind) controls whether or
                         not the resource is protected.

3.2 DEFINING THE KINDS OF OBJECTS—CLASSES

Now we must translate the English-language description of null locks
and simple locks into the language of CLOS. The translation illustrates

- Designing a program that uses inheritance
- Using slots to store state information
- Defining classes with the `defclass` macro
- Requesting methods for reading and writing slots
- Giving a slot a default initial value

Choosing the Classes to Represent Locks

Although at first glance it seems that we should define two classes (one
to represent simple locks and the other to represent null locks), we can
make better use of inheritance by defining three classes in the organization shown in Fig. 3.1.

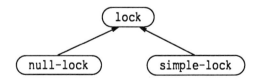

Figure 3.1 Organization of lock classes.

The classes `simple-lock` and `null-lock` include `lock` in their definition;
we say that they are *built on* the class `lock`. They both inherit from the
class `lock`. Here is a terminology reminder:

lock is a direct superclass of null-lock.
lock is a direct superclass of simple-lock.

null-lock is a direct subclass of lock.
simple-lock is a direct subclass of lock.

We call lock a *basic class*. The term "basic class" does not have any specific technical significance (the class lock acts just like any other class), but it describes the purpose of the class. The lock class is intended to be the foundation of all locks; its purpose is to contribute the characteristics that all locks have in common. The principal characteristic that all locks share is the fact that they are locks. By building all lock classes on the class named lock, we can use (typep *object* 'lock) to find out whether an object is a lock.

Also, both simple locks and null locks have names, so the "name characteristic" is provided by the class lock and is inherited by all kinds of locks. Another reason for providing a basic class is to make it convenient to define *default methods*. A method attached to a basic class is a default method. Any class that inherits from the basic class can choose to use the default method, provide a method to override the default method, or support additional behavior by providing a before-method or an after-method to work with the default method. In summary, we define the class lock for three reasons:

- It enables us to use (typep *object* 'lock) to check whether an object is a lock
- It contributes the name characteristic to all locks
- It supports the default behavior of all locks

We do not intend this class to stand alone, in that we do not expect to create instances of it. The class lock will not have a complete set of methods for supporting the locking protocol.

Using defclass

We define the class lock as follows:

```
(defclass lock ()
      ((name :initarg :name :reader lock-name))
   (:documentation "The foundation of all locks."))
```

Evaluating this form creates a new class named lock with one slot called `name`. It also creates the generic function `lock-name`, and a method for `lock-name` that allows you to read the value of the `name` slot of any object whose type is `lock`. Here we examine each portion of the class definition and see what it does:

`defclass`   The macro for defining a new class.

`lock`   The name of the new class.

`()`   The list of direct superclasses. The list here is empty because we have not specified any superclasses for `lock`.

`((name :initarg :name :reader lock-name))`
                The list of slot specifiers. Each slot specifier can be given as a symbol (the name of the slot) or a list (the name of the slot followed by *slot options*). Here we have a single slot named `name`, with these two slot options:

> `:initarg :name`
> This option makes it possible to initialize the value of this slot when creating instances. To initialize the `name` slot, we can give the `:name` keyword argument to `make-instance`. (Note that `make-instance` is the CLOS function for creating new instances; we discuss it in "Using make-instance or Constructors," page 24.)

> `:reader lock-name`
> This option makes it possible to read the value of this slot by using the generic function `lock-name`. This slot option causes the CLOS system to generate a method for `lock-name`. `lock-name` is called a *reader generic function*.

`(:documentation "The foundation of all locks.")`
                This is a *class option*; it pertains to the class as a whole. The `:documentation` class option provides a documentation string describing the purpose of the class. You can retrieve the documentation string of a class by calling the `documentation` function.

Inheriting from a Superclass

The definition of null-lock illustrates how to define a class that is built
on a superclass. Here the class null-lock is built on one superclass, the
class lock.

```
(defclass null-lock (lock)
      ()
   (:documentation "A lock that is always free."))
```

The class null-lock inherits the following from its superclass lock:

name slot   Each instance of null-lock has a slot named name.

:initarg :name slot option
            You can initialize the name slot when making an instance of
            null-lock.

lock-name method
            You can use the reader lock-name on instances of null-lock
            to read the value of the name slot.

Accessors

We now define the class simple-lock. A simple lock keeps track of
whether it is busy or free. The definition of simple-lock provides the
slot owner, which indicates whether the simple lock is busy or free by re-
membering which process currently owns the lock. A free lock has its
owner slot set to nil, and a busy lock has its owner slot set to the process
that currently owns the lock.

```
(defclass simple-lock (lock)
      ((owner :initform nil :accessor lock-owner))
   (:documentation "A lock that is either free or busy."))
```

The class simple-lock inherits exactly the same characteristics and behavior from lock as does null-lock. Note that the class simple-lock inherits the slot name from its superclass, and that it adds a slot of its
own, the owner slot. The definition of simple-lock also includes two new
slot options:

:initform nil
            This slot option allows you to give a default initial value
            for a slot. Here, the default initial value of the owner slot is
            nil. This means that, when a simple lock is created, it is
            free.

```
:accessor lock-owner
```
> This slot option enables you to access the slot owner for either reading or writing the value of the slot. CLOS generates two generic functions: a *reader generic function* called lock-owner and a corresponding *writer generic function.* CLOS also defines methods for each of these generic functions. Thus, you can read the value of the slot owner by using the reader generic function lock-owner, and you can write the value of the slot by using setf with lock-owner.

The name of this reader generic function is the symbol lock-owner. To call a reader, use normal function-calling syntax, such as:

> (lock-owner *lock-object*)

The name of the writer generic function is the list (setf lock-owner). This list is not a form to be evaluated; it is the name of the function—in other words, it is the "function specifier." To call the writer, use the setf syntax as follows:

> (setf (lock-owner *lock-object*) *new-value*)

The slot options :reader and :accessor are similar. The :reader slot option generates a method for a reader generic function only. The :accessor slot option generates two methods: one for a reader and one for a writer. The term *accessor generic function* is an umbrella term that includes both readers and writers. Usually you define a reader if you want to read the slot, and both kinds of accessors if you want to read and write the slot. It is possible to define only a writer (with the :writer slot option), but this is rarely done.

Slots Used in Lock Classes

Here we review how we intend to use the name and owner slots, and relate that to the slot options chosen for the slots:

name
> Each lock has a name. We initialize the name when we create a lock, by giving it as an argument to make-instance. We do not provide a default initial value for the name slot because that would not make sense; each lock needs a name suited to its purpose, so no default name would be appropriate in enough cases to make defaulting worthwhile.

We can use the reader lock-name to determine the name of a lock. We have not provided a means for changing the name of the lock; there is no writer method for lock-name.

owner

Each simple lock has an owner. The owner slot is always initialized to nil when a simple lock is created. We have not allowed the slot to be initialized by an argument to make-instance, because we want all newly created simple locks to be free.

We can use the reader lock-owner to find out the owner of a simple lock. We can use the writer method corresponding to lock-owner to change the owner of a simple lock. The name of the writer is (setf lock-owner). This writer method will be useful inside the seize methods, but we do not intend it to be part of the interface.

Despite the similarity in the names :initform and :initarg, these slot options are intended for different purposes. The :initarg option lets you provide an argument to make-instance for initializing the value of a slot. Thus, using this slot option enables callers of make-instance to specify an initial value for the slot. We used :initarg for the name slot.

In contrast, :initform provides a default initial value for the slot. The slot is initialized to the value specified in the :initform option, instead of being initialized by an argument to make-instance. We used :initform for the owner slot.

3.3 CREATING NEW OBJECTS—INSTANCES

The code we have written will feel more real if we create some locks and manipulate them. In the following sections, we create instances of simple-lock and null-lock and experiment with them.

Using make-instance or Constructors

The function for creating new instances is make-instance. Here we use make-instance to create a null lock and to initialize its name slot to be "Null lock":

```
(setq *null-lock*
      (make-instance 'null-lock :name "Null lock"))
=> #<NULL-LOCK 802335>
```

Here we use `make-instance` to create a simple lock and to initialize its name slot to be "Simple Lock":

```
(setq *simple-lock*
      (make-instance 'simple-lock :name "Simple lock"))
=> #<SIMPLE-LOCK 802393>
```

You can use `make-instance` to make an instance of a class. The first argument is the name of the class. The following arguments are initargs followed by values. Here the initarg `:name` is used to initialize the `name` slot with a value.

We recommend that you define constructor functions to be used by the clients to make instances. A constructor is a tailored way to make an instance of a given class; its name usually describes the kind of instance that it creates. A constructor provides a more abstract external interface than does `make-instance`, because its name describes its higher-level purpose (make a null lock) instead of its internal implementation (make an instance of the class `null-lock`).

Another advantage is that a constructor can have required arguments. In contrast, all arguments to `make-instance` except for the first are optional. We might prefer to require that users initialize the name of a lock.

You can define a constructor by using `defun`, and calling `make-instance` in the body of the function. For example, here we define two constructors, one for making a null lock, and the other for making a simple lock:

```
(defun make-null-lock (name)
  (make-instance 'null-lock :name name))

(defun make-simple-lock (name)
  (make-instance 'simple-lock :name name))
```

We shall advertise `make-null-lock` and `make-simple-lock` as part of the interface to be used by clients when creating new locks. Thus, instead of using `make-instance`, clients use the constructors:

```
(make-null-lock "Null lock")
(make-simple-lock "Simple lock")
```

Using the Accessors

We can experiment with the reader and writer generic functions which were automatically generated through the :reader and :accessor options to defclass.

We have a reader generic function lock-name, and a method for it. That method is attached to the lock class, and is inherited by both null-lock and simple-lock, because they are both built on lock.

```
(lock-name *null-lock*)                    => "Null lock"
(lock-name *simple-lock*)                  => "Simple lock"
```

We also have a reader generic function named lock-owner, and a corresponding writer generic function named (setf lock-owner). Each of these accessors has a method for it attached to the simple-lock class. We can use these accessors on instances of simple-lock.

In the following example, we use lock-owner on the newly created simple lock, which shows that the initial value of the owner slot is nil. We then call the writer generic function to set the value of the slot to 3401, and call the reader again to see that the value is indeed 3401.

```
(lock-owner *simple-lock*)                 => nil
(setf (lock-owner *simple-lock*) 3401)     => 3401
(lock-owner *simple-lock*)                 => 3401
```

We cannot use lock-owner or (setf lock-owner) on instances of null-lock. No method is attached to null-lock for these generic functions, and null-lock does not inherit any method for them. Therefore, if we try to use these generic functions on an instance of null-lock, CLOS will signal the "no applicable method" error.

```
(lock-owner *null-lock*)
ERROR:  No applicable method for LOCK-OWNER
for the argument #<NULL-LOCK 802335>

(setf (lock-owner *null-lock*) 3401)
ERROR:  No applicable method for (SETF LOCK-OWNER)
for the argument #<NULL-LOCK 802335>
```

Querying a Lock for Its Type

Now that we have instances, we can demonstrate that CLOS is neatly integrated with the existing COMMON LISP type hierarchy. The names of all classes are COMMON LISP type specifiers, so you can use type-of and typep to query a LISP object about its type. The type of an instance is its class.

```
(type-of *null-lock*)                    => NULL-LOCK
(type-of *simple-lock*)                  => SIMPLE-LOCK

(typep *simple-lock* 'simple-lock)       => t
(typep *simple-lock* 'lock)              => t
(typep *simple-lock* 't)                 => t
```

We use typep as shown to indicate that the lock *simple-lock* is not only of the type simple-lock, but it is also of the type lock and the type t. This is entirely analogous to how typep works for other COMMON LISP type specifiers, when one type is a subtype of another. For example, an object of type integer is also of type number, because integer is a subtype of number. Similarly, all objects are of type t.

The significance of this is related to inheritance. The instance *simple-lock* is of the types simple-lock, lock, and t. That means that each of those classes can contribute structure and behavior to *simple-lock*. So we can use typep to find out whether the behavior of an instance is affected by a particular class.

Similarly, to find out the relationship of one class to another, we can use subtypep with classes:

```
(subtypep 'simple-lock 'lock)            => t t
(subtypep 'null-lock 'lock)              => t t
(subtypep 'null-lock 'simple-lock)       => nil t
```

The results confirm what we already knew: simple-lock is a subtype of lock, null-lock is a subtype of lock, and null-lock is not a subtype of simple-lock.

The first value of subtypep tells whether the first argument is a subtype of the second argument. The second value of subtypep indicates the certainty of the first value. If the relationship between the two types is not known, the values will be nil nil. This can happen for COMMON LISP types, but it can never happen for two classes. When both arguments to subtypep are class names, the second value will always be t.

3.4 DEFINING THE INTERFACE—GENERIC FUNCTIONS

We have already completed one part of the interface, by giving clients a means of creating new locks. Each kind of lock has its own constructor for creating a new lock. The constructor make-simple-lock creates a simple lock and make-null-lock creates a null lock. Constructors are ordinary functions, not generic functions.

Once a lock has been created, it must support two locking operations: seize and release. We shall implement these operations as generic functions.

Using defgeneric to Document the Interface

We can document the interface of each generic function by using a defgeneric form. The interface comprises three concepts, each of which is represented in the defgeneric form:

Interface	Described by defgeneric
Expected arguments	Parameters in the lambda-list
What it does	The documentation string
Returned values	The documentation string

You can use defgeneric to document the generic function for the benefit of programmers who call it or define additional methods for it. A defgeneric form also sets guidelines for the generic function that must be followed by any future extensions to the program.

A defgeneric form describes the generic function as a whole. The defgeneric forms for seize and release provide English text in the documentation string describing the overall purpose of the generic function. The documentation string is not a functional piece of the program; it does not actually do anything. However, without that documentation, people who wanted to read the code and learn how a program works would have to look at the method definitions and try to discern the overall purpose of the generic function based on the set of methods.

```
(defgeneric seize (lock)
  (:documentation
"Seizes the lock.
Returns the lock when the operation succeeds.
Some locks simply wait until they can succeed, while
other locks return NIL if they fail."))

(defgeneric release (lock &optional failure-mode)
  (:documentation
"Releases the lock if it is currently owned by this process.
Returns T if the operation succeeds.
If unsuccessful and failure-mode is :no-error, returns NIL.
If unsuccessful and failure-mode is :error, signals an error.
The default for failure-mode is :no-error."))
```

In LISP, a lambda-list is the portion of a function that specifies names for the parameters of the function. The defgeneric form for seize specifies one required parameter (whose name is lock), and the defgeneric form for release specifies one required parameter named lock and one optional parameter named failure-mode.

The documentation strings look somewhat awkward as shown, but there is a reason for aligning them at the left margin. If we indented them, the documentation function would indent them, which is not what we want. It is not necessary to align the first line of a documentation string at the left margin, but we choose that style for strings that are longer than one line, just to be consistent with the lines that follow.

Creation of a Generic Function

A defgeneric form creates a new generic function. Using defgeneric is not the only way to define a generic function. The other way is to define a method. If you define a method for a generic function and the generic function itself does not yet exist, CLOS automatically creates it. The lambda-list of the generic function is derived from the lambda-list of the method. You can use defgeneric later to specify the lambda-list of the generic function, a documentation string, and any other options; CLOS modifies the existing generic function according to your new definition.

Although is not necessary to document the interface explicitly by means of defgeneric, as we do here, doing so often makes it easier for other people to learn how your program works, and provides guidelines for programmers who wish to extend the program.

Establishment of the Parameter Pattern

A defgeneric form establishes a parameter pattern that must be followed by all methods for that generic function. Thus, the lambda-list of a defgeneric form is a functional piece of the program. CLOS requires that the lambda-lists of all methods and the defgeneric form for a generic function have the same "shape" or be "congruent." The lambda-lists must have the same number of required parameters and the same number of optional parameters. Special rules state what congruence means for &key parameters. For full details, see "Congruent Lambda-Lists," page 132.

Naming Issues

The names of the parameters of a generic function should imply the class of objects on which the generic function can operate. Here, we use the name "lock" to indicate that the generic function can be used on any lock. It happens that "lock" is also the name of a class, but there is no requirement that parameter names of a generic function be class names.

The same guideline applies to the name of a generic function. The name should tell us something about the function's purpose and should answer the question, "How generic is it?" For example, we might later add a generic function to the protocol for resetting a lock, which would be useful for debugging; a process could reset the lock owned by another process. The name "reset-lock" would be better than merely "reset", which is too general. One potential pitfall of an overly general name for a generic function is related to the requirement that all methods for a generic function must have congruent lambda-lists. If we name a generic function "reset" and several different programs want to write methods to reset different kinds of devices, it is likely that the different programs will want to establish different argument patterns, which is not allowed.

The Locking Protocol

A generic function defines the interface of a single operation. This is a valuable concept in the initial design phase, because it helps you focus on the interface while leaving the details of the implementation until later. It is also valuable during the maintenance of the program. A set of defgeneric forms appearing at the beginning of a program can go a long way toward documenting the roles of the individual pieces of the program.

The generic functions taken together can be called a *protocol*. A protocol encompasses the complete behavior of the objects in the program. For example, the basis of the *locking protocol* is as follows:

> There must be a means for creating new locks, and all existing locks must support the seize and release operations.

The locking protocol must convey more information on the semantics of each operation: its arguments, what it does, and its returned values. For the generic functions, this information is contained in the individual defgeneric forms.

The idea of a protocol gives us another perspective on an application program. The question "What is a lock?" can be answered with "A lock is an object that obeys the locking protocol." We now have an operational definition of locks. This perspective allows for a natural and accurate description of a null lock: "A null lock obeys the locking protocol, without actually protecting anything against simultaneous access." Note that an instance of the basic class lock is not a lock by this definition, because it does not obey the locking protocol.

When we define locks by the protocol that they obey, we are taking an external point of view. We could take an internal point of view by defining a lock as "an instance of any class that includes the class lock." Each of these perspectives is valid and useful in its own right. Software developers who use locks benefit by the external point of view. The implementor of locks takes the internal point of view when defining the classes and methods that constitute the locking program. However, the implementor cannot neglect the external point of view, because the implementation must ensure that the locks follow the advertised locking protocol.

We are discussing not a formalized concept of a protocol, but rather an informal notion that programmers find useful when designing and describing object-oriented programs. CLOS does not include any mechanism for enforcing protocols.

3.5 DEFINING THE IMPLEMENTATION—METHODS

In this section, we define the methods for null locks and simple locks. We discuss methods in detail, including when a method is called, what arguments it receives, and how a method can provide a default value for an argument. Throughout this discussion, keep in mind the distinction between the terms *argument* and *parameter*. You provide arguments to a LISP function when you call it, and you name the parameters of the function when you define it. In the body of a function, you can refer to an argument by using the corresponding parameter. Thus, a parameter is a variable that is bound to an argument during the execution of a function. For details on the different kinds of parameters, see Steele's *Common LISP: The Language*, pages 59-61.

Generic functions and methods use the same terminology. The lambda-list of a defgeneric form names the parameters of the generic function, and the lambda-list of a defmethod form names the parameters of the method.

Methods for Null Locks

The purpose of implementing null locks is to disable locking in a program that performs locking operations. The program follows its normal seizing and releasing routine, without a need for a special "debug mode" that turns locking off in exceptional circumstances. The methods exist so that a null lock can be used wherever a program expects a lock.

The methods for the locking operations on null locks are simple. They are primary methods and they do all the work of the generic functions they implement. Each method adheres to the interface of its generic function. Since these methods do not actually seize or release anything, they are always successful and they always return the value indicating success.

```
(defmethod seize ((1 null-lock))
  1)                                ;return lock, no waiting

(defmethod release ((1 null-lock) &optional failure-mode)
  (declare (ignore failure-mode))   ;never fails for null locks
  t)
```

A Method's Lambda-List

In an object-oriented program, it is important to understand the scope of a method. When is this method applicable? The lambda-list states the method's scope by using *specialized parameters*, which attach the method to one or more classes. A method is applicable when the arguments to the generic function fulfill the requirements of the specialized parameters in the lambda-list.

Figure 3.2 shows the lambda-list of the `release` method, which has one specialized parameter.

```
((1 null-lock) &optional failure-mode)
 specialized
 parameter
```

Figure 3.2 Specialized parameter in a lambda-list.

The lambda-list of a method is an ordinary lambda-list with one difference. It distinguishes between two kinds of parameters:

- A specialized parameter indicates the applicability of the method by stating the class of the argument for which this method applies. A specialized parameter is a list containing a variable and a class name. The parameter is said to be *specialized* on that class. You can specialize any of the required parameters, but not &optional, &key, or &rest parameters.

- An ordinary parameter does not indicate the applicability of the method; it simply gives a variable to be bound to the argument to the generic function.

Although a specialized parameter has the same syntax as a defaulted parameter, there is no ambiguity. In methods, required parameters may be specialized but may not have default values. Optional parameters may not be specialized but may have default values.

The Applicability of a Method

When a generic function is called, CLOS selects the set of *applicable methods*. A method is applicable if the arguments to the generic function match that method's specialized parameters. For an argument to match, it must be *of the type* indicated by the class. This includes instances of the class itself and instances of classes built on that class (subclasses).

In the lambda-list in Fig. 3.2, only the first parameter is specialized. The parameter specializer is the class named null-lock, indicating that the method is applicable when the first argument to the generic function is an instance of null-lock or some class built on it. In other words, the following expression must be true:

(typep *argument* 'null-lock)

Sometimes we speak of a class "inheriting a method." This is a natural way to describe the fact that an instance can use a method that is attached to a superclass of its class. This model allows us to picture a link between a class and a method attached to that class.

It is important to keep in mind that a method can contain any number of specialized parameters. A method can have links to more than one class; it is linked to all the classes that are used as parameter specializers. We discuss this style of programming in "Multi-Methods," page 75. For methods that have more than one specialized parameter, the model of "method applicability" is more appropriate than is the model of "inheriting a method." We can express the rule of method applicability in one sentence:

> **Rule of method applicability:**
>
> A method is applicable if each of its specialized parameters is satisfied by the corresponding argument to the generic function.

Many methods have only one specialized parameter. Accessor methods fall into this category, as do all the methods we define in the locking program. We shall continue to use the model of "inheriting a method" for methods that have only one specialized parameter.

The Arguments Passed to a Method

When CLOS chooses the implementation of a generic function and calls the methods, it passes all the arguments supplied to the generic function to each method. The variables in the lambda-list are bound to the arguments. Within the method body, you can use the variables bound to the objects by using generic functions or ordinary functions to manipulate them.

For example, when `release` is called on an instance of `null-lock`, the method we defined for `release` is called. The variable `l` is bound to the first argument to the generic function, the lock.

The variable `failure-mode` is bound to the second argument. The method chooses to ignore this variable, because it has no need to use it. Even though the method does not use this argument, it must explicitly allow it by including a parameter for it in the lambda-list. This is necessary because the method receives all arguments passed to the generic function.

Locks and Processes

Before defining the methods for simple locks, we need to discuss processes further. Our example assumes that processes do not actually execute concurrently, but rather are interleaved, as happens when a single time-sliced processor is used.

Since COMMON LISP does not currently include functions for dealing with processes, for the purposes of this example we assume three primitives that support multiple processes in a shared address space. These primitives are not part of CLOS or COMMON LISP.

`without-process-preemption` &body *body*

> The body of this special form runs without risk of the process being preempted by the scheduler. In other words, the body is an atomic operation with respect to process scheduling.

`process-wait` *reason function* &rest *arguments*
> This function is the primitive for waiting. The current process waits until the application of *function* to *arguments* returns non-`nil`. At that time `process-wait` returns the values of applying *function* to *arguments*. The argument *reason* is a string describing the reason for waiting.

`*current-process*`
> The value of this variable is an identifier of the process that is currently executing.

We now define the macro `setf-if`, which we shall use in the `seize` and `release` methods. The macro `setf-if` compares the value of a generalized variable to an expected value. If these values are the same, `setf-if` sets the value of the variable to a new value and returns t; otherwise, it does not change the value and it returns nil. `setf-if` uses `without-process-preemption` to ensure that the operations happen atomically, to ensure that another process cannot change the variable between the time `setf-if` tests the variable and the time it changes it.

```
;; If value of place is old-value, set it to new-value
;; Return t if the setf worked, nil otherwise
(defmacro setf-if (place old-value new-value)
  '(without-process-preemption          ;do atomically
     (cond ((eql ,place ,old-value)
            (setf ,place ,new-value)
            t)
           (t nil)))))
```

Note that a real multiprocessing system would include its own definition for a `setf-if` operation, which would no doubt be more efficient and would deal better with order of evaluation issues.

Methods for Simple Locks

First, we define `check-for-mylock` to check for the common mistake in which a process tries to seize a lock it already owns. The following method for `check-for-mylock` signals an error in this situation. We shall use `check-for-mylock` in the `seize` method.

```
(defmethod check-for-mylock ((l simple-lock) process)
  (when (eql (lock-owner l) process)
    (error "Can't seize ~A because you already own it." l)))
```

The following `seize` method iterates with `do` until the `setf-if` succeeds. On each iteration, `setf-if` determines whether the lock is free by using `lock-owner` to find out if the `owner` slot is `nil`. If the lock is free, `setf-if` sets its owner to the current process, thus seizing it. (This is done atomically by `setf-if`.) If the lock is not free the first time around, `process-wait` is called to wait until `lock-owner` returns `nil`, which indicates that the lock is currently free. Then the `setf-if` form tries again.

```
(defmethod seize ((l simple-lock))
  (check-for-mylock l *current-process*)
  (do ()
      ((setf-if (lock-owner l) nil *current-process*))
    (process-wait "Seizing lock"
                  #'(lambda () (null (lock-owner l)))))
  l)
```

Note that the body of the `do` is not necessary, because without it the end-test itself would iterate repeatedly until the `setf-if` succeeds. The problem is that the `setf-if` might use a good deal of machine time before it finally succeeds. In contrast, using `process-wait` in the body of the `do` allows other processes to run, and tries the `setf-if` only when it is likely to succeed.

The following `release` method uses `setf-if` as a convenient way to make sure that the process trying to release the lock is the current owner of the lock. If not, `setf-if` does not release the lock.

```
(defmethod release ((l simple-lock)
                     &optional (failure-mode :no-error))
  (or (setf-if (lock-owner l) *current-process* nil)
      (ecase failure-mode
        (:no-error nil)
        (:error (error "~A is not owned by this process" l)))))
```

Defaulting Optional Parameters of Methods

The lambda-list of the `release` method for `simple-lock` gives a default value for the optional parameter `failure-mode`. A method lambda-list may provide default values for any optional parameters, but not for required parameters. The `defgeneric` form may not provide a default value for any parameter in its lambda-list.

3.6 SPECIALIZING THE BEHAVIOR OF LOCKS

At this point, we have completed the requirements of the locking application. The interface is defined and the implementation is complete. In this section, we add some final touches by specializing the printed representation and description of locks. We describe the system-supplied default methods for printing and describing objects and discuss why it is often useful to provide a method to override the default behavior. We also show how methods can have different roles and work together cooperatively.

Controlling How Locks Print

The printed representations of null locks and simple locks look something like this:

```
#<NULL-LOCK 738592>
#<SIMPLE-LOCK 220478>
```

This output gives the type of the lock and the address in memory where the instance is stored. However, it does not give the name of the lock. We might decide to change the way that locks are printed so that the printed representation of a lock contains its name as well as its type and address in memory:

```
#<NULL-LOCK "Debug lock" 738592>
#<SIMPLE-LOCK "Database lock" 220478>
```

CLOS specifies that LISP always calls the generic function `print-object` whenever one of the printing functions is called, such as `print`, `prin1`, `princ`, `write`, `format`, and so on. This generic function offers a hook for programs to use to control the printed representation of various classes of objects.

Each CLOS implementation supplies a default method for `print-object`. The default method is inherited by all user-defined classes. However, any class can provide a method to override the default method.

We use this hook by *specializing* `print-object`. Conceptually, specializing a generic function means causing that generic function to behave in a customized manner for a given set of arguments. We specialize a generic function by defining a method for it. In this case, we shall provide a method to override the inherited method, so locks will be printed in a customized way.

Before writing a method, you must understand the interface of the generic function. The interface of `print-object` is documented in the

CLOS specification. CLOS specifies that the generic function `print-object` prints an object on a stream and then returns the object. It accepts two required arguments, an *object* and a *stream*. When LISP calls `print-object`, the *stream* argument will be a real stream, not t or nil. (This is different from `print`, which does accept t or nil as the *stream* argument.)

Specializing print-object for Locks

We want the method to be selected if the first argument is a lock. In other words, we want all objects whose type is `lock` to inherit this method. Since only the first argument will be used for method selection, the lambda-list of the method has one specialized parameter and one ordinary parameter.

```
(defmethod print-object ((l lock) stream)
  (format stream "#<~S ~A ~D>"
          (type-of l)
          (if (slot-boundp l 'name)
              (lock-name l)
              "(no name)")
          (sys:%pointer l))
  l)
```

Once this method is defined, it will be used whenever a lock is printed, and the result is exactly what we want.

The function `sys:%pointer` is not part of COMMON LISP; it is a function that returns the address of an object in memory in some implementations. It is useful for `print-object` methods to print the address of the object because it distinguishes this object from other objects, which can be helpful for debugging. The address of the object can change, however, due to garbage collection.

Methods for `print-object` should not signal errors; it should be possible to get a printed representation of any LISP object without error. The `print-object` method for `lock` uses `slot-boundp` to check that the lock has a name before calling `lock-name`. If the `name` slot were unbound, the `lock-name` accessor would signal an error; see "Reading Unbound Slots," page 75.

It is important to keep in mind the scope of this method. We know it is attached to the class `lock`, and can therefore use knowledge of the internal details of that class. We also know it is inherited by the classes `simple-lock` and `null-lock` and will be used for instances of `simple-lock` and `null-lock`. This method cannot use knowledge of any classes built on lock. For example, this method can use the reader generic function lock-name, because the class lock has a method for it; however, it cannot use the reader generic function lock-owner, because the only class that has a method for lock-owner is simple-lock. If this method did use lock-owner, and the argument to print-object were a null lock, an error would be signaled at run time to indicate that there is no applicable method for lock-owner.

Although this method must restrict itself to knowledge of the lock class, we know that the method is inherited by other classes. A common error people make when first learning to write object-oriented programs is to assume that the method will be called only for instances of lock, and not for instances of classes that are built on lock. This method could have made that incorrect assumption and produced output stating that the instance is a lock, instead of recognizing that the object might be an instance of a class built on lock. By querying the object for its type with type-of, however, we are recognizing that several different classes will inherit this method.

What Is a Default Method?

The system's method for print-object is a default method for objects of all user-defined classes. We have provided a method for print-object for the class lock. This is a default method for all locks, because all locks are built on lock.

Like the term "basic class," the term "default method" does not have a technical meaning. These terms simply describe the intended purpose of the class or method. A basic class is usually intended to be the foundation of a set of classes. A default method is intended to be inherited by a set of classes. Many basic classes provide default behavior; thus, default methods usually are attached to basic classes.

Specializing describe for Locks

In addition to controlling the printed representation of locks, it would be beneficial to provide a way for people to examine a lock in more detail.

One way to do this is to specialize the describe generic function. An alternative would be to write a method for a new generic function, such as show-lock. Either way would accomplish the same thing, but often it is preferable to extend a familiar COMMON LISP function rather than to introduce a new function. This approach works only if the function is a generic function.

Like `print-object`, `describe` is a generic function that is provided by
CLOS so users can specialize its behavior for a given class of object. A
system-supplied default method is available, but you can provide a
method to override it.

The interface for `describe` states that it takes a single argument,
prints a description of its argument to standard output, and returns no
values. This method specializes `describe` for locks:

```
(defmethod describe ((l lock))
  (format t "~&~S is a lock of type ~S named ~A."
          l (type-of l)
          (if (slot-boundp l 'name)
              (lock-name l)
              "(no name)"))
  (values))
```

This primary method is applicable for all locks. It is inherited by null
locks and simple locks. We use `slot-boundp` to ensure that the `describe`
method does not signal an error if the `name` slot is unbound.

An After-Method for Describing Simple Locks

The primary method for `describe` does not give an adequate description
of a simple lock. A crucial element of a simple lock is its owner, if it is
currently busy. The `describe` method supplied by `lock` cannot give this
information, because it would be overstepping its bounds. The class `lock`
does not have an owner.

We want to specialize the behavior of `describe` for `simple-lock` so that
it will give the same information as does the `describe` method for `lock`,
but also describe the owner of the simple lock.

We could supply a primary method for `describe` attached to the class
`simple-lock` to override the method inherited from the class `lock`. Of
course, we would have to duplicate the code for displaying the lock's
type and name, and for ensuring that no values are returned. However,
duplication of code is antithetical to the object-oriented programming
style. Instead of overriding the method, we should seek to inherit it and
add behavior to it.

We can do this by providing an *after-method* for the class
`simple-lock`. The after-method takes care of describing the owner of the
simple lock.

When the generic function `describe` is called on a simple lock, the
generic dispatch procedure first calls the primary method supplied by
the class `lock`, and then calls the after-method supplied by the class

simple-lock. The generic function returns the values returned by the primary method, which is just what we want. Any values returned by an after-method are ignored. After-methods are used to perform side effects, not to return values. An after-method has the keyword :after as its *method qualifier*. This method qualifier gives the *role* of the method. Until now, we have seen only primary methods, which have no method qualifiers. If a method has any qualifiers, they appear immediately after the name of the generic function.

```
(defmethod describe :after ((l simple-lock))
   (let ((owner (lock-owner l)))
      (format t (if owner
                     "~&It is now owned by process ~A.~%"
                     "~&It is now free.~%")
              owner)))
```

When the describe generic function is called for a simple lock, two methods are called. When the describe generic function is called for a null lock, only one method is called. describe has only one interface, but it has various implementations. This is the meaning of the term *generic function*.

In this method, we assume that the owner slot is bound. If it is not, this method will signal an error. The semantics of ordered locks require that the owner slot be either a process or nil.

The System's Default describe Method

The behavior of the default method for describe is implementation dependent. Typically, the default method gives the type of the object and the names and values of its slots. Why is the default method undesirable for describing locks?

Instead of merely displaying the names and values of the slots, our method goes a step further and conveys the semantics behind the slots and their values. Our describe method provides output that gives an English-language, conceptual description of the lock. The output of our describe method looks like this:

```
#<SIMPLE-LOCK File lock 2417> is a lock of type
SIMPLE-LOCK named File lock.
It is now owned by Process 3299.
```

The output of a typical system-supplied default method for describe looks like this:

```
#<SIMPLE-LOCK "File lock" 2417> is of type SIMPLE-LOCK,
with slots:
                NAME:              "File lock"
                OWNER:             3299
```

There is another advantage to supplying a describe method customized for a class of object. Often, it is desirable to conceal the details of the implementation of the object. The default method has no way to describe the object other than by laying bare its implementation. By supplying a describe method, you can control how users view your object.

3.7 ANALYZING THE INHERITANCE OF LOCKS

So far, we have been programming with an implicit understanding of how inheritance should work. At this point it is worth examining inheritance in greater detail and making explicit some of the mechanisms behind it.

Overriding Inherited Traits

Our organization of locks includes the basic class lock, and two classes built on lock. Both simple-lock and null-lock inherit from the class lock. Also, all user-defined classes inherit from the class standard-object.

The class standard-object is a predefined class whose purpose is to support default behavior. That is, several system-supplied default methods are attached to the class standard-object.

Consider what happens when the print-object generic function is called with an instance of null-lock as its argument. The class null-lock has two applicable primary methods for print-object: the method attached to lock and the method attached to standard-object.

Class	Method for print-object
lock	primary
standard-object	primary

Here we see two superclasses of null-lock offering competing traits; that is, primary methods for the same generic function. This is a conflict, but its resolution is simple and obvious. One of the methods is *more specific* than the other. The precedence of a method is directly related to the precedence of the classes for which it is applicable. In the class precedence list of null-lock, the class lock precedes standard-object, so the method supplied by lock overrides the method supplied by standard-object.

The reason that lock is more specific than standard-object is that a class has precedence over its superclasses. The class standard-object is a superclass of the class lock.

Class Precedence Lists of Null and Simple Locks

The class precedence list is the arbiter of conflicting traits. CLOS determines the class precedence list for every class, based on the organization of classes that the programmer has set up. During this process, CLOS must answer two questions:

- *From what classes does this class inherit?* A class inherits from itself and all its superclasses. This includes its direct superclasses, each of their direct superclasses, and so on. CLOS derives this information from the set of class definitions.

- *What is the precedence order among these classes?* The answer to this question is also derived from the class definitions. CLOS uses an algorithm to determine the precedence, and the algorithm always obeys the following class precedence rule:

> **Rule 1 of class precedence:**
>
> A class always has precedence over its superclasses.

We have mentioned that all user-defined classes have standard-object as a superclass. In addition, all classes have the class t as a superclass. The class t is the root of all classes. Just as all types are subtypes of t, all classes are subclasses of t.

Consider the example of simple-lock. This class inherits from itself, simple-lock, and its superclasses, lock, standard-object, and t. When CLOS applies Rule 1 to each of these class definitions, the result is a set of ordering constraints:

```
simple-lock has precedence over lock
simple-lock has precedence over standard-object
simple-lock has precedence over t
lock has precedence over standard-object
lock has precedence over t
standard-object has precedence over t
```

The class precedence list must satisfy all these constraints. The resulting class precedence list for `simple-lock` is

    `(simple-lock lock standard-object t)`

Similarly, the class precedence list of `null-lock` is

    `(null-lock lock standard-object t)`

It is a simple matter to determine the class precedence lists for these two classes. It is more difficult for classes that have more than one direct superclass. We introduce another class precedence rule to address that situation, in "Class Precedence Lists of Ordered Locks ," page 48.

The Generic Dispatch Procedure

When a generic function is called, CLOS takes charge of selecting the implementation that is appropriate to the arguments. This entails finding the applicable methods, then sorting them by order of precedence, and finally calling one or more of them. This procedure is called *generic dispatch*. It happens automatically whenever a generic function is called.

    You are responsible for defining the classes and methods in the first place, with an understanding of how the generic dispatch works. CLOS takes care of the mechanics behind the generic dispatch.

What You Do	*What CLOS Does*
Define the classes.	Computes the class precedence list based on the class definitions.
Define the methods.	Saves the methods for use when a generic function is called.
Call generic functions.	Determines the types of the arguments. Locates the set of applicable methods. Sorts the methods from most specific to most general, based on the class precedence list. Calls before-methods. Calls the most specific primary method. Calls after-methods. Returns the value(s) of the primary method.

Although calling a generic function sounds like a slow and complex process, good CLOS implementations optimize it, precomputing many of the steps. In fact, in some implementations, calling a generic function is nearly as fast as calling an ordinary function. Such optimizations can make CLOS efficient enough for use in an operating system, for example.

We discuss the order of execution of before-methods and after-methods in "Order of Before- and After-Methods," page 50.

3.8 EXTENDING THE LOCKING PROGRAM

The design of the locking application is now complete, and the implementation of simple locks and null locks is done. We now want to add a new kind of lock to the existing locking application. In this section, we illustrate defining a "mixin class" to be used as a building block and "aggregate classes" built on the mixin and another class.

Avoiding Deadlock with Ordered Locks

Some operations require you to access more than one shared resource. You might want to delete an item from one data structure and add it to another data structure. If the data structures are shared resources with locks protecting them against simultaneous access, you must own the locks on both resources while you do the adding and deleting operations.

Here is another scenario: To obtain butter you need to be holding both the butter dish and the butter knife at the same time. When you hold the butter dish and knife, you are protecting them from simultaneous use by other people (in other words, you "own the locks" on the two butter resources).

When you need to own two locks at the same time, there is a risk of deadlock. Suppose one person holds the butter dish and is waiting for the butter knife. Meanwhile, another person holds the butter knife and is waiting for the butter dish. Neither person can obtain butter until the other has finished. In this case, both people will realize that deadlock has occurred, and one person will probably release one of the resources in contention. This allows the other person to obtain butter and then to release both resources for other people to use. In this solution, the people detect the deadlock and resolve it.

When a process needs to seize more than one simple lock, there is the risk of deadlock. Remember that, if a simple lock cannot immediately seize a resource, it waits until the resource is free.

Instead of implementing deadlock detection and resolution, we can seek to *avoid* deadlock. We use a technique in which all processes must seize a group of locks in a prescribed order. We could apply this approach at the dinner table by making a rule that to obtain butter, you must pick up the butter dish before picking up the butter knife. If all people obey this rule, no person will be holding the butter knife and waiting for the butter dish, so no deadlock will happen.

We can invent a new kind of lock, called an *ordered lock*, to assist programmers in using this technique. This enables you to assign a locking order to a set of locks. The ordered locking mechanism is a programming tool that provides run time error-checking to make sure that the order is not violated. It checks running code to see whether the program runs the risk of deadlock, and signals an error in that case.

Thus, if we anticipate that processes need to seize both lock-A and lock-B before doing an operation, we can use ordered locks. Each ordered lock has a lock level. The ordered locking mechanism enforces the rule that a process cannot seize an ordered lock if the process already owns a lock at a higher level. We might assign a lock level of 1 to lock-A and a lock level of 2 to lock-B to ensure that lock-A must be seized before lock-B. In this scheme, all programs should be written to seize lock-A, then seize lock-B, perform the operation, and finally release both locks. If any process owns lock-B and attempts to seize lock-A, the ordered locking mechanism signals an error at run time. This approach ensures that no process can be in the state of owning lock-B and waiting for lock-A.

Defining a Mixin Class

We anticipate needing both ordered null locks and ordered simple locks. The behavior that these two classes will have in common is the ordered locking behavior. Here it is useful to create a *mixin class* that supports the ordered locking behavior. We call that class `ordered-lock-mixin`.

This mixin class is not expected to stand alone; we do not create instances of it. Instead, we define two *aggregate classes* that combine this mixin class with other lock classes, and create instances of them. The aggregate classes are named `ordered-null-lock` and `ordered-lock`. The terms "mixin" and "aggregate" are informal designations that describe the intended purpose of the class.

We do not specify any superclasses for `ordered-lock-mixin`. There is a single slot named `level`. We can initialize that slot when creating instances and use a reader function to read its value. We do not expect to change the level of an ordered lock once the lock has been created, so there is no writer provided for the `level` slot. Our implementation allows a process to seize an ordered lock only if the process does not own another ordered lock at a higher level.

```
(defclass ordered-lock-mixin ()
      ((level :initarg :level
              :reader lock-level
              :type integer))
      (:documentation "Avoids deadlock by checking lock order."))
```

The purpose of a mixin class is to customize the behavior of the classes built on it. Generally, mixins do not interfere with or override inherited behavior. Instead, mixins usually supply before-methods and after-methods to augment inherited primary methods with customized behavior. Mixins might also provide primary methods for additional generic functions.

Notice the new slot option :type. This slot option declares that you expect the value of the slot to be of a certain type. Type declarations on slots are ignored by some implementations, whereas other implementations gain efficiency when declarations are used. Type declarations are also a way of documenting the slot. You cannot, however, depend on CLOS doing type checking when a value is stored in the slot. Although some CLOS implementations might choose to do type checking, they are not required to do so. This behavior is consistent with COMMON LISP itself, which has a loose type-checking behavior.

Defining Aggregate Classes

Here we define two aggregate classes by including the desired set of superclasses:

```
(defclass ordered-lock (ordered-lock-mixin simple-lock)
      ()
      (:documentation
      "Avoids deadlock by ensuring that a process seizes
      locks in a specific order.
      When seizing, waits if the lock is busy."))

(defclass ordered-null-lock (ordered-lock-mixin null-lock)
      ()
      (:documentation
      "Avoids deadlock by ensuring that a process seizes locks
      in a specific order.   Does not actually seize anything,
      but does check that the lock ordering is obeyed."))
```

An aggregate class includes a set of superclasses that together make up a complete whole, a class that can stand alone. Here, the aggregate class `ordered-lock` derives most of its behavior from the class `simple-lock` and customizes it with the ordered lock behavior of the class `ordered-lock-mixin`. Only rarely does an aggregate class provide additional methods, because that would make the program less modular. Ideally, all the slots and methods are provided by the basic class or by the mixins. The aggregate classes here do not need any further modification.

We need to define constructors for these two new kinds of locks:

```
(defun make-ordered-null-lock (name level)
  (make-instance 'ordered-null-lock :name name
                                    :level level))

(defun make-ordered-lock (name level)
  (make-instance 'ordered-lock :name name
                               :level level))
```

Class Precedence Lists of Ordered Locks

For null locks and simple locks, CLOS could determine the class precedence list by referring only to Rule 1: A class always has precedence over its superclasses.

When a class has more than one direct superclass, however, this rule is not sufficient for determining the class precedence list. Rule 1 does not indicate how to rank the direct superclasses. For example, when determining the class precedence list for `ordered-lock`, does `ordered-lock-mixin` have precedence over `simple-lock`, or is it the other way around? CLOS uses another rule in this situation:

Rule 2 of class precedence:

Each class definition sets the precedence order of its direct superclasses.

The order of the direct superclasses in the `defclass` form states their relative precedence. For example, the class definition of `ordered-lock` includes two direct superclasses: `ordered-lock-mixin` and `simple-lock`. Since `ordered-lock-mixin` appears first (leftmost) in the list, it is more specific than `simple-lock`.

When we take into account the two rules, we can determine the class precedence list for the two aggregate classes. The class precedence list of `ordered-lock` is

```
(ordered-lock ordered-lock-mixin simple-lock lock standard-object t)
```

The class precedence list of `ordered-null-lock` is

```
(ordered-null-lock ordered-lock-mixin null-lock lock standard-object t)
```

Specializing describe for Ordered Locks

Before delving into the implementation of ordered locks, we specialize `describe` to display the lock level of an ordered lock. Because the lock level is a critical aspect of an ordered lock, it is important for `describe` to give that information.

```
(defmethod describe :after ((1 ordered-lock-mixin))
  (format t "~&Its lock level is ~D." (lock-level 1)))
```

When we try to `describe` an instance of `ordered-lock`, CLOS finds the following applicable methods:

Class	Method for describe
ordered-lock-mixin	after
simple-lock	after
lock	primary
standard-object	primary

There are two applicable primary methods. The primary method supplied by `lock` is the more specific of the two, so it is called.

There are two applicable after-methods. Both of them are called. They are called in *most-specific-last* order. Here, the after-method for `simple-lock` is called first because it is the less specific of the two. When it returns, the after-method for `ordered-lock-mixin` is called.

Here we create an ordered lock and call `describe` on it, to show the effect of the generic dispatch on this set of methods:

```
(setq *lock-C* (make-ordered-lock "C" 3))
=> #<ORDERED-LOCK C 29451>

(describe *lock-C*)
#<ORDERED-LOCK C 29451> is a lock of type ORDERED-LOCK named C.
It is now free.
Its lock level is 3.
=> no values
```

Order of Before- and After-Methods

The generic dispatch procedure finds all applicable methods, which might include several before-methods, primary methods, and after methods. The generic dispatch procedure calls the following methods:

1. *All before-methods in most-specific-first order.* This allows a more specific class to do an operation *before anything else happens*, where "anything else" includes inherited before-methods, the primary method, and after-methods.

2. *The most specific primary method.* This allows a more specific class to override an inherited primary method, if desired.

3. *All after-methods in most-specific-last order.* This allows a more specific class to do an operation *after everything else happens*, where "everything else" includes before-methods, the primary method, and inherited after-methods.

In other words, a class can do something in advance of the behavior inherited from less-specific classes; it can also do something after the behavior inherited from less-specific classes occurs. This kind of nesting should feel natural to programmers familiar with LISP.

Imagine that the classes `ordered-lock-mixin`, `simple-lock`, and `lock` all provide a before-method and an after-method. Figure 3.3 shows the order in which the methods would be called.

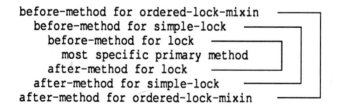

```
before-method for ordered-lock-mixin
   before-method for simple-lock
      before-method for lock
         most specific primary method
      after-method for lock
   after-method for simple-lock
after-method for ordered-lock-mixin
```

Figure 3.3 Nesting of before- and after-methods.

In practice, any of these before- or after-methods can be present or absent. When a generic function is called, the only requirement is that there must be at least one applicable primary method. If there is none, an error is signaled.

Implementing Ordered Locking Behavior

We shall implement ordered locking behavior by keeping track of which ordered locks are owned by a process. When a process tries to seize an ordered lock, we shall first check to see whether the process already owns an ordered lock at a higher level. If so, the lock is considered "out of order" and invalid; an error is signaled and we do not allow the process to seize that lock. Otherwise, the lock is considered "in order" and valid, so we do allow the process to seize it.

We use a hash table to keep track of the ordered locks owned by each process. The first two functions are used to update the table when a process seizes or releases an ordered lock; the second two functions examine the table.

```
(defvar *process-lock-table* (make-hash-table)
  "Each key is a process identifier;
   value is a list of ordered locks it owns")

(defun add-process-lock (process lock)
  (without-process-preemption
    (push lock
          (gethash process *process-lock-table*))))

(defun delete-process-lock (process lock)
  (without-process-preemption
    (let ((hash-entry
            (gethash process *process-lock-table*)))
      (setf (gethash process *process-lock-table*)
            (delete lock hash-entry)))))

(defun get-process-locks (process)
  (without-process-preemption
    (gethash process *process-lock-table*)))

(defun get-highest-lock (process)
  (first (get-process-locks process)))
```

In this code, we assume that the gethash and setf of gethash operations are not atomic, so we use without-process-preemption around the use of those functions. Note that get-highest-lock depends on the first lock being the highest lock. We rely on the caller of add-process-lock always adding a higher level of lock; this is what ordered locking is all about. The function delete-process-lock can delete any lock from a given process, but it does not change the order of the remaining locks.

The hash table is a simple and effective way of storing the association between a process and the ordered locks it owns. In some LISP implementations, the process itself would be implemented as an instance of a class. In these cases, each process might have a slot in which it stores a list of its ordered locks; this would replace the hash-table mechanism.

The functions defined here are the interface to the association between processes and their lists of ordered locks. We shall use that interface within the methods that implement ordered locking. Nothing prevents us from someday switching from the hash table to another representation. We could redefine these functions to do their work differently without affecting the callers of the functions. For example, we could change them from ordinary functions to generic functions and methods without changing the callers.

Methods for Ordered Locks

Before we allow a process to seize an ordered lock, we check that it does not currently own a lock with a higher level. We do this by defining a before-method for **seize**. If the before-method determines it is valid for the process to seize the lock, it simply returns. This method does not do any actual locking, but assumes that another method will take care of that. If the before-method determines that it is invalid for the process to seize this lock, it signals an error. Since **error** never returns, no other method is called. The invocation of the **seize** generic function is aborted by a nonlocal exit caused by the call to **error**. Thus, this method can prevent the lock from being seized, if necessary.

```
(defmethod seize :before ((l ordered-lock-mixin))
  "Checks validity of this process seizing this ordered lock.
   If invalid, signals an error.
   If valid, does nothing and allows primary method to run."
  ;; First check for the mylock mistake to give the specific
  ;; error for that case, instead of the "Out of order" error.
  (check-for-mylock l *current-process*)
  ;; Now check for a possible infraction of ordered locking.
  (let ((highest-lock (get-highest-lock *current-process*)))
    (when (and highest-lock
               (<= (lock-level l) (lock-level highest-lock)))
      (error "Out of order:  Can't seize ~A while owning ~A"
             l highest-lock))))
```

After a process has seized an ordered lock, it is necessary to update the ***process-lock-table*** to associate this lock with the process. We do this update with an after-method for `seize`:

```
(defmethod seize :after ((l ordered-lock-mixin))
  "Adds the lock to the *process-lock-table*"
  (add-process-lock *current-process* l))
```

Similarly, after releasing an ordered lock, we must update the *process-lock-table*. We need another after-method to take care of this update:

```
(defmethod release :after ((l ordered-lock-mixin)
                           &optional failure-mode)
  "Deletes a lock from the *process-lock-table*"
  (declare (ignore failure-mode))
  (delete-process-lock *current-process* l))
```

The class `ordered-lock-mixin` provides a before-method that checks for a situation (in fact, for both the "mylock" and the "out of order" mistakes) and an after-method that notes a situation (the new association between the lock and the process). These are typical uses of before- and after-methods.

This is a simplified implementation of ordered locks, since this code does not deal with the possibility of aborts happening at a bad time, leaving the process table inconsistent with the actual state of the lock. These details are omitted because they are irrelevant to the discussion of object-oriented programming.

3.9   HOW CLIENT PROGRAMS USE LOCKS

So far, our locks have not been connected with any shared resource. One way to make a resource lockable is to incorporate a lock into the data structure representing the resource. You then write functions for accessing the data structure that first seize the lock, then access the data structure, and finally release the lock.

Locking a Shared Queue

Consider how a print spooler might work. When a user requests a hardcopy printout, the print spooler stores the print request in a queue until the printer is ready, then sends the request to the printer. The print spooler maintains a queue of print requests. Several processes can access this queue, so it is important to guarantee that the queue is updated in a consistent way. This is a good candidate for a client program of our locking application.

A simple lock is the right kind of lock here. These processes will not need to own more than one lock at a time, so deadlock should not be a problem.

We can implement our queue of print requests by defining a class that includes a slot for the lock and a slot for the list of print requests:

```
(defclass print-request-queue ()
        ((lock :accessor print-queue-lock
                  :initform (make-simple-lock "Print Queue"))
         (requests :accessor print-requests :initform nil))
     (:documentation "Queue of pending print requests."))

(defun make-print-queue ()
   (make-instance 'print-request-queue))
```

Here we create the print-request queue and define the constructor make-print-queue. The constructor takes no arguments, so the two slots are initialized to their default initial values. The lock slot is initialized with a simple lock named "Print Queue" and the requests slot is initialized to the empty list.

```
(defvar *print-queue* (make-print-queue))
```

The following functions for modifying the queue take care of seizing the lock, modifying the data structure, and releasing the lock. The unwind-protect ensures that the lock gets released even if the operation is aborted.

```
(defun enqueue-print-request (r)
   (let ((lock (print-queue-lock *print-queue*)))
      (unwind-protect
          (progn (seize lock)
                  (push r (print-requests *print-queue*)))
        (release lock :no-error))))
```

The dequeue-print-request function takes a request as an argument instead of simply popping the first request off the list. This allows the caller—the print spooler—to choose which request to print first.

```
(defun dequeue-print-request (r)
  (let ((lock (print-queue-lock *print-queue*)))
    (unwind-protect
        (progn
          (seize lock)
          (setf (print-requests *print-queue*)
                (delete r (print-requests *print-queue*))))
      (release lock :no-error)))))
```

Supporting the Typical Use of Locks: with-lock

When we step back and look at the first client program, we see that both enqueue-print-request and dequeue-print-request demonstrate the canonical use of locks: first seizing the lock, then performing an operation, then releasing the lock.

We can add a with-lock macro to the locking application to make it more convenient for programs to use locks:

```
(defmacro with-lock ((lock) &body body)
  (let ((lock-var (gensym)))
    `(let ((,lock-var ,lock))
       (unwind-protect
           (progn (seize ,lock-var)
                  ,@body)
         (release ,lock-var :no-error)))))
```

This macro allows the developer of the client program to simplify the two functions considerably:

```
(defun enqueue-print-request (r)
  (with-lock ((print-queue-lock *print-queue*))
    (push r (print-requests *print-queue*))))

(defun dequeue-print-request (r)
  (with-lock ((print-queue-lock *print-queue*))
    (setf (print-requests *print-queue*)
          (delete r (print-requests *print-queue*)))))
```

Specializing describe for Print-Request Queues

It is good style for the client program to specialize describe for the class print-request-queue. Notice that this method does not seize the print-request queue before describing it. This means that, if the queue has an owner, that process might be presently modifying the queue, so the pending print requests might be changing.

The reason we do not seize the queue is that we believe it is more valuable for describe to show the owner of a lock if it is busy, rather than waiting until the queue is free. If we waited for the queue to become free, it would be impossible to use describe for debugging in cases where one process waits while owning the lock, because describe would also wait.

```
(defmethod describe ((queue print-request-queue))
  (let ((owner (lock-owner (print-queue-lock queue)))
        (requests (print-requests queue)))
    (if owner
        (format t "~&Process ~A owns queue.~%" owner))
    (format t (if (null requests)
                  "~&There are no print requests.~%"
                  "~&Pending print requests:~%"))
    (dolist (x requests)
      (format t "~&~A " x))))
```

3.10 REVIEWING THE LOCK CLASSES

Imagine that you are going to describe the structure of the locking program to another programmer. When describing the organization of an object-oriented program, you would probably need to answer questions like these:

What is the set of classes?
What does each class contribute to the whole?
How do the classes interact?

Once we have collected this information, we shall take a close look at the class ordered-lock, to see how it works.

What Is the Set of Classes?

The first two classes are building blocks that are not intended to stand alone. The remaining four classes support the complete locking protocol and can stand alone. This distinction is important.

Class	*Description*
lock	Foundation of all locks.
ordered-lock-mixin	A mixin that supports ordered locking behavior; an integral part of all ordered locks.
simple-lock	A lock that is either busy or free. When busy, it stores its owner. Constructor is make-simple-lock.
null-lock	A lock that is always free. It obeys the locking protocol without seizing anything. Constructor is make-null-lock.
ordered-lock	A lock that supports ordered locking and is either busy or free. Constructor is make-ordered-lock.
ordered-null-lock	A lock that supports ordered locking but is always free. It does not seize anything. Constructor is make-ordered-null-lock.

What Does Each Class Contribute?

A class can contribute slots and methods. Also, slot options are inherited; that is, they affect the classes built on the class that gives the slot option. For example, the slot options :initarg and :initform are inherited by subclasses. If a class provides accessor methods, they are applicable for subclasses as well. Here we concentrate on the slots and the methods that support the locking protocol. We start by listing the slots that each class supplies:

Class	Slots
lock	name
ordered-lock-mixin	level
simple-lock	owner
null-lock	*none*
ordered-lock	*none*
ordered-null-lock	*none*

We now list the methods for seize and release:

Class	seize	release
lock	*none*	*none*
ordered-lock-mixin	before, after	after
simple-lock	primary	primary
null-lock	primary	primary
ordered-lock	*none*	*none*
ordered-null-lock	*none*	*none*

We now list the methods for describe and print-object. Notice that we include the class standard-object here, because it supplies methods for these generic functions:

Class	describe	print-object
standard-object	primary	primary
lock	primary	primary
ordered-lock-mixin	after	*none*
simple-lock	after	*none*
null-lock	*none*	*none*
ordered-lock	*none*	*none*
ordered-null-lock	*none*	*none*

How Do the Classes Interact?

The interaction of classes happens via inheritance. The key to understanding how one class inherits from its superclasses is the class precedence list of that class. We have catalogued what each class contributes to the whole. Now we can describe any one class in detail by looking at its class precedence list and collecting the contributions of each class in the list.

The class precedence list of each class includes the class itself and all of its superclasses, ordered from most to least specific. Although all user-defined classes have `standard-object` and `t` at the end of their class precedence lists, we omit these system-supplied classes here, because they are a given.

Class	Class Precedence List
lock	(lock)
ordered-lock-mixin	(ordered-lock-mixin)
simple-lock	(simple-lock lock)
null-lock	(null-lock lock)
ordered-lock	(ordered-lock ordered-lock-mixin simple-lock lock)
ordered-null-lock	(ordered-null-lock ordered-lock-mixin null-lock lock)

Examining Ordered Locks

We use the information gathered in the previous sections to take a closer look at the class `ordered-lock`. What slots does it have? Look at each class in its class precedence list to see what slots they provide. The following table shows that `ordered-lock` has three slots: `level`, `owner`, and `name`. (The classes `standard-object` and `t` have no slots and are not shown.)

Class	Slots
ordered-lock	*none*
ordered-lock-mixin	level
simple-lock	owner
lock	name

How does the class `ordered-lock` implement the `seize` generic function? Look at the classes in its class precedence list to see what methods they provide for `seize`:

Class	Method for `seize`
`ordered-lock`	*none*
`ordered-lock-mixin`	before, after
`simple-lock`	primary
`lock`	*none*

When `seize` is called on an instance of `ordered-lock`, the following methods are called:

1. The before-method provided by `ordered-lock-mixin`, which checks the validity of allowing this process to seize this ordered lock

2. The primary method provided by `simple-lock`, which stores the process identifier in the `owner` slot

3. The after-method provided by `ordered-lock-mixin`, which updates the `*process-lock-table*` to note that this process now owns this ordered lock

We can go through this same procedure to inspect any lock class, to find out what slots it has and how it implements any of these generic functions.

3.11 THE EXTERNAL AND INTERNAL PERSPECTIVES

We originally intended to write the methods that would support the locking protocol. In the course of developing the program, we defined additional methods, a macro, and several functions. Here we categorize each of these LISP operations according to their purpose: Which are part of the external interface, and which are internal?

External Locking Protocol

The external locking protocol consists of the constructors and the locking operations. Client programs are expected to create their own locks by using these constructors and to use `seize` and `release` to manipulate the locks.

```
seize                   release
make-simple-lock        make-null-lock
make-ordered-lock       make-ordered-null-lock
```

Support for Other Protocols

These methods are intended for external use, but they are not part of the locking protocol. Both `describe` and `print-object` have protocols of their own, which our methods follow.

     `describe`   `print-object`

Support for Using Locks

This macro is intended for external use. It is a syntactic extension to the locking protocol.

     `with-lock`

For Internal Use Only

We defined methods for generic functions, a macro, a special variable, and several functions that are not part of the external interface to locking. They are used within the implementation of locking or for debugging. The following are intended for internal use only:

`lock-name`	`lock-level`
`lock-owner`	`(setf lock-owner)`
`setf-if`	`get-process-locks`
`get-highest-lock`	`add-process-lock`
`delete-process-lock`	`*process-lock-table*`

There is no guarantee to the clients of the locking program that internal functions like these will always exist or always work in the same way they work now. Similarly, the definitions of the classes could be modified later. For example, the names of the slots can change, and slots can be added or removed. These purely internal details are in the domain of the implementor, who is free to change them for any reason.

Distinguishing the Internal from the External

CLOS does not enforce the distinction between the external and internal perspectives. It is up to the programmer to design a program with this separation as a design goal. The documentation of the program should advertise only the external interface.

You can distinguish internal from external names with packages by setting up a package for your program and exporting from the package only those symbols that are intended to be external names. COMMON LISP provides convenient ways for a program to use the exported symbols of a package without encountering the other symbols; these techniques include `use-package` and the single-colon syntax for symbols. Using packages is a general COMMON LISP technique, and we do not cover it further in this book.

3.12 GUIDELINES ON DESIGNING PROTOCOLS

We have been quite strict with our definition of the locking protocol. This strictness benefits the users, who can depend on the protocol's working as advertised, and the implementor, who can modify the implementation without disrupting the user community. CLOS offers the framework for defining a protocol, but it is the responsibility of the programmer to invent a protocol for a new application. In addition to recommending using packages, we provide these guidelines to help you keep the internal functions separate from the external protocol:

- *Restrict the user's access to the internal data structures.* Our `describe` methods give a good English description of simple locks and ordered locks. The output does not reveal the names of the slots, which is an internal implementation detail. The default method for `describe` probably would display the names and values of the slots, but our methods avoid displaying that internal view of the locks.

- *Provide constructor functions for creating the data structures.* There are two ways to create instances: use a constructor function or use `make-instance`. In either case, the end result is the same, but a constructor function encourages users to think of the object in more abstract, conceptual terms. In contrast, `make-instance` gives away details of the implementation. First, it publicizes that the conceptual object is implemented as an instance of a class. If `make-instance` were part of the advertised protocol, it would be awkward to change some aspects of the implementation. It would be impossible to change the name of the class or its initargs, or to switch to a `defstruct` representation of data, without changing the advertised protocol.

- *Design the protocol to anticipate the needs of the users.* When the protocol offers all the power and flexibility that is needed by the user community, there is little temptation for people to delve into the implementation. But sometimes a protocol is sufficient for the majority of its users, while frustrating a small number of users by the lack of a needed feature. These users might be motivated to search for an internal function that supports that feature. If users begin to depend on an internal function, the implementor is no longer free to change it. The valuable distinction between interface and implementation becomes muddied.

For example, our original design for locking anticipates the needs of programs (the operations for creating, seizing, and releasing) and the needs of people (hence the methods that print and describe locks). This design seems quite adequate on paper, but one day we might find a user who wants to change the name of a lock. A persistent user could investigate the implementation, find out that the name is stored in a slot, and use the primitive `slot-value` to change the value of that slot. (Even when there is no accessor for a slot, you can access a slot by calling `slot-value`. We discuss this in "Accessors Versus slot-value," page 72.)

- *Allow the protocol to evolve to meet the reasonable needs of users.* Realistically, it is usually impossible to anticipate all needs of the users in advance. When you hear of a need for a feature, you can consider adding a new interface to the protocol. Some requests for features are reasonable, such as changing the name of a lock or adding a "reset-lock" generic function to the locking protocol. You might judge some as unreasonable, such as wanting to convert a simple lock into an ordered lock. If you decide the feature should be available, you can extend the protocol in a compatible and controlled way.

We have said that there are two choices for users who find the existing protocol useful but not exactly appropriate for their applications: They can dive into the internals and make use of them at their own risk, or they can submit a request to the implementor to add new features. The first avenue is not recommended, and the second might involve a delay or even a refusal by the implementor.

There is another alternative. You can offer a lot of flexibility and power by designing the protocol so that other people can extend it. This is an entirely different approach; it entails designing and documenting a set of classes to be building blocks for user programs. This goal is more ambitious and requires careful design work to achieve, but the benefits can be valuable. We add one final guideline that describes this approach.

- *Design some protocols to be extensible by the user.* The usual way for a user to extend an existing protocol is to define new classes that include some combination of the existing classes. This way users can take advantage of the existing modules and tailor them to their own purposes. Users should not interfere with the workings of the classes provided by the protocol; instead of writing methods for the advertised classes, users write methods for their own customized classes.

This last approach paves the way for future extensions of the program, whether those extensions are done by other in-house programmers or by customers of the product.

Consider how this approach can be used by people who develop and sell computer systems for others to program. The original developer supplies documented modules that use knowledge of the internals of the machine (including hardware and microcode) and exploit the machine's power to best advantage. The users can define new classes built on the advertised modules and can customize the new, aggregate classes; they are freed from writing the lower level of code themselves. Meanwhile, the developers retain the freedom to change the underlying mechanism, to track upgrades to the internals of the machine. Developers have only two requirements: they must document the interface, and then adhere to it.

One portion of the locking example illustrates leaving a hook in the code for future extensibility. We defined a method for check-for-mylock for the class simple-lock; the method signals an error if the process attempting to seize a lock already owns that lock. It would be an easy matter to define a new class of lock built on simple-lock that does not signal an error in the mylock situation. We could define the new class and give it exactly one method: a primary method for check-for-mylock that does not do anything. This method would override the method for simple-lock and thus prevent an error from being signaled. Note that, if we had defined check-for-mylock as an ordinary function, it would not be a hook, because clients could not specialize it for a given class.

4

Programming with Methods

The locking program illustrated the central features of CLOS. This chapter describes additional useful techniques, including how to write methods to do the following:

- Represent information without storing it in slots
- Add behavior to an accessor generic function
- Specialize on more than one argument
- Specialize on COMMON LISP types such as strings and arrays
- Specialize on an individual LISP object

We use three examples in this chapter. The first example represents triangles as instances of classes and demonstrates different ways to store information associated with triangles. The second example is an installation program designed to install various software products on different operating systems; shows how to write methods that specialize on more than one argument. The third example is a program supporting remote evaluation, which illustrates methods that specialize on COMMON LISP types and on individual LISP objects.

4.1 IMPLEMENTATION CHOICES: METHODS VERSUS SLOTS

CLOS supports more than one way to represent certain kinds of information associated with an instance or a class. This section introduces the concept of a shared slot and discusses the pros and cons of representing information in slots versus in methods.

Local and Shared Slots

There are two kinds of slots. A *local slot* stores information about the state of a particular instance. Each instance maintains its individual copy of the slot with its own value. This is the default kind of slot. All the slots mentioned previously in this book are local slots.

A *shared slot* stores information on the state of the class as a whole. There is only one value of a shared slot; it is associated with the class and shared by all instances of the class. If one instance changes the value of the shared slot, the new value will be seen by all instances if they read the slot.

For example, we might define a class named `triangle`. Each instance stores the length of its three sides in local slots named `side-a`, `side-b`, and `side-c`. These must be local slots, so that each instance can keep track of its own dimensions.

Suppose the triangle class is one of several classes in a program that handles geometric shapes. The shape protocol states that the generic function `number-of-sides` returns the number of sides of a given shape. For the `triangle` class, we can store that information in a shared slot named `number-of-sides` and provide a reader method for it. A shared slot is appropriate, because all instances of the `triangle` class have the same number of sides.

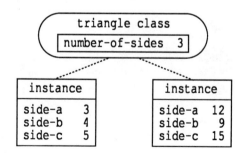

Figure 4.1 Local and shared slots.

Figure 4.1 shows that each instance stores its individual values for the local slots side-a, side-b, and side-c, but there is only a single value for the shared slot number-of-sides. Local slots are stored inside each instance, and shared slots are stored inside the class itself.

The defclass form defines the slots and controls whether the slot is local or shared. The :allocation slot option specifies whether a slot is local or shared. The default is :allocation :instance, which means the slot is local. To specify that a slot should be shared, you give the :allocation :class slot option.

The following defclass form defines three local slots and one shared slot for the triangle class:

```
(defclass triangle (shape)
      ((side-a :accessor side-a :initarg :side-a)
       (side-b :accessor side-b :initarg :side-b)
       (side-c :accessor side-c :initarg :side-c)
       (number-of-sides :reader number-of-sides
                        :initform 3
                        :allocation :class)))
```

The reader number-of-sides can be used on any instance of triangle. The reader method returns the value of the slot named number-of-sides, which is shared by all instances of the triangle class.

Useful Triangle Functions

In the examples that follow, we label each angle of the triangle according to its opposite side. Angle-A is opposite side-a, and adjacent to side-b and side-c. Figure 4.2 shows how the angles and sides are related to one another.

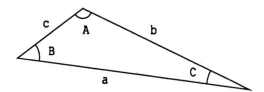

Figure 4.2 Angles and sides of a triangle.

Here we define two useful functions for dealing with triangles, which we use in the examples that follow:

```
;;; Return the area of a triangle, given three sides.
;;; Algorithm is: area = ab(sin C)/2
(defun area-of-triangle (a b c)
  (let ((angle-C (three-sides-to-angle c a b)))
    (* a b (sin angle-C) .5)))
```

```
;;; Return the angle A between adjacent sides b and c
;;; and opposite side a, given all sides of a triangle
;;; Law of Cosines:  a^2 = b^2 + c^2 - 2bc(cos A)
(defun three-sides-to-angle (a b c)
  (acos (/ (- (+ (expt b 2) (expt c 2))
             (expt a 2))
          (* 2 b c))))
```

We expand on the triangle example in "Example of Redefining CLOS
Elements," page 144.

Representing Information About an Instance

In the shape program, we might need to determine the area of a given
shape. There are two ways to represent the area of a shape: calculate it
in a method, or store the area in a local slot. For example, here are the
ways to represent the area of a triangle:

Method
: Define a method that calculates the area based on the
lengths of the sides of the triangle.

```
;;; Return the area of a triangle.
(defmethod area ((tri triangle))
  (area-of-triangle (side-a tri)
                    (side-b tri)
                    (side-c tri)))
```

Local slot
: Define a local slot named area that stores the area of
each triangle and a reader method for the slot.

```
(defclass triangle (shape)
  ((side-a :accessor side-a :initarg :side-a)
   (side-b :accessor side-b :initarg :side-b)
   (side-c :accessor side-c :initarg :side-c)
   (number-of-sides :reader number-of-sides
                    :initform 3
                    :allocation :class)
   (area :reader area :initarg :area)))
```

We must calculate the area when the triangle is first created. One effective way to do this is to define a constructor called `make-triangle`, which initializes the area:

```
(defun make-triangle (side-a side-b side-c)
  (make-instance 'triangle
                 :side-a side-a
                 :side-b side-b
                 :side-c side-c
                 :area (area-of-triangle
                         side-a side-b side-c)))
```

Since many programs need to do initialization such as this, CLOS provides a technique especially intended for this purpose, called *initialization methods*; we discuss them in "Controlling Initialization with Methods," page 159.

It is also necessary to recalculate the area whenever any of the side lengths change, which we demonstrate in "Defining Auxiliary Methods for Accessors," page 71.

Regardless of which implementation choice you make, the client gets the area the same way: by calling the `area` generic function. The choice of internal representation is up to the programmer. The effects of using a method to calculate the area each time are that: less storage space is needed and object-creation and updating of the side length are faster, but the `area` query is slower. The effects of storing the area in a slot are that: the `area` query is faster, but more storage space might be needed, and object-creation and updating of the side length are slower.

Representing Information About a Class

We have already mentioned the need to represent information associated with a class, such as the number of sides of triangles. CLOS offers two ways to do this:

Method   Define a method that returns the information. The number of sides is "stored" only in the method body and not in a slot.

```
(defmethod number-of-sides ((tri triangle))
  3)
```

Shared slot   Define a shared slot and a reader method for the generic
               function `number-of-sides`. The two `defclass` forms for
               `triangle` given earlier show how to define a shared slot
               (use the `:allocation :class` slot option) and a reader
               method (specify the `:reader number-of-sides` slot option).

Here the tradeoff is between speed of the query and the convenience of
updating the information associated with the class. When a method
stores the information, the query is probably faster, because no slot access is required. This technique might also save storage space, since the
information is stored in one method, rather than in a slot and a reader
method. However, the only way to change the information is to redefine
the method. This approach works, but it requires programming (locat-
ing the method's definition, editing it, and compiling it), rather than
just using a program (calling a writer generic function). In some applications, you can reasonably assume that the information associated with
a class will never change, so updating is not a problem. For example, we
know that the number of sides of a triangle will always be 3, and there
is no need ever to update that information. In other contexts, however,
the information associated with the class might need to be changed.

When the information is stored in a shared slot, you can conveniently
change it by using a writer generic function. However (depending on
the CLOS implementation), the query might be slower and more storage space might be used.

4.2 PROGRAMMING WITH ACCESSORS

This section describes how to modify the behavior of an accessor generic
function and discusses the various ways to access slots.

Automatically Generated Accessors

By giving the `:accessor` slot option to `defclass`, you ask CLOS to generate a method for a reader generic function and a method for a writer
generic function. The reader method simply returns the value of the
slot, and the writer method writes a new value into the slot.

These are primary methods that behave just like any other primary
method, which means you can write auxiliary methods to perform additional computation. That is, you can define before-methods and after-
methods to augment the behavior of primary methods for reader and
writer generic functions.

Defining Auxiliary Methods for Accessors

Here we continue to use the triangle example. Recall that the definition
of the triangle class gives the :accessor slot option to generate methods
for a reader named side-a and the corresponding writer named (setf
side-a).

Earlier, we mentioned the possibility of storing the area of a triangle
in a slot and recalculating the area every time a side length of the triangle changes. To use this approach, we need a method to run every time
a new value is stored in any of the slots side-a, side-b, or side-c. We
can do this by defining after-methods for the writer generic functions
(setf side-a), (setf side-b), and (setf side-c).

You can use defmethod to write an auxiliary method for a reader
generic function or a writer generic function. The first argument is the
name of the generic function, which for a reader is a symbol, and for a
writer is a list such as (setf *symbol*). In methods for writer generic
functions, the first parameter in the lambda-list is the parameter for the
new value to be written into the slot. For example:

```
(defmethod (setf side-a) :after (new-length (tri triangle))
   (setf (area tri)
         (area-of-triangle new-length
                           (side-b tri)
                           (side-c tri)))))
```

This is an after-method, which runs after the primary method for (setf
side-a). This method calculates the area of the triangle and stores it in
the area slot every time the writer function (setf side-a) is called. We
would need to write similar after-methods for (setf side-b) and (setf
side-c) to ensure that the area is updated whenever any of the side
lengths change.

Defining Primary Methods for Accessors

The :accessor, :reader, and :writer slot options are convenience features of CLOS. You could implement primary methods for reading and
writing a slot yourself, by using defmethod. The body of a reader method
would use the primitive slot-value to read the value of the slot, whereas a writer method would use setf with slot-value.

For example, in our previous definition for the triangle class, we
gave the :accessor option to define a reader and writer for side-a. Alternatively, we could define primary methods for the readers and writers by hand.

```
;;; Defining the reader side-a
(defmethod side-a ((tri triangle))
  (slot-value tri 'side-a))

;;; Defining the writer (setf side-a)
(defmethod (setf side-a) (new-side-a (tri triangle))
  (setf (slot-value tri 'side-a) new-side-a))
```

Usually, there is no advantage to defining a primary method of an accessor by hand, because in almost all cases you want the primary method simply to read or write the value of the slot. When you need to do something special, you can provide a before-method or after-method to work in conjunction with the primary method, rather than providing a special-purpose primary method.

Accessors Versus slot-value

The implementation of primary methods for accessors (regardless of whether the method is automatically generated by CLOS or is defined by hand) is done in terms of slot-value. You can read the value of any slot with slot-value, and you can write the value of a slot by using setf with slot-value. It is important to understand the difference between using slot-value and using an accessor.

Clients of a program are expected to use accessors to read and write slots, because the accessors are usually the advertised interface. In contrast, slot-value is the underlying implementation of accessors and is not intended to be used in other contexts. To call slot-value, you need to know the name of the slot, which is strictly an internal detail of the program. Consider what happens if the developer changes the internal representation of that information by changing the name of the slot or by storing the information in a method instead of a slot: presumably the developer defines new methods for the generic functions to replace the accessor methods, so callers of the advertised generic functions continue to work. However, any callers of slot-value for that slot will be invalidated.

slot-value accesses the slot directly, without calling any accessor methods. This is a disadvantage if the program depends on accessor methods to do necessary work related to accessing the slot. Recall that the triangle example uses after-methods for the writers of the side length slots to update the area; if you use setf of slot-value to write the value of a side length, the value of the area slot will be incorrect because no accessor methods will be called.

You should use `slot-value` for two purposes: if you want to define an accessor by hand, or if you want to access a slot without calling any accessor methods. The latter use of `slot-value` can be helpful when debugging a program.

Using with-accessors and with-slots

Another way to access slots is to use `with-accessors` or `with-slots`, two macros that allow you to access slots by using variable names. Within the body of `with-accessors`, using the variable has the same effect as calling the corresponding accessor generic function. In contrast, `with-slots` translates use of the variable to a call to `slot-value`, so no accessor methods are called.

The purpose of these macros is to simplify bodies of code that access slots frequently, by supporting a shortcut syntax. Thus, using `with-accessors` is a shortcut for calling the accessors, and using `with-slots` is a shortcut for calling `slot-value`. Using these macros can result in more concise code, especially when the bodies of the methods use either accessors or `slot-value` frequently.

In the triangle example, we might need a method for returning angle A, which is opposite to side a, and adjacent to sides b and c. Here, we show two equivalent ways to access the sides.

Calling the readers to get the sides:

```
(defmethod angle-A ((tri triangle))
  (three-sides-to-angle (side-a tri)
                        (side-b tri)
                        (side-c tri)))
```

Using `with-accessors` to get the sides:

```
(defmethod angle-A ((tri triangle))
  (with-accessors ((a side-a)
                   (b side-b)
                   (c side-c))
                  tri
    (three-sides-to-angle a b c)))
```

You can also write the value of a slot by using `setq` or `setf` with the variable. The following table shows how variables can be used in the body of the `with-accessors` form in method shown:

This Form	Translates to This Form
a	`(side-a tri)`
`(setq a` *value*`)`	`(setf (side-a tri)` *value*`)`
`(setf a` *value*`)`	`(setf (side-a tri)` *value*`)`

The `with-accessors` macro requires you to specify a variable (such as `a`) for each accessor (such as `side-a`). Although you can specify that the variable should be the same symbol as the accessor, there is no brief syntax for it; you always have to list both the variable and the accessor names.

The `with-slots` macro does have a brief syntax: You list the slots you want to access, and then you can access them by their names. Here we show two equivalent ways to access the slots directly—calling `slot-value` and using `with-slots`:

```
;;; Using slot-value to access the slots
(defmethod angle-A ((tri triangle))
  (three-sides-to-angle (slot-value tri 'side-a)
                        (slot-value tri 'side-b)
                        (slot-value tri 'side-c)))

;;; Using with-slots to access the slots
(defmethod angle-A ((tri triangle))
  (with-slots (side-a side-b side-c)
              tri
    (three-sides-to-angle side-a side-b side-c)))
```

The following table shows how variables can be used in the body of the `with-slots` form in the method shown:

This Form	Translates to This Form
a	`(slot-value tri 'side-a)`
`(setq a` *value*`)`	`(setf (slot-value tri 'side-a)` *value*`)`
`(setf a` *value*`)`	`(setf (slot-value tri 'side-a)` *value*`)`

Note that, when you use `with-slots` or `with-accessors`, the instance form gets evaluated only once.

Reading Unbound Slots

If a slot is not initialized, and no value has been stored in it by means of a writer, the slot is unbound. If you try to read the value of an unbound slot, an error is signaled.

The default behavior (signaling an error) is supported by the generic function `slot-unbound`. That is, if you try to read an unbound slot, CLOS calls the exception handler `slot-unbound`. The generic function `slot-unbound` has a system-supplied default method that signals an error; you can specialize this generic function if you want to change what happens when unbound slots are read in instances of a certain class.

4.3 MULTI-METHODS

Many object-oriented programs can be written with methods that specialize only one parameter. However, sometimes it is useful to write methods that specialize more than one parameter. These are called *multi-methods*.

The technique of using multi-methods is intended for operations whose implementation truly depends on the type of more than one argument.

We introduce multi-methods by discussing an installation scenario. Suppose a company sells various software products, each of which can run on a variety of operating systems. The installation procedure depends on the type of the software product and on the type of the operating system. This company wants to provide a generic installation program to automate the installation process.

Currently, the company supports two software products, Life and Adventure, on two operating systems, GENERA and UNIX. The company plans to support additional software products and operating systems in the future, so the installation program should be extensible. In this example, we use the following representation of the software products and operating systems:

- The software products are represented by the classes `life` and `adventure`
- All software products are built on the class `basic-product`
- The operating systems are represented by the classes `genera` and `unix`
- All operating systems are built on the class `basic-os`

Checking Arguments with Multi-Methods

We want to provide one top-level function for installing any of our supported products on any of our supported operating systems. We can do this with a generic function `install`, which expects a software product as its first argument and an operating system as its second argument:

```
(defgeneric install (software-product operating-system)
  (:documentation "Installs software on the operating system."))
```

Method 1 is applicable when both arguments are valid; that is, the first argument is of the type `basic-product`, and the second argument is of the type `basic-os`:

```
;;; Method 1
(defmethod install ((sw basic-product) (os basic-os))
  body)
```

Method 1 is a multi-method; it specializes two parameters. This method is applicable only when both arguments are valid. The body of this method will perform an installation. (We leave the body of the method blank for now.)

What if the user calls `install` with invalid arguments? That is, what if the first argument is not a software product, or the second argument is not an operating system, or both? CLOS will look for applicable methods, find none, and signal an error along the lines of "No applicable method."

Such an error message does not make it clear whether the error was caused by a bug in the program or by the wrong kind of input given by the user. For an installation tool, we should give the user a more informative error message. We can supply three methods to do this job.

```
;;; Method 2
(defmethod install ((sw basic-product) non-os)
  (error "Cannot install because ~A is not
          a recognized operating system." non-os))

;;; Method 3
(defmethod install (non-product (os basic-os))
  (error "Cannot install because ~A is not a
          recognized software product."  non-product))
```

```
;;; Method 4
(defmethod install (non-product non-os)
  (error "Cannot install because ~A is not a
          recognized software product and ~A is not
          a recognized operating system."
         non-product non-os))
```

We intend that, for any pair of arguments, only one method is called. If both arguments are valid, method 1 should be called to perform the installation. Otherwise, the most appropriate method of methods 2, 3, and 4 should be called, to give an informative message.

The methods are correctly written to fulfill their intended purposes. Since they are all primary methods, we know that only the most specific applicable method is called. CLOS selects that method by first finding the set of applicable methods, and then ranking these methods in order of precedence. The next two sections discuss the applicability and precedence order of multi-methods.

Applicability of Multi-Methods

CLOS allows methods for the same generic function to specialize any of the required parameters. The methods for `install` take advantage of that flexibility:

Method	Lambda-list
Method 1	((sw basic-product) (os basic-os))
Method 2	((sw basic-product) non-os)
Method 3	(non-product (os basic-os))
Method 4	(non-product non-os)

When `install` is called, CLOS looks for the applicable methods. A method is applicable if each specialized parameter is satisfied by the corresponding argument to the generic function. "Satisfied" means that the argument is of the type of the parameter specializer; it is an instance of the class itself or an instance of a subclass.

An unspecialized parameter is equivalent to the class t being the parameter specializer. Since all objects are of type t, an unspecialized parameter is always satisfied by the argument. Thus, method 4 is applicable for any two arguments, no matter what their types.

Suppose `install` is called with two valid arguments. Here, `*life*` is an instance of `life`, and `*genera*` is an instance of `genera`.

```
;;; Here install is called with two valid arguments.
(install *life* *genera*)
```

Both methods 1 and 2 are applicable, as seen by the following tests:

```
;;; Method 1 is applicable because these forms are true.
(typep *life* 'basic-product)
(typep *genera* 'basic-os)

;;; Method 2 is applicable because these forms are true.
(typep *life* 'basic-product)
(typep *genera* 't)
```

Similarly, methods 3 and 4 are applicable:

```
;;; Method 3 is applicable because these forms are true.
(typep *life* 't)
(typep *genera* 'basic-os)

;;; Method 4 is applicable because these forms are true.
(typep *life* 't)
(typep *genera* 't)
```

Earlier, we stated that a method is applicable if each specialized parameter is satisfied by the corresponding argument to the generic function.
This rule holds for multi-methods too. We can clarify this statement by
noting that all required parameters must be satisfied, and that any unspecialized required parameters are treated as though they had the class
named t as their parameter specializers.

Rule of applicability of multi-methods:

A method is applicable if each of its required parameters is satisfied by the corresponding argument to the generic function.

An unspecialized required parameter is equivalent to a parameter that specializes on the class named t.

When CLOS finds more than one applicable primary method, only the
most specific one is called. Thus, CLOS must rank the applicable methods in order of precedence. We continue this example and rank methods
1 through 4 in order of precedence.

Precedence Order of Multi-Methods

CLOS ranks two applicable methods in order of precedence by considering the required arguments of the method from left to right, with respect to their parameter specializers. Mathematicians call this *lexicographic order*.

Here, we show the class of the parameter specializer of the first required parameter, for the four methods:

Method	First Parameter is Specialized by
Method 1	basic-product
Method 2	basic-product
Method 3	t
Method 4	t

The class precedence list of the corresponding argument to the generic function determines which of these classes is more specific. The class of the first argument, *life*, is life, and its class precedence list is

    (life basic-product t)

Since basic-product is more specific than t, methods 1 and 2 are more specific than methods 3 and 4. To rank the precedence of method 1 versus method 2, CLOS proceeds to the next required parameter and compares the pair of parameter specializers:

Method	Second Parameter is Specialized by
Method 1	basic-os
Method 2	t

The class of the second argument, *genera*, is genera, and its class precedence list is

    (genera basic-os t)

Since basic-os is more specific than t, method 1 is more specific than method 2. Using the same procedure, we find that method 3 is more specific than method 4. Thus, the precedence order of the methods is

    (method-1 method-2 method-3 method-4)

Just by looking at the lambda-lists of the methods, it probably feels right that method 1 is the most specific (because it specializes both parameters), and that method 4 is the least specific (because it does not specialize either parameter). It is not intuitively obvious, however, which of methods 2 and 3 is more specific:

Method	Lambda-list
Method 2	((sw basic-product) non-os)
Method 3	(non-product (os basic-os))

CLOS ranks method 2 as more specific than method 3 because of the left-to-right order for comparing parameter specializers. That is, the order of the parameters in the lambda-list affects the precedence of the methods. Since the leftmost parameter specializer of method 2 is more specific than the leftmost parameter specializer of method 3, method 2 is more specific than method 3. The remaining parameter specializers are not considered.

The left-to-right precedence order of parameters is an arbitrary default. You can change it by using the :argument-precedence-order option to defgeneric; see "Summary of Method Inheritance," page 98.

The Implementation of install

Usually, the installation of a software product requires several distinct steps, which must be performed in a certain order. We might find that all installations consist of four separate steps:

1. Restoring the software from tape
2. Compiling the software system
3. Configuring the site to know about the new software
4. Verifying the installation of the software product

We can implement install to call four generic functions. This framework makes it convenient to write code in sharable modules.

```
;;; Method 1
(defmethod install ((sw basic-product) (os basic-os))
  (restore-product sw os)
  (compile-product sw os)
  (configure-site sw os)
  (verify-product sw os))
```

Here we consider what methods are needed for each of the four installation operations.

Restore   This probably uses a system-dependent function for restoring data from tape. Since this operation depends on only the type of operating system, it can be implemented by one primary method for each type of operating system:

```
(defmethod restore-product (sw (os genera)) body)
(defmethod restore-product (sw (os unix)) body)
```

The sw argument is used for describing which product to restore from tape. The only part of restore-product that depends on both the type of the product and the type of the operating system is the pathname where the source file should be stored. The bodies of the restore-product methods call get-source-pathname for this information:

```
(defgeneric get-source-pathname (product os)
  (:documentation "Returns a string."))

(defmethod get-source-pathname ((sw life) (os unix))
  "/bin/games/life.lsp")

(defmethod get-source-pathname ((sw adventure) (os unix))
  "/bin/games/adventure.lsp")

(defmethod get-source-pathname ((sw life) (os genera))
  "sys:games;life.lisp")

(defmethod get-source-pathname ((sw adventure) (os genera))
  "sys:games;adventure.lisp")
```

Compile   This operation can probably be done with one default method.

```
(defmethod compile-product (sw os)
  (compile-file (get-source-pathname sw os)))
```

Configure   This step configures the site to understand about the new software package. It might include updating some configuration files, such as designating a location for storing any error messages generated by the software. This step probably depends on both the type of software product and the type of operating system:

```
(defmethod configure-site ((sw life) (os genera)) body)
(defmethod configure-site ((sw adventure) (os genera)) body)
(defmethod configure-site ((sw life) (os unix)) body)
(defmethod configure-site ((sw adventure) (os unix)) body)
```

Verify   This runs a test suite on the software product to ensure
              that the installation was successful. Since the internal tests
              work the same way for a given software product regardless
              of the type of operating system, the methods specialize on-
              ly the software product parameter:

```
(defmethod verify-product ((sw life) os) body)
(defmethod verify-product ((sw adventure) os) body)
```

At this point, the design of the program is done and only the implementation remains. We have sketched out an implementation based entirely
on primary methods. It might happen that this sketch does not account
for every piece of the installation. If we identify behavior that must be
added to this sketch, we can always use before- and after-methods.

This design makes for a reasonable protocol. To add support for a
new software product or another operating system, we need only implement methods for a subset of the installation operations. This design effectively separates the complexities of the operating system from the
software product:

- We could add a new software product by defining methods for
  configure-site, verify-product, and get-source-pathname

- We could support a new operating system by defining methods for
  configure-site, restore-product, and get-source-pathname

4.4 METHODS FOR COMMON LISP TYPES

CLOS provides classes corresponding to some (but not all) of the standard COMMON LISP types. The name of such a class is the same as the
name of the type. For example, there is a class named array corresponding to the type array. These classes are provided for a single reason: to
enable you to write methods that specialize on COMMON LISP types.

Classes Corresponding to COMMON LISP Types

We have already seen one example of a class corresponding to a COMMON LISP type—the class t, which corresponds to the type t. The class t appears as the last (least specific) class in all class precedence lists, including classes defined by users and classes provided by CLOS.

Table 4.1 lists the classes corresponding to COMMON LISP types and the class precedence list of each class. This table is adapted from "Common Lisp Object System Specification" with permission from the authors.

Class	Class Precedence List
array	(array t)
bit-vector	(bit-vector vector array sequence t)
character	(character t)
complex	(complex number t)
cons	(cons list sequence t)
float	(float number t)
integer	(integer rational number t)
list	(list sequence t)
null	(null symbol list sequence t)
number	(number t)
ratio	(ratio rational number t)
rational	(rational number t)
sequence	(sequence t)
string	(string vector array sequence t)
symbol	(symbol t)
t	(t)
vector	(vector array sequence t)

Table 4.1 Precedence of classes corresponding to COMMON LISP types.

These classes have multiple inheritance. The class/subclass relationships among them parallel the type/subtype relationships described in Steele's *Common LISP: The Language.* Consider the type vector:

- The type vector is a subtype of sequence and array
- The class vector is a subclass of sequence and array

For each class corresponding to a COMMON LISP type, if *Common LISP: The Language* specifies a type/subtype relationship, the class/subclass relationship is determined accordingly. In some cases, however, no type/subtype relationship was specified, and the CLOS working group decided on the precedence order. For example, the type `string` is a subtype of both `array` and `sequence`, but COMMON LISP does not specify a type/subtype relationship between `array` and `sequence`. The CLOS working group decided that `array` should precede `sequence` in the class precedence list for `string`,

There must be a completely specified class precedence list for each class, in order for CLOS to choose the precedence of methods. One reason why the CLOS working group did not specify that all COMMON LISP types should have corresponding classes is that some types have ill-defined relationships to other types, and it would be difficult to decide the precedence orders of the types. For example, consider what happens if the argument is the instance 7, and two methods are applicable: one specializes on `(integer 0 10)` and the other specializes on `(integer 5 15)`—which method should be deemed more specific? Since the semantics of some types do not lend themselves to a strict precedence order, those types do not have corresponding classes.

If a COMMON LISP type does not have a corresponding class, you cannot define a method that specializes on that type. CLOS does not support classes for type specifiers that are lists, such as

```
(integer 0 10)
(string 25)
(not number)
(vector (mod 256))
```

Built-in Classes

Usually, classes corresponding to COMMON LISP types are implemented as "built-in classes," which means they do not have all the properties of classes defined with `defclass`. Built-in classes are implemented in a special, system-dependent way, to take advantage of a machine's architecture, or for other reasons. For the most part, it does not make sense to implement these classes with `defclass`, because they do not neatly fit into that model.

The decision of how to implement classes corresponding to COMMON LISP types is made by each CLOS implementation. Any of these classes could be implemented as a built-in class or as a user-defined class.

Although built-in classes follow the CLOS model in some ways (they have multiple inheritance; they have instances; they inherit from the class t, and you can define methods that specialize on them), they diverge from the model in other ways. These are the significant differences between built-in classes and user-defined classes:

- *Structure.* The structure of a user-defined class is in the form of slots. However, the internal structure of built-in classes is usually not represented by slots. For example, the value of a symbol is probably not stored in a slot in most CLOS implementations.

- *Creation of instances.* To create instances of user-defined classes, you can use `make-instance`. However, CLOS does not allow using `make-instance` to create instances of built-in classes. You use an independent mechanism for creating instances, such as using the `cons` function to create an instance of `cons`.

- *Use as a superclass.* CLOS does not allow you to include a built-in class as a direct superclass of any user-defined class. The only exception to this rule is the class named `t`, which is automatically a superclass of every class.

- *Inheritance from* `standard-object`. Recall that `standard-object` is implicitly included as a superclass of user-defined classes. In contrast, `standard-object` is not a superclass of built-in classes. This distinction makes it possible for implementations to provide default methods intended for user-defined classes only.

The CLOS specification defines a set of requirements for implementations to follow with regard to built-in classes, but it also allows implementations to support extensions in this area. Here are two extensions that you might encounter:

- CLOS implementations may provide classes for other COMMON LISP types, in addition to those required. This might include classes for `pathname`, `package`, or others. All such classes must adhere to the precedence implied by their type/subtype relationships defined in Steele's *Common LISP: The Language.*

- As mentioned earlier, CLOS implementations can choose to implement the class for any COMMON LISP type either as a built-in class (which follows the restrictions noted) or as a user-defined class. For example, a CLOS implementation is free to define the class `string` by using `defclass`. When this is done, you can do anything with the class `string` that you can do with other classes defined by `defclass`.

Note that programs that depend on extensions to CLOS are not readily portable to other CLOS implementations.

Examples of Methods for COMMON LISP Types

We can illustrate defining methods for COMMON LISP types by implementing a simple network protocol for performing remote evaluation. This program enables a user to send a LISP form to another machine over a network and receive the result of evaluating that form. The machine that sends the form is called the *client machine*, and the machine that performs the evaluation and returns the result to the client is called the *server machine*.

The portion of this program pertaining to COMMON LISP types lies in the sending and receiving of LISP objects over the network. A LISP object lives in one LISP world, and it is not possible or desirable to transmit the actual object. Instead, the client machine encodes a LISP object into a representation suitable for sending over the network. On the other side, the server machine decodes the representation and creates or obtains a LISP object equivalent to the object that was encoded. The result of the evaluation is then encoded by the server, transmitted, and decoded by the client machine.

Figure 4.3 shows the interaction between the client and the server machines during a remote evaluation.

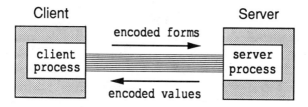

Figure 4.3 Remote evaluation.

Decoding and encoding are analogous to the LISP reading and printing operations: The LISP reader takes a typed-in representation of an object and generates a LISP object; the printer takes a LISP object and generates a representation of it suitable for printing. Like the printer and reader, the decoding and encoding methods preserve only the "simple" characteristics of objects. For example, the contents of an array are encoded, but any fill pointer is not.

The implementation of encoding takes advantage of classes corresponding to COMMON LISP types. The remote-evaluation program supports the transmission of simple LISP objects, such as lists, integers, characters, strings, symbols, and vectors. We provide methods for encoding these objects; these methods specialize on the classes corresponding to the various types of objects. It is possible to extend this model to send instances of user-defined classes as well, by providing encoding and decoding methods for those classes.

Although the main point of this example is to show the encoding and decoding, for the sake of completeness we also describe the top-level functions that call the encoding and decoding generic functions.

A Sample Remote Evaluation Session

We begin by describing how to use the remote evaluation program. We create a `remote-eval-stream` and call the `remote-eval` function to send forms to the stream and receive the results. Finally, we close the stream:

```
(setq *my-stream* (make-remote-eval-stream server-machine))

(remote-eval *my-stream* "hello") => "hello"
(remote-eval *my-stream* '(+ 1 23)) => 24

(close *my-stream*)
```

The Top-Level Functions

`make-remote-eval-stream` creates a network connection to the server machine and returns a bidirectional binary eight-bit byte stream. Once the stream has been created, a process is started on the server to run the `eval-server` function (defined below). Closing this stream kills the server process and closes the network connection. Since the implementation of `make-remote-eval-stream` is necessarily specific to the operating system, it is not given here.

`remote-eval` implements the client side; it sends a form to the server, receives the result of evaluating that form, and returns the result. The form is evaluated in the server's environment, and any side effects happen in that environment. This example does not transmit printed output, transmit multiple return values, or handle errors generated by the evaluation of the form on the server; any of these features could be added.

```
;;; This must be defined on the client machine.
(defun remote-eval (stream form)
   (encode form stream)
   (force-output stream)
   ;; Read the return value
   ;; The first byte is a control byte
   (decode (read-byte stream) stream))
```

eval-server implements the server side; it continually reads forms sent to it, evaluates the forms, and returns the results. When the stream is closed, this process is killed.

```
;;; This must be defined on the server machine.
(defun eval-server (stream)
   (loop (encode
             (eval (decode (read-byte stream) stream))
             stream)
         (force-output stream))))
```

The Encoding and Decoding Protocol

The bulk of the program lies in the encoding and decoding of Lisp objects. We shall use a simple protocol for this purpose. To encode an object, we first transmit on the stream a control byte that declares the type of object. (A control byte is an eight-bit byte.) We then encode and transmit the representation of the object itself; the implementation of this varies, depending on the type of object. When decoding, we read a control byte from the stream; this byte indicates what type of object is being transmitted. We then decode the bytes that follow and convert the encoded representation into a Lisp object. The implementation of decoding an object depends on the type of object.

The method for encoding any one kind of object (such as symbols) works together with the method for decoding that kind of object. Those methods must use the same technique for encoding and decoding. However, the methods for encoding and decoding another type of object (such as characters) can use an entirely different technique for encoding and decoding from the technique used for symbols. The only requirement is that the decoding method for any given type of object must understand how the encoding method for that type of object works.

Our protocol consists of two generic functions:

```
(defgeneric encode (object stream)
   (:documentation
 "Encode object and send the result to stream."))

(defgeneric decode (code stream)
   (:documentation
 "Based on the code, read an encoded representation
from the stream, decode, and create an object."))
```

This is an extensible protocol; it is a straightforward matter to extend it to support additional types of objects. To do so, we would supply methods for encoding and decoding. There is no need to change the code that calls encode and decode. This is one clear benefit of using generic functions instead of having the callers use a typecase to select the code for encoding and decoding the various types of objects.

This example shows how to encode and decode a handful of types of objects. Each type of object has a corresponding control byte. These control bytes are

```
(defconstant %positive-integer 1)
(defconstant %negative-integer 2)
(defconstant %character 3)
(defconstant %symbol 4)
(defconstant %string 5)
(defconstant %list 6)
(defconstant %vector 7)
```

Encoding Integers

To encode an integer, we send the control byte indicating positive or negative integer, then the length of the integer, then the absolute value of the integer itself. The length of the integer is always sent in one byte.

```
(defmethod encode ((num integer) stream)
  (cond ((minusp num)
          (write-byte %negative-integer stream)
          (setq num (abs num)))
        (t
          (write-byte %positive-integer stream)))
  (let ((n-bytes (ceiling (integer-length num) 8)))
    (write-byte n-bytes stream)
    (dotimes (i n-bytes)
      (write-byte (ldb (byte 8 0) num) stream)
      (setq num (ash num -8)))))
```

To decode integers, we will need one method for decoding positive integers and another method for decoding negative integers. The method that decodes positive integers will be called when the code is %positive-integer. That method will read the length of the integer and then the integer itself; it can then create (read) the integer and be finished. The next byte on the stream is a new control byte, which is the start of a new encoded object.

By sending the length of integers in one byte, we have implicitly placed a limitation on the value of integers transmitted: No value of num for which (> (ceiling (integer-length (abs num)) 8) 255) is true can be transmitted, which means the maximum integer length is 2040. Using the definition of integer-length on page 224 of Steele's *Common LISP: The Language*, the maximum positive integer is (1- (expt 2 (* 8 255))) and the most negative integer is the negative of that. The limit is therefore very large, a bit over 10 raised to the 614th power.

The decoding methods are given in the next section, "Methods for Individual LISP Objects," page 94.

Encoding Characters

To encode a character, we send the control byte indicating character and then the ASCII code of the character in the next byte. This method sends only the character's code, and ignores any font or bits.

To allow for differences in the native character sets of the server and client machines, we convert the character to its ASCII code when encoding, and convert it from ASCII to the corresponding code in the native character set when decoding. The function char-to-ascii is implementation dependent and is not provided here. It is necessary that char-to-ascii return a value less than 256 so it will fit within an eight-bit byte.

```
(defmethod encode ((char character) stream)
  (write-byte %character stream)
  (write-byte (char-to-ascii char) stream))
```

Encoding Lists and Vectors

To encode a list or vector, we determine the appropriate control byte, then call encode-sequence to send the control byte, the length of the sequence, and the encoded representation of each element of the sequence.

```
(defmethod encode ((list list) stream)
  (encode-sequence list stream %list))

(defmethod encode ((vector vector) stream)
  (encode-sequence vector stream %vector))

(defun encode-sequence (seq stream code)
  (let ((length (length seq)))
    (write-byte code stream)
    (encode length stream)
    (dotimes (i length)
      (encode (elt seq i) stream))))
```

The two methods call the encode-sequence function to do the sharable part of the work. This is a modular design that uses an ordinary function instead of a generic function. There is no advantage in implementing encode-sequence as a generic function in this context.

Encoding Strings

A string is a vector, so the method for encoding vectors is applicable for strings, and it would work fine for them. However, we are going to provide a method for string for efficiency reasons. It is easy to optimize the encoding of strings because we know that each element of a string is a character and will fit in one byte. When we encode a string, there is no need to encode each character of the string. In contrast, there is no way of knowing what the elements of a vector are, so each element must be encoded.

To encode a string, we send the control byte indicating string, then the length of the string, then each character of the string. Any fill pointers, bits, or fonts are not encoded.

```
(defmethod encode ((string string) stream)
  (let ((length (length string)))
    (write-byte %string stream)
    ;; careful to allow strings greater than 256 chars
    (encode length stream)
    (dotimes (i length)
      (write-byte (char-to-ascii (aref string i)) stream))))
```

When encode is called with a string as its first argument, two methods are applicable: the method that specializes on string, and the method that specializes on vector. To determine which method is more specific, CLOS consults the class precedence list of string, which is

```
(string vector array sequence t)
```

Since the class string has precedence over the class vector, the method that specializes on string is more specific than the method that specializes on vector.

Encoding Symbols

To encode a symbol and its package, we send the control byte indicating symbol, the encoded representation of the symbol's name, and the encoded representation of the symbol's package. Note that the value, function definition, and any properties of the symbol are not transmitted. Also, the package must exist on the server side.

```
(defmethod encode ((symbol symbol) stream)
  (write-byte %symbol stream)
  (encode (symbol-name symbol) stream)
  (encode (package-name (symbol-package symbol)) stream))
```


Design and Efficiency Considerations

Note that the method for character is quite efficient; it sends one control byte, then the ASCII character code. In contrast, the method for symbol results in a lot of overhead. That method sends the control byte indicating symbol, then the encoded representation of the symbol's name, then the encoded representation of the symbol's package. Table 4.2 shows the encoded representation of the symbol + in the package lisp.

Datum	Meaning
4	%symbol
5	%string
1	%positive-integer
1	length of the integer
1	length of the string
43	ASCII character code of +
5	%string
1	%positive-integer
1	length of the integer
4	length of the string
76	ASCII character code of L
73	ASCII character code of I
83	ASCII character code of S
80	ASCII character code of P

Table 4.2 Encoding of the symbol + in the lisp package.

The encoded representation of symbols uses five control bytes. This is a result of using encode on both the symbol's name and its package. If speed is important, we can devise a more efficient strategy for encoding symbols. However, the current strategy has two benefits. First, it allows for error checking on the decoding side: the decode method expects a symbol to contain a string (the symbol's name) followed by another string (the symbol's package). Second, this method calls the method that specializes on string instead of duplicating the work accomplished by that method.

The overall design of encoding and decoding is simple, modular, and effective. This design easily accommodates improvements and additions to the program in several areas:

- Tuning for greater efficiency
- Transmitting multiple return values
- Transmitting printed output
- Handling errors encountered in the evaluation of the form on the server
- Extending this protocol for transmitting additional types of objects

4.5 METHODS FOR INDIVIDUAL LISP OBJECTS

So far, we have seen methods that specialize on the class of the arguments to the generic function. That is, the parameter specializers are classes. Sometimes, it is useful to write a method that specializes on an individual LISP object. A method that specializes one of its parameters on an individual LISP object is called an *individual method*.

Applicability and Precedence of Individual Methods

Suppose you have an operation that works a certain way when the argument is a number, but should work differently if the argument is the integer 0. Method 2 is an individual method. Its second parameter is specialized on the integer 0. The parameter specializer is the list (eql 0).

```
;;; Method 1
(defmethod divide ((dividend number) (divisor number))
  (/ dividend divisor))

;;; Method 2
(defmethod divide ((dividend number) (zero (eql 0)))
  (error "Cannot divide by zero."))
```

The lambda-list of an individual method contains a parameter such as

(*var* (eql *form*))

The parameter specializer is (eql *object*), where *object* is the result of evaluating the *form*. The *form* is evaluated only once, when the method is defined.

When divide is called with 0 as its second argument, both methods are applicable. The rule of applicability of individual methods follows. Note that since the test for applicability uses eql, method 2 is applicable for only the integer 0, and not for 0.0.

> ### Rule of applicability of an individual method:
>
> For a parameter specializer of the form (eql *object*), the argument to the generic function satisfies the parameter specializer if the argument is eql to the *object*. In other words, this expression must be true:
>
> (eql *argument* 'object)

Method 2 is more specific, as you would expect. The rule of precedence of individual methods follows.

Rule of precedence of an individual method:

When two parameter specializers are compared, a parameter specializer of the form (eql *object*) is always more specific than a class.

Examples of Individual Methods

Consider the job of decoding the encoded representations of LISP objects. Each LISP object is encoded and decoded according to its type, so it makes sense to write separate methods for encoding and decoding each different type of object.

The encoder has a LISP object as its argument, so those methods can specialize on the classes of objects. However, the decoder does not have LISP objects as arguments; instead it reads from a stream and is alerted to the type of an object by the control byte preceding the object in the stream. Thus, the decoder cannot supply methods that specialize on classes, but it can use individual methods that specialize on each of these control bytes.

The generic function decode is repeated here:

```
(defgeneric decode (code stream)
  (:documentation
"Based on the code, read an encoded representation
from the stream, decode, and create an object."))
```

Each method for decode specializes its first argument, and exactly one method is applicable for each different control byte. Recall that decode is called with one byte as its first argument (this is the control byte) and a stream as its second argument. The definition of remote-eval is repeated here to illustrate how decode is called:

```
(defun remote-eval (stream form)
  (encode form stream)
  (force-output stream)
  ;; Read the return value
  ;; The first byte is a control byte
  (decode (read-byte stream) stream))
```

Decoding Integers

We need two methods to decode integers, because the method for encoding integers sends two different control bytes, depending on whether the integer is positive or negative. The first method is applicable when the first argument is the control byte indicating positive integer. Similarly, the second method is applicable when the first argument is the control byte indicating negative integer.

```
(defmethod decode ((code (eql %positive-integer)) stream)
  (decode-integer stream))


(defmethod decode ((code (eql %negative-integer)) stream)
  (- (decode-integer stream)))


(defun decode-integer (stream)
  (let ((num 0)
        (n-bytes (read-byte stream)))
    (dotimes (i n-bytes)
      (setq num (dpb (read-byte stream) (byte 8 (* i 8)) num)))
    num))
```

%positive-integer and %negative-integer are evaluated exactly once, at the time these methods are defined.

The function decode-integer does the sharable part of the work; it is called by both methods. There is no advantage in implementing decode-integer as a generic function.

Decoding Characters

To decode a character, we read one byte and convert it from the ASCII code to the corresponding character code in the native character set. The function ascii-to-char is implementation dependent and is not provided here.

```
(defmethod decode ((code (eql %character)) stream)
  (ascii-to-char (read-byte stream)))
```

Decoding Lists and Vectors

To decode a list or vector, we read the length of the sequence, then decode each element in the sequence. Again, we can use a function to do the sharable part of the work.

```
(defmethod decode ((code (eql %list)) stream)
  (decode-sequence stream 'list))

(defmethod decode ((code (eql %vector)) stream)
  (decode-sequence stream 'vector))

(defun decode-sequence (stream type)
  (let* ((length (decode (read-byte stream) stream))
         (seq (make-sequence type length)))
    (dotimes (i length)
      (setf (elt seq i)
            (decode (read-byte stream) stream)))
    seq))
```

Decoding Strings

To decode a string, we read the length of the string, then each character of the string.

```
(defmethod decode ((code (eql %string)) stream)
  (let* ((length (decode (read-byte stream) stream))
         (string (make-string length)))
    (dotimes (i length)
      (setf (aref string i) (ascii-to-char (read-byte stream))))
    string))
```

Decoding Symbols

To decode a symbol, we first decode the name and then decode the package. Note that this method does not create a package if it does not already exist.

```
;;; Does not create the package.
(defmethod decode ((code (eql %symbol)) stream)
  (let ((code (read-byte stream)))
    (when (/= %string code)
      (error "The symbol's name must be a string."))
    (let ((symbol-name (decode code stream)))
      (setq code (read-byte stream))
      (when (/= %string code)
        (error "The symbol's package name must be a string."))
      (let* ((pkg-name (decode code stream))
             (pkg (find-package pkg-name)))
        (when (null pkg)
          (error "Package named ~A not found." pkg-name))
        (intern symbol-name pkg)))))
```

4.6 SUMMARY OF METHOD INHERITANCE

The inheritance of methods involves two separate mechanisms. Both happen automatically as part of the generic dispatch.

1.   Selecting the set of applicable methods
2.   Ranking the applicable methods in order of precedence

To select the set of applicable methods, CLOS requires knowledge of the arguments to the generic function, and the methods defined for the generic function. The following general rule takes into account all kinds of methods, including methods that specialize only one parameter, multi-methods, and individual methods:

General rule of method applicability:

A method is applicable if each of its required parameters is satisfied by the corresponding argument (*arg*) to the generic function.

Required Parameter	Test
(*var* (eql *form*))	(eql *arg* '*object*)
(*var* *class-name*)	(typep *arg* '*class-name*)
var	(typep *arg* 't)

In the first case, the *object* is obtained by evaluating *form* once, at the time the method is defined. In the last case, the required parameter is unspecialized, which is equivalent to being specialized on the class t. Any argument satisfies an unspecialized parameter, because every LISP object is of the type t.

To rank applicable methods in order of precedence, CLOS requires knowledge of the following:

- The set of applicable methods
- The class precedence list of the class of each required argument to the generic function
- The *argument precedence order* of the generic function

When ranking the precedence of two methods, CLOS compares the parameter specializers of the methods. An unspecialized parameter is equivalent to the class named t being the parameter specializer.

Normally, the argument precedence order is left to right, meaning that CLOS starts by comparing the first (leftmost) parameter specializer of method A to the first parameter specializer of method B. If the two parameter specializers are different, CLOS uses the following rule to determine which parameter specializer is more specific and ranks the methods on that basis, without considering any other parameter specializers. If the two parameter specializers are the same, however, CLOS cannot rank the precedence of the methods on that basis. CLOS proceeds to the next pair of parameter specializers, and so on, until it finds a pair of parameter specializers that are different; then the methods are ranked on the basis of that pair of parameter specializers.

If two methods have all the same parameter specializers, they must have different qualifiers. In this case, it does not matter which method is more specific.

Rule of ranking parameter specializers:

A parameter specializer of (eql *object*) is more specific than a class.

When both parameter specializers are classes, they are ranked according to the class precedence list of the class of the corresponding argument to the generic function. The class precedence list indicates which class is more specific than the other.

Argument Precedence Order

The precedence of methods depends on the *argument precedence order* of the generic function. By default, CLOS uses left-to-right argument precedence order, which means the first argument (the leftmost) is more important in ranking precedence than the following arguments. You can use the :argument-precedence-order option to defgeneric to specify a different order.

The argument precedence order is important when CLOS ranks two methods that specialize different parameters or methods that specialize more than one parameter. Consider the following methods:

```
;;; Method A
(defmethod install ((sw basic-product) non-os)
  body)
```

```
;;; Method B
(defmethod install (non-product (os basic-os))
  body)
```

Method A specializes its first parameter but leaves its second parameter unspecialized. Method B specializes its second parameter but leaves its first parameter unspecialized. If we consider the first parameters in isolation, method A is more specific, because any specialized parameter takes precedence over an unspecialized one. However, if we consider the second parameters in isolation, method B is more specific. The argument precedence order resolves this conflict by stating which of the arguments should be considered first.

5

Controlling the Generic Dispatch

All the sample programs we have written so far rely on before-methods, primary methods, and after-methods. We can call these techniques the "core framework" of CLOS. This chapter describes how to use several advanced techniques that expand the core framework or replace it entirely.

5.1 THE CORE FRAMEWORK

In the core framework, the flow of control is as follows:

1. All applicable before-methods are called in most-specific-first order
2. The most specific applicable primary method is called
3. All applicable after-methods are called in most-specific-last order

In the core framework, any values of before- or after-methods are ignored, and the generic function returns the values of the primary method. If there is no applicable primary method, an error is signaled.

5.2 DECLARATIVE AND IMPERATIVE TECHNIQUES

Within the context of the core framework, you *declare* the role of a method (by its qualifier). We call this a *declarative technique*. You assign a role to a method and rely on the generic dispatch procedure to call the applicable methods according to their roles within the core framework.

This declarative technique works well for programs that fit naturally into the core framework. However, sometimes you need to control the generic dispatch procedure more directly. CLOS offers some *imperative techniques* that enable you to control explicitly which method is called next. The imperative techniques are

- Providing an *around-method* to "wrap around" the core framework
- Calling a shadowed primary method

CLOS also provides additional declarative techniques, both involving a departure from the familiar method roles of the core framework. You can specify that the generic dispatch should support different method roles and use a different framework entirely.

CLOS supplies a set of built-in frameworks, which are called *method combination types*. The method combination type controls what method roles are supported, the order in which the various kinds of methods are called, and how the values of the generic function are generated. You can either use one of the built-in method combination types or invent a new one. Thus, the new declarative techniques are

- Using a built-in method combination type
- Inventing and using a new method combination type

5.3 AROUND-METHODS

An around-method expands the core framework by wrapping a layer of code around it. An around-method usually performs some computation and calls `call-next-method` to invoke the methods of the core framework. To specify that a method is an around-method, include the keyword `:around` as the method qualifier in the `defmethod` form.

Around-methods offer a new kind of power that can be useful. They can set up an environment to be in effect during the execution of the other methods. For example, an around-method can set up a `catch` or bind a special variable. An around-method can use `with-lock` to seize and hold a lock while the other methods are called. Although you could use a before-method to seize a lock and an after-method to release it, that would not have the same effect as using with-lock in an around-method: using with-lock ensures that the lock is released even if an abort occurs.

When only one around-method is applicable, CLOS calls that around-method first and returns its values as the values of the generic function. (This is an important distinction from before- and after-methods, whose values are ignored.) If that around-method calls call-next-method, the entire core framework is called, and call-next-method returns the values of the core framework to the around-method.

Around-methods are different from the methods we have seen so far, because around-methods control which method is called next. If an around-method uses call-next-method, the "next method" is called. If an around-method does not use call-next-method, however, no other methods are called. Thus, an around-method can prevent other methods from being called.

In the general case, any number of around-methods can be applicable. In summary, the generic dispatch works like this:

1. CLOS calls the most specific around-method; its values are the values of the generic function.

2. When an around-method calls call-next-method

    • If there are other applicable around-methods, the next most specific around-method is called, and its values are returned by call-next-method.

    • If not, the entire core framework (before-methods, the primary method, and after-methods) is called, and its values are returned by call-next-method.

Example of an Around-Method

As a simple example, we might provide an around-method to keep track of how long an installation process takes. The role of the around-method is well suited to the task of timing an installation. The following method is applicable to all supported products and operating systems, and its role in the generic dispatch ensures that it wraps around the entire installation. This method ordering allows it to start the timing before the other methods run, and finish the timing after the other methods return.

```
(defmethod install :around
           ((sw basic-product) (os basic-os))
   (declare (ignore sw os))
   (let* ((start-time (get-internal-real-time))
          (result (call-next-method)))
      (if (null result)                  ; normal completion
          (format t "~&Installation completed in ~A seconds."
                    (round (- (get-internal-real-time)
                              start-time)
                           internal-time-units-per-second))
          (format t "~&Installation failed."))
      result))
```

The timing example illustrates some interesting aspects of around-methods:

- This method uses the value returned by `call-next-method`. This shows a means for communication between methods that we have not seen in the core framework. The around-method uses the result of the core framework to decide which output to produce, and then returns the result. It is customary, although not required, for around-methods to return the value or values of `call-next-method`.

- This method works correctly only if there is no other applicable around-method. If there were a more specific around-method, it would be called before this one, so this method would not be timing the complete installation. This is one example of how around-methods can be tricky; often, you need explicit knowledge of the other applicable methods in order to write an around-method. Thus, using around-methods can lead to nonmodular code.

- This around-method specializes on two basic classes, yet it is the first method called by the generic dispatch (since there are no other applicable around-methods). An around-method allows you to define code associated with less specific classes to perform some computation in advance of the other kinds of methods provided by more specific classes.

- Although this method always calls `call-next-method`, it is possible for an around-method to choose not to call `call-next-method`. Therefore, an around-method can prevent before-methods, the primary method, and after-methods from being called. In contrast, a before-method cannot prevent other methods from being called without using `error` or another function that abandons the current computation.

5.4 CALLING A SHADOWED PRIMARY METHOD

This section describes the second imperative technique. CLOS allows you to expand the second step of the core framework: the calling of the primary method. In the core framework, only the most specific primary method is called. Any other applicable primary methods are "shadowed" by the most specific one. However, the most specific primary method can call `call-next-method` to invoke the next most specific primary method. The shadowed method can return values, and its caller can continue to execute and make use of those values.

CLOS signals an error if a generic function is called and there is no applicable primary method. Also, if a method calls `call-next-method` and there is no next method, CLOS signals an error. You can use `next-method-p` within the body of a method to find out whether there is another applicable primary method.

Any primary method can call `call-next-method`, which results in the calling of the next most specific primary method. Actually, a primary method can call `call-next-method` more than once, and each time the same "next method" is called.

5.5 USING A DIFFERENT METHOD COMBINATION TYPE

CLOS enables you to specify that the generic dispatch should use an entirely different framework and recognize different method roles. Each generic function has a *method combination type*, which defines the framework that the generic dispatch follows. The method combination type controls

- The method qualifiers that are supported and what their roles are
- The order in which the methods are called
- The way the values of the generic function are generated

At one point in the generic dispatch, CLOS takes the set of applicable methods and combines them into the LISP code that is the implementation of the generic function. This LISP code is called the *effective method*. CLOS calls the effective method and returns its values to the caller of the generic function. The method combination type controls how the applicable methods are combined into the effective method.

The Default Method Combination Type: standard

The default method combination type is named `standard`. It supports
methods with no qualifiers (primary methods) and methods with any
one of these qualifiers: `:before`, `:after`, or `:around`. The `standard` method
combination type supports using `call-next-method` in around-methods
and in primary methods. We have already discussed the order in which
the methods are called and how the values are generated, and we summarize this information in "Summary of the Standard Method Combination Type," page 113.

We can give a rough idea of the effective method of a generic function that uses standard method combination. Suppose the set of applicable methods includes two before-methods, two primary methods, and
two after-methods. In this example, there are no applicable around-
methods, and `call-next-method` is not used. The effective method calls
the before-methods in most-specific-first order, the most specific primary
method, and the after-methods in most-specific-last order. The values of
the primary method are returned. Thus, the effective method resembles
this:

```
(multiple-value-prog1
   (progn (most-specific-before-method args)
          (least-specific-before-method args)
          (most-specific-primary-method args))
   (least-specific-after-method args)
   (most-specific-after-method args))
```

The progn Method Combination Type

Suppose we need to implement a function for cleanly shutting down a
computer resource, such as a network interface. The network interface
is an instance of a class, which is constructed from several superclasses.
The `shutdown` generic function should allow each class the opportunity to
do cleanup work in preparation for the shutdown. One class might turn
off the hardware, and other classes might clear the pending input and
output queues and inform the higher layers of the network that the device is no longer operational.

For this generic function it is reasonable to use a framework that
calls all applicable primary methods in most-specific-first order. This
framework allows any class to provide a method for `shutdown`. You can
visualize such a framework as a LISP form that uses `progn` to call all applicable primary methods:

```
(progn (method-1 args)      ; inform higher layers
       (method-2 args)      ; flush pending queues
       (method-3 args))     ; turn off hardware
```

CLOS offers a set of built-in method combination types, and `progn` is one of them. Except for the `standard` method combination type, none of the built-in method combination types recognize before- or after-methods.

Using the progn Method Combination Type

To specify that a generic function should use a different type of method combination, we use the `:method-combination` option to `defgeneric`, as shown here:

```
(defgeneric shutdown (interface)
  (:method-combination progn))
```

To write primary methods that are intended to be used with the `progn` method combination type, we supply the symbol `progn` as the method qualifier:

```
(defmethod shutdown progn ((interface interface))
  body)
```

CLOS signals an error if you define a method whose qualifier is not recognized by the method combination type in use by the generic function.

5.6 BUILT-IN METHOD COMBINATION TYPES

In addition to `standard` (the default method combination type), CLOS provides the following built-in method combination types:

+	and	append
list	max	min
nconc	or	progn

Notice that these method combination types have the same names as LISP functions or special forms; we call them *operator method combination types*. Each one defines a framework that combines the applicable primary methods inside a call to the LISP operator of the same name.

The primary methods are combined in most-specific-first order. For example, if there are three primary methods, numbered from most to least specific, the effective method resembles this:

> (*operator*   (*primary-method-1 args*)
>   (*primary-method-2 args*)
>   (*primary-method-3 args*))

The semantics of operator method combination types are defined by the LISP operator of the same name. For example, when the `progn` method combination type is used, the operator is the `progn` special form. Thus, the framework follows the semantics of `progn`: all the methods are called, and the values of the last method are returned. Similarly, when the `list` method combination type is used, the result is a list of the values of all the methods.

Primary Methods in Operator Method Combination Types

In `standard` method combination, an unqualified method is a primary method. This is not so, however, when operator method combination types are used; they do not accept unqualified methods. A primary method intended to be used with an operator method combination type must have the method qualifier that is the name of the method combination type.

For example, the generic function `total-electric-supply` uses the `+` method combination type:

```
(defgeneric total-electric-supply (region)
  (:method-combination +))
```

A primary method for `total-electric-supply` must have the symbol `+` as its method qualifier:

```
(defmethod total-electric-supply + ((city city))
  body)
```

The operator method combination types do not support using `call-next-method` in primary methods.

Around-Methods in Operator Method Combination Types

The operator method combination types support around-methods, and the use of `call-next-method` in them. A method with the keyword `:around` as its qualifier is an around-method. In the effective method, any around-methods surround the call to the operator.

Usually, when you use an operator method combination type, you supply only primary methods. However, around-methods are supported for the same reason that they are supported in standard method combination: to allow you an extra degree of control over the generic dispatch procedure. For example, you might provide one method that prints an English description of the result and then returns the result:

```
(defmethod total-electric-supply :around ((region region))
  (let ((supply (call-next-method)))
    (format t "Available electricity in ~A is: ~A"
            region supply)
    supply)))
```

Usually, around-methods return whatever values are returned by call-next-method, although this is not required.

Summary of Operator Method Combination Types

The operator method combination types do the following:

- Support primary methods and around-methods, but not before- or after-methods

- Support the use of call-next-method in around-methods, but not in primary methods

- Call any around-methods in the same way as does the standard method combination type

- Combine all applicable primary methods inside a call to the LISP operator whose name is the same as the name of the method combination type, and call these methods in most-specific-first order

- Require at least one primary method and signal an error if none exists

5.7 DEFINING A NEW METHOD COMBINATION TYPE

CLOS makes it easy to define a new operator method combination type—a framework that combines all applicable primary methods inside a LISP function, macro, or special form. The macro define-method-combination has a short form and a long form. The short form has a simple syntax and is adequate for defining many of the commonly used types of method combination.

Short Form of define-method-combination

The short form of `define-method-combination` defines an operator
method combination type. Any of the built-in operator method combination types could have been defined using the short form of `define-
method-combination`. For example, if the `progn` method combination type
were not already defined, we could define it as follows:

```
(define-method-combination progn
  :operator progn
  :identity-with-one-argument t)
```

The first argument is the name of the method combination type. The
`:operator` keyword specifies the operator that receives the values of the
methods. It is often reasonable to give the method combination type the
same name as the operator. The `:identity-with-one-argument` t option
means "this is an identity when it is called with one argument." This
option requests the compiler to optimize for cases when there is only
one applicable method; it indicates that the value of that method should
be returned as the value of the generic function, rather than calling the
operator. This makes sense for operators such as `progn`, `and`, `+`, `max`, and
all the other built-in operator method combination types.

Operator method combination types support primary methods and
around-methods, but not before- and after-methods. Around-methods
may use `call-next-method`, but primary methods may not. Primary
methods must have a method qualifier that is the same symbol as the
name of the method combination type. For related information, see
"Built-in Method Combination Types," page 107.

Long Form of define-method-combination

The long form of `define-method-combination` supports a rich and powerful syntax for defining a new framework. You can use it when none of
the built-in method combination types (including `standard`) are appropriate, and the framework cannot be defined with the short form of
`define-method-combination`. Because we believe that most applications
will fit well with one of the built-in method combination types, we do
not cover the syntax of the long form of `define-method-combination` in
this book. See the CLOS specification for more information.

5.8 GUIDELINES ON CONTROLLING THE GENERIC DISPATCH

The declarative technique relies on a consistent framework in which the methods are called according to their roles within the framework; the role of a method is declared by its qualifier. The generic dispatch automates the process of calling the appropriate applicable methods. You can predict the order of the methods without looking at the code in the bodies of the methods.

In contrast, the imperative technique allows the methods themselves to alter the course of the generic dispatch by calling `call-next-method`. This technique offers a different kind of power, while adding a considerable degree of complexity to the program. Usually, you need to understand the implementation of inherited behavior in order to use `call-next-method`; in a sense, this is a violation of modularity. However, you cannot write some programs without resorting to the imperative technique. We recommend that you use around-methods and `call-next-method` only when that power is truly necessary.

In the `shutdown` example, we used the declarative technique of using the `progn` type of method combination. We could have written the program differently, however, using the `standard` method combination type. Here, we describe two alternate implementations of `shutdown` and discuss the design considerations that led us to choose `progn` instead of the `standard` method combination type.

- *Imperative Technique:* `call-next-method`. Each class could supply a primary method that does whatever computation is desired and then calls `call-next-method` to pass control to the next most specific primary method. The least specific method must return without calling `call-next-method`.

  This scheme has several disadvantages. It is necessary to examine all the methods to understand the implementation. Any one method can break the implementation by not calling `call-next-method`. Also, this is not a consistent model; it requires the least specific method *not* to call `call-next-method`, whereas all other methods *must* call `call-next-method`. (Each method should use `next-method-p` to determine whether there is a less specific method to call.) Finally, this scheme probably requires several extra function calls, which add overhead.

- *Declarative technique: before-methods.* Each class could provide a before-method. Before-methods run in most-specific-first order, so the desired order of methods can be achieved this way. Since the standard method combination requires a primary method, at least one class must provide a primary method. The primary method does not have to do anything; it can simply return nil.

The disadvantage here is that the declared roles of the methods do not accurately reflect their purposes. We expect a primary method to do the bulk of the work, but this primary method is not essential to the implementation; it simply fulfills a requirement of the standard method combination. Usually, a before-method does auxiliary work before the primary method, but these before-methods are not auxiliary to the implementation; they *are* the implementation. This scheme tries to force a program into the standard method combination framework even though that framework is not appropriate to the program.

These techniques rely on ad hoc conventions that all methods must follow. The first convention relies on call-next-method, and the second relies on before-methods. Both conventions treat one method differently from the others.

In this example, the declarative technique of defining a new framework has one great advantage: It eliminates the need for an ad hoc convention that must be maintained by each method, in favor of a concrete and consistent framework that is automatically maintained by the generic dispatch procedure.

5.9 SUMMARY OF THE GENERIC DISPATCH PROCEDURE

When a generic function is called, the generic dispatch procedure takes charge of choosing the implementation that is appropriate for the arguments of the generic function. This process involves four steps:

1. Selecting the set of applicable methods
2. Ranking the applicable methods by precedence order
3. Combining the methods into an effective method, according to the roles of the methods and the method combination type
4. Calling the effective method and returning its values

For a complete summary of the first and second steps of this procedure, see "Summary of Method Inheritance," page 98.

In the third step, CLOS chooses the final implementation of the generic function, by combining the methods into a single body of code called the effective method. The input to the third step includes the set of applicable methods ranked by precedence order, and the method combination type. The method combination type describes how to combine the methods, based on their qualifiers. By default, a generic function uses standard method combination type. When you define and use a new type of method combination, you can customize the third step. The method combination type has no effect on any of the other steps.

CLOS implementations are free to optimize the generic dispatch procedure such that some of these steps are precomputed and thus are not performed on each generic function call.

5.10 SUMMARY OF THE STANDARD METHOD COMBINATION TYPE

The standard method combination type is the default. All generic functions use this framework, unless the defgeneric form uses the :method-combination option to specify another method combination type.

This section summarizes how the standard method combination type works, including what method roles it supports, how the various methods are combined into an effective method, and how the values are handled.

Recognized Method Roles

The standard method combination type recognizes four roles for methods, based on their qualifiers:

Qualifier	Method Role
none	A primary method
:before	Called before the primary method
:after	Called after the primary method
:around	Wrapped around all other kinds of methods

The standard method combination type supports call-next-method in around-methods and in primary methods.

Flow of Control

Figure 5.1 shows the flow of control of methods in the standard method combination. Each step poses a question; the answer to the question determines where the flow of control goes next. Notice that in the around

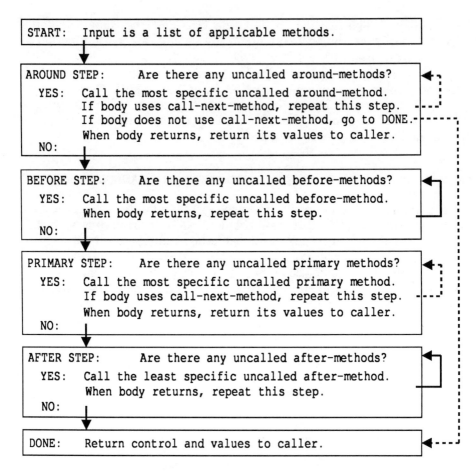

Figure 5.1 Flow of control of standard method combination.

and primary steps, there is a question that can be answered only by executing the body of the method: Does the body of this method use call-next-method? If so, the "next method" is called. For an around-method, the "next method" is the next most specific around-method if there is one; otherwise, it is the entire core framework. For a primary method, the "next method" is the next most specific primary method.

The dashed lines in Fig. 5.1 show decisions that are controlled by the use of call-next-method. For example, if there is an around-method and call-next-method is *not* used in the body, the flow of control goes directly to DONE, without calling any before-methods, primary methods, or after-methods.

If the body of a method uses `call-next-method` more than once, the same "next method" is called each time.

Errors

Figure 5.1 does not show the possible error situations. CLOS signals an error if

* There is no applicable primary method
* A primary method uses `call-next-method`, and there is no "next method" to call
* A before- or after-method uses `call-next-method`

Values

In summary, this is how the values of the methods are handled:

* Any values of before-methods and after-methods are ignored
* Each primary and around-method returns its values to its caller
* If there are no applicable around-methods, the final values of the generic function are the values returned by the most specific primary method
* If there are any applicable around-methods, the final values of the generic function are the values returned by the most specific around-method

6

Class Inheritance

CLOS uses the class precedence list to determine the precedence, or dominance, of any competing traits. This chapter describes how the class precedence list is determined and how it controls the inheritance of slots and slot options. We also discuss the classes that are implicitly included as superclasses: standard-object and t.

6.1 INHERITANCE FROM DEFAULT CLASSES

All classes implicitly include t as a superclass. This is true for user-defined classes (those we define with defclass) and built-in classes (such as array and integer). The only exception is the class t itself, which has no superclasses. One effect of inheriting from t is that every LISP object is of the type t. The type t is the root of the COMMON LISP type system, and the class t is the root of the CLOS class system.

All user-defined classes also implicitly include standard-object as a superclass, but built-in classes do not. The existence of standard-object enables CLOS implementations to define default behavior that is inherited by all user-defined classes. For example, primary methods for the class standard-object implement the print-object and describe generic functions. The classes t and standard-object do not have slots.

All classes have t as the last (least specific) class in their class precedence lists. All user-defined classes have standard-object as the second-to-last class in their class precedence lists. This is something you can take for granted; it is always true.

6.2 THE CLASS PRECEDENCE LIST

CLOS calculates the class precedence list of each class. The class precedence list contains the class itself and all its superclasses; it does not contain any duplicate classes. The order of the classes in the class precedence list is significant; it goes from most specific to least specific. If one class is more specific than a second class, that class has precedence over the second class.

The two rules governing the precedence order of classes are:

> **Rule 1 of class precedence:**
>
> A class always has precedence over its superclasses.

Rule 1 allows a class to override or modify aspects of behavior supplied by its superclasses.

> **Rule 2 of class precedence:**
>
> Each class definition sets the precedence order of its direct superclasses.

For Rule 2, the ordering constraints on the direct superclasses are obtained by the order of superclasses listed in the defclass form. That is, each class is more specific than the classes that follow it in this list.

By considering Rule 1 alone, we know the most specific class and the least specific class in any class precedence list. The class itself is always the most specific class in its own class precedence list, and the class t the least specific class in any class precedence list. (Since every class has t as a superclass, t cannot precede any class and is therefore always last in all class precedence lists.) For user-defined classes, standard-object is the second-to-last class in the class precedence list. In the examples that follow, we do not explicitly mention the ordering constraints of standard-object or t, because the constraints are always the same.

When CLOS determines the class precedence list of a class, it starts with the definition of the class. CLOS applies both rules to the class definition and obtains a set of local ordering constraints. CLOS then applies the rules to the definitions of each of the direct superclasses, each of their direct superclasses, and so on, until all paths end in the root class t. The result is a set of ordering constraints on the classes.

The next step is to find a total ordering that satisfies all the ordering constraints. CLOS does this by sorting the set of ordering constraints topologically. In other words, each of the constraints is a partial order, and the class precedence list is achieved by doing a topological sort on the set of partial orders. The result is one of these three possibilities:

Case 1. Exactly one total ordering satisfies the constraints
Case 2. Several total orderings satisfy the constraints
Case 3. No total ordering satisfies the constraints

In either of the first two cases, CLOS produces a class precedence list. In the third case, it signals an error.

We present examples of each of these cases. The examples show definitions of various stream classes that have superclasses but no slots. We do not intend to describe the semantics of these classes, but rather to focus on the mechanics of class precedence lists. (In "Developing an Advanced CLOS Program: Streams," page 171 we develop a stream example based on an organization of a large number of classes.)

Case 1: Exactly One Total Ordering Satisfies the Constraints

In this case, when CLOS applies the two class precedence rules to the class definitions of the class and all its superclasses, the result is only one possible ordering. This becomes the class precedence list.

Here is an example. Our goal is to determine the class precedence list for the class char-input-stream, given the following class definitions:

```
(defclass stream () ())
(defclass input-stream (stream) ())
(defclass char-stream (stream) ())

(defclass char-input-stream
     (char-stream input-stream)
     ())
```

The following chart gives the set of ordering constraints for char-input-stream. The symbol >> is shorthand for "precedes." Each constraint is the result of applying one of the class precedence rules to one of the class definitions. Thus, the first entry in the chart means "The class input-stream precedes the class stream, which is the result of applying Rule 1 to the input-stream class definition." Similarly, the last entry means "The class `char-stream` precedes the class `input-stream`, which is the result of applying Rule 2 to the `char-input-stream` class definition."

Constraint	Rule	Class
`input-stream >> stream`	1	`input-stream`
`char-stream >> stream`	1	`char-stream`
`char-input-stream >> char-stream`	1	`char-input-stream`
`char-input-stream >> input-stream`	1	`char-input-stream`
`char-stream >> input-stream`	2	`char-input-stream`

Exactly one total ordering satisfies the constraints, so the class precedence list for the class `char-input-stream` is

```
(char-input-stream char-stream input-stream stream
  standard-object t)
```

Although the class `stream` is included by two different classes (it is a direct superclass of both `char-stream` and `input-stream`), there are no duplicate classes in the class precedence list.

Case 2: Several Total Orderings Satisfy the Constraints

For many programs, the two class precedence rules do not yield a single class precedence order. That is, some pairs of classes might not have an ordering constraint based on the rules. This can happen when neither class is a superclass of the other (Rule 1 does not constrain their relative precedence), and no class includes both classes as direct superclasses (Rule 2 does not constrain their relative precedence). This does not pose a problem for three reasons:

- *The lack of constraints implies no conflict.* When no ordering constraint on two classes is given, this implies that their relative precedence order is not important. If the order of two classes is important, the programmer can and should set an ordering constraint by explicitly including them as direct superclasses of the new class.

- *CLOS chooses one of the possible orderings.* CLOS uses an algorithm that always yields a deterministic ranking of classes. This guarantees that all implementations of CLOS choose the same class precedence list, given the same set of class definitions. The details of the algorithm are not important, but the guarantee that the algorithm is deterministic provides a safety net for situations where a working CLOS program depends on a certain order without explicitly stating the dependency in a class definition. Such a program is portable to another CLOS implementation.

- *CLOS tries to keep family trees together in the class precedence list.* Consider a class and its superclasses to be a "family tree." When applying the algorithm to choose one ordering from the set of possible orderings, CLOS uses this guideline: The entire "family tree" of each direct superclass is kept together in the class precedence list, if that would not violate either of the two class precedence rules.

  Consider a class `ascii-disk-stream` that has two direct superclasses, `ascii-stream` and `disk-stream`. The class `ascii-stream` precedes `disk-stream`, and (if possible) all the superclasses of `ascii-stream` precede `disk-stream` in the class precedence list. The effect is that you can treat `ascii-stream` as a "black box" of behavior; `disk-stream` cannot override behavior supplied by `ascii-stream` or any of its superclasses. In cases where other ordering constraints prevent CLOS from following this guideline (that is, the result would violate one or both of the rules) CLOS chooses an ordering that keeps the members of each family tree as close together as possible.

Here we give an example of the case when several total orderings satisfy the constraints. We determine the class precedence list for the class `ascii-disk-stream`, given the following class definitions:

```
(defclass stream () ())

(defclass buffered-stream (stream) ())
(defclass disk-stream (buffered-stream) ())

(defclass char-stream (stream) ())
(defclass ascii-stream (char-stream) ())

(defclass ascii-disk-stream
      (ascii-stream
       disk-stream)
      ())
```

The set of ordering constraints for `ascii-disk-stream` is as follows:

Constraint	Rule	Class
buffered-stream >> stream	1	buffered-stream
disk-stream >> buffered-stream	1	disk-stream
char-stream >> stream	1	char-stream
ascii-stream >> char-stream	1	ascii-stream
ascii-disk-stream >> ascii-stream	1	ascii-disk-stream
ascii-disk-stream >> disk-stream	1	ascii-disk-stream
ascii-stream >> disk-stream	2	ascii-disk-stream

There are no constraints on the precedence of char-stream with respect to buffered-stream, or on the precedence of char-stream with respect to disk-stream. Here, we show three total orderings that satisfy the constraints. The middle line of each class precedence list shows where the changes occur:

```
(ascii-disk-stream ascii-stream
 char-stream disk-stream buffered-stream
 stream standard-object t)

(ascii-disk-stream ascii-stream
 disk-stream buffered-stream char-stream
 stream standard-object t)

(ascii-disk-stream ascii-stream
 disk-stream char-stream buffered-stream
 stream standard-object t)
```

In this case, CLOS chooses the first total ordering. Here, we see an illustration of the guideline that family trees are kept together. The family tree of ascii-stream precedes the family tree of disk-stream, except for the class stream, which is a superclass of both ascii-stream and disk-stream.

Sometimes it is not possible to keep family trees intact, but if two superclasses have a "common tail," it is moved to the end of the class precedence list. Suppose class A has direct superclasses B and C, and the class precedence list of B and C are as follows:

Class	Class Precedence List
B	(B B1 B2 B3 B4 D D1 D2 standard-object t)
C	(C C1 C2 D D1 D2 standard-object t)

The classes B and C have a common tail, because starting at D the two class precedence lists are equal. Prior to class D, the class precedence lists are disjoint. In the class precedence list of A, the common tail is moved to the end:

```
(A B B1 B2 B3 B4 C C1 C2 D D1 D2 standard-object t)
```

There is no need for concern if several orderings satisfy the constraints unless, in fact, the program does depend on one of the orderings. If so, you should make the ordering dependency explicit, as shown next.

How to Add Ordering Constraints

To continue the previous example, suppose some aspect of the program depends on the class disk-stream preceding the class char-stream, and on the class char-stream preceding buffered-stream. That is, you want the third of the possible total orderings to be chosen.

In this example, it is hard to conceive of any semantic reason why the stream program should have the dependencies mentioned, because there should be no interaction between the classes whose order is unconstrained. In other programs, however, there might well be interaction among various classes.

You can add the constraints mentioned by defining class ascii-disk-stream in a different way:

```
(defclass ascii-disk-stream
       (ascii-stream disk-stream
        char-stream buffered-stream)
       ())
```

The previous constraints mentioned still hold, and there are two new constraints:

Constraint	Rule	Class
disk-stream >> char-stream	2	ascii-disk-stream
char-stream >> buffered-stream	2	ascii-disk-stream

These additional constraints result in exactly one possible total ordering:

```
(ascii-disk-stream ascii-stream
 disk-stream char-stream buffered-stream
 stream standard-object t)
```

Case 3: No Total Ordering Satisfies the Constraints

No total ordering satisifies the constraints when a class is included by more than one class definition and the local constraints set by the class definitions are in direct conflict with each other.

CLOS cannot resolve such a conflict, so it signals an error. You can then edit the class definitions to remove some of the conflicting ordering constraints. Here is an example of a class organization in which no total ordering is possible. We try to determine the class precedence list for the class ascii-disk-stream, given the following class definitions:

```
(defclass stream () ())

(defclass buffered-stream (stream) ())
(defclass disk-stream (buffered-stream) ())

(defclass char-stream (stream) ())
(defclass ascii-stream (char-stream) ())

(defclass ascii-disk-stream
      (ascii-stream buffered-stream disk-stream)
      ())
```

Two of the class definitions result in a conflict. Here we present only the conflicting constraints:

Constraint	Rule	Class
disk-stream >> buffered-stream	1	disk-stream
buffered-stream >> disk-stream	2	ascii-disk-stream

In this case, CLOS signals an error because it cannot produce a class precedence list consistent with the ordering constraints.

It is clear that this class organization is flawed. The class ascii-disk-stream depends on buffered-stream preceding disk-stream, but the class disk-stream depends on disk-stream preceding buffered-stream.

This particular problem might have been caused by a misunderstanding of the class organization. It seems likely that the constraint set by the disk-stream definition is a semantic constraint that is necessary to the correct working of disk streams, but that the constraint set by ascii-disk-stream is simply a programmer error. Probably, there was no need to include buffered-stream as a direct superclass of ascii-disk-stream.

If the class `ascii-disk-stream` really does depend on `buffered-stream` preceding `disk-stream`, however, then the problem lies somewhere in the class organization. The solution is to rethink the semantics of the class organization.

Opposing Constraints Are Possible

It is possible to define two classes that contain opposing ordering constraints, as long as you do not try to define a class that is built on both of them.

```
(defclass stream () ())
(defclass input-stream (stream) ())
(defclass buffered-stream (stream) ())

(defclass disk-stream (buffered-stream input-stream) ())

(defclass tape-stream (input-stream buffered-stream) ())
```

Note that class `disk-stream` requires `buffered-stream` to precede `input-stream`, but the class `tape-stream` requires `input-stream` to precede `buffered-stream`.

These class definitions do not conflict, because as yet there is no connection between the classes `disk-stream` and `tape-stream`. However, CLOS would signal an error if you tried to define a class built on both `disk-stream` and `tape-stream`:

```
(defclass disk-emulating-tape-stream (disk-stream tape-stream) ())
```

6.3 GUIDELINES ON DESIGNING CLASS ORGANIZATIONS

This section discusses how the class precedence rules affect programming practice. An important aspect of the two class precedence rules is that the programmer controls the ordering constraints locally, by deciding which direct superclasses to include and what their order should be. If all the local ordering constraints are correct, the resulting class precedence list will be appropriate. When designing a class organization, you should concentrate on the effect of the two rules on each class definition, without being concerned about the final class precedence list.

> **Rule 1 of class precedence:**
>
> A class always has precedence over its superclasses.

Rule 1 suggests that you should define one or more basic classes and build more specialized classes on them. This style of programming allows the specialized classes to inherit desired behavior and override unwanted behavior.

Rule 2 of class precedence:

Each class definition sets the precedence order of its direct superclasses.

Rule 2 has implications for classes built on more than one direct superclass. In some cases, each direct superclass makes a distinct contribution, and there is no conflict between them; then it does not matter how you order them in the list of superclasses. In other cases, however, two superclasses offer competing traits. For example, they both might have a primary method for the same generic function. In this case, you should decide which of the two primary methods is more appropriate for the new class and order the two direct superclasses accordingly.

Rule 2 also encourages the style of programming that uses mixin classes. In this style, each mixin class supports a separate, well-defined aspect of behavior. The goals of a mixin are to support that behavior completely and not to collide with other classes. For example, a mixin might provide before-methods and after-methods that modify the behavior of primary methods provided by other classes. When a mixin does not compete with other classes, its precedence order is not important. Usually a mixin has the root class as its only superclass, so its ordering constraints are minimal. This allows a class to be built from a set of many mixins.

Note that the final class precedence list always satisfies the two rules—and, in most cases, it also follows the guideline of keeping nonintersecting family trees together. In most cases, a program can consider each of the direct superclasses as a black box, and can rely on all the superclasses of the first direct superclass preceding the second direct superclass and all its superclasses. In cases where CLOS cannot follow the guideline (due to other ordering constraints), the resulting class precedence list allows a superclass of the second direct superclass to precede a superclass of the first direct superclass.

As mentioned earlier, if a program depends on one class being more specific than another, you should make that ordering constraint explicit.

6.4 INHERITANCE OF SLOTS AND SLOT OPTIONS

A class can define a slot by providing a slot specifier, which includes the name of the slot and possibly some slot options. In addition to the slots that the class defines locally in its defclass form, the class inherits slots and slot options defined by its superclasses.

Modifying Inherited Aspects of a Slot

A class can modify or override aspects of a slot that would otherwise be inherited, by providing a local slot specifier for a slot with the same name. For example:

```
(defclass basic-lock ()
      ((name :initarg :name)))

(defclass simple-lock (basic-lock)
      ((name :initform "Simple Lock")))
```

The class basic-lock provides a slot specifier for a slot named name and the :initarg :name slot option.

The class simple-lock, which is built on basic-lock, inherits the name slot and the :initarg :name slot option. It also provides a local slot specifier for the name slot and the :initform slot option. This does not override any of the inherited traits, but it adds a default initial value form to the slot. It is often useful for a class to supply a default initial value form for a slot that is inherited from a superclass.

Each instance of simple-lock has only one slot with the name name. The characteristics of that slot come from all classes in the class precedence list that supply a slot specifier for name. Instances of simple-lock receive the following slot characteristics from these classes:

Slot Characteristics	From Class
the name slot itself	basic-lock
:initarg :name	basic-lock
:initform "Simple Lock"	simple-lock

Inheritance Behavior of Each Slot Option

Here we describe how each slot option is inherited. The slot options have different inheritance behavior. It is important to note that each slot option is inherited independently of the other slot options.

Each class in the class precedence list can affect the characteristics of a slot by providing a slot specifier for the slot with that name. CLOS gathers together the slot specifiers and ranks them from most specific to least specific, based on the class precedence list. In other words, the precedence of the slot specifier is controlled by the precedence of the class that provides it.

These rules determine the final set of characteristics of the slot:

`:accessor, :reader, :writer`   Not inherited

> These slot options create methods but do not affect the slot itself. Although these slot options themselves are not inherited, the accessor methods are inherited in the same way that any other method is inherited.

`:allocation`   Inherited by shadowing

> The allocation of a slot is controlled by the most specific class that provides a slot specifier for the slot, whether or not the `:allocation` slot option is provided.

> If the most specific slot specifier provides `:allocation` `:instance`, or does not provide the `:allocation` slot option at all, this slot is a local slot. If the most specific slot specifier provides `:allocation` `:class`, this is a shared slot. (In this case, a new class slot is created for this class, which is accessible to all its instances and to instances of any subclasses that do not provide or inherit a more specific slot specifier for the slot.)

`:documentation`   Inherited by shadowing

> The documentation of a slot is controlled by the most specific slot specifier that provides the `:documentation` slot option for this slot. Any less specific slot specifiers that provide the `:documentation` slot option are ignored.

`:initarg`   Inherited by union

A slot can have more than one initarg. If several classes in the class precedence list provide the `:initarg` slot option for the same slot, the slot can be initialized by using any of the initargs.

`:initform`   Inherited by shadowing

The initform of a slot is controlled by the most specific slot specifier that provides the `:initform` slot option for this slot. Any less specific slot specifiers that provide an `:initform` are ignored.

`:type`   Inherited by "and"

The type of a slot is controlled by all slot specifiers that provide the `:type` slot option. The value of the slot must satisfy all the type constraints provided. For example, if three classes in the class precedence list specify the type as being `number`, `rational`, and `integer`, then the value of the slot must satisfy

(typep *value* '(and number rational integer))

This implies that a class cannot relax any inherited type constraints on a slot, but it can make the type constraint more stringent.

6.5 GUIDELINES ON USING INHERITANCE OF SLOT OPTIONS

The inheritance behavior of slots and slot options probably sounds complicated. Each slot option is inherited independently and by different rules. The inheritance behavior of each slot option offers a feature that can be useful in some contexts, but most programs do not need all these features.

Almost all CLOS programs make use of the fact that slots are inherited. The basic class provides a small number of slots that are appropriate for all classes built on it, and the more specialized classes can include additional slots.

Many CLOS programs take advantage of the inheritance of the :initform slot option. In some cases it is appropriate to inherit a default initial value from a superclass. In other cases, it is useful to override an inherited default initial value.

Many CLOS programs also take advantage of the inheritance of the :initarg slot option. Usually, the class that provides the slot also provides the initarg, if the slot is intended to be initialized. Occasionally it is useful for a subclass to provide the :initarg slot option to give the slot another initarg.

When :type is used, typically the class that provides the slot also specifies the slot's type. Subclasses generally inherit the type without a need for constraining it further.

Generally, subclasses do not choose to override the allocation of a slot. It is unusual for a class to change the allocation of a slot from :class to :instance or vice versa, because the semantics of a shared slot versus a local slot are so different. The most common example of overriding the allocation occurs when one class specifies a :class slot, and its subclass chooses not to share that particular slot, but rather to create a new :class slot to be shared among the instances of the subclass (and instances of its subclasses, unless they also create a new :class slot).

7

Defining CLOS Elements

In this chapter, we describe what happens when you define classes, methods, and generic functions. We discuss the following topics: the order in which you should define CLOS elements, the congruence rules for lambda-lists of a generic function and its methods, the LISP objects that represent the CLOS elements, and the relationships between these objects and their names.

7.1 ORDER OF DEFINING CLOS ELEMENTS

CLOS is quite flexible in allowing you to define CLOS elements in various orders:

- When designing a class organization, you can define the classes in any order; you can define a class before defining its superclasses.

- You can define methods and generic functions in any order. If you define a method before defining the generic function, CLOS automatically creates the generic function. The lambda-list of the generic function is derived from the method's lambda-list; all other aspects of the generic function are defaulted. If you use `defgeneric` later, the existing generic function is modified.

There are, however, some ordering dependencies:

- Before you make an instance of a class, that class and all its super-classes must be defined

- Before you define a method that specializes on a class, that class itself must be defined

7.2 CONGRUENT LAMBDA-LISTS

When a `defgeneric` form is evaluated and no methods for the generic function exist, the `defgeneric` form establishes a parameter pattern that must be followed by all the methods. If a method is defined before a `defgeneric` form has been evaluated, that method establishes the pattern. The parameter pattern is derived from the lambda-list of the `defmethod` or `defgeneric` form. It specifies the number of required parameters, the number of optional parameters, and whether `&rest`, `&key`, or both are used.

Once the pattern is established, if any `defmethod` form or `defgeneric` form is evaluated that does not match the pattern, CLOS signals an error. To match the pattern, the following CLOS congruence rules must be obeyed:

- The number of required parameters must be the same as in the established pattern.

- The number of optional parameters must be the same as in the established pattern. Methods can supply default values for optional parameters, but the `defgeneric` form cannot.

- If the established pattern uses `&rest` or `&key`, all methods and the `defgeneric` form must use `&rest`, or `&key`, or both.

Keyword parameters are treated specially. A `defgeneric` form can state a requirement regarding `&key` parameters, whether or not the parameter pattern was established before the `defgeneric` form was evaluated. We state the rules for keyword parameters here, and then explain them further.

- If a `defgeneric` form specifies `&key`, its set of keyword parameters must be accepted by each of the methods. In other words, the `defgeneric` form states the minimum set of keywords that must be accepted by all the methods. The methods can accept the keywords by naming them explicitly with &key, by using &rest and not &key, or by specifying &allow-other-keys.

- Each method can name &key parameters in addition to the set specified by the defgeneric form; the only requirement is that all methods must accept the minimal set specified by the defgeneric.

For generic functions that use &key parameters, the keyword arguments are checked for validity when the generic function is called. The set of accepted keywords is controlled by the defgeneric form and the applicable methods. A keyword argument is accepted by the generic function call if it is accepted by the defgeneric form or by one or more applicable methods.

In general, a generic function passes all its arguments to each method it calls. Nevertheless, no error is signaled if a generic function calls a method with a keyword argument that is not explicitly accepted by the method. The generic function checks the validity of keyword arguments; this checking is not done by the individual methods.

If the defgeneric form or any method for the generic function uses &allow-other-keys, all keyword arguments are accepted when the generic function is called.

In general, CLOS signals an error if a method or generic function is defined that does not adhere to these congruence rules. This can happen in the following situations:

- A defmethod or defgeneric form is evaluated that does not match the established pattern

- A defmethod form is evaluated that does not accept the minimal set of keyword arguments specified by the defgeneric form

- A defgeneric form is evaluated and an existing method does not accept the minimal set of keyword arguments specified by the defgeneric form

7.3 LISP OBJECTS REPRESENTING CLOS ELEMENTS

When you use defclass, the returned value is a *class object*. Similarly, defgeneric returns a *generic function object* and defmethod returns a *method object*. These LISP objects are the internal representation of CLOS classes, generic functions, and methods.

When writing application programs, you usually do not need to deal directly with the LISP objects representing the CLOS elements. Instead, you refer to these objects by their names. For example, when you use defclass, you create a class object and give it a name. Later, you refer to the class by its name—for example, when using make-instance. Similarly, you refer to a generic function by its name when defining it (using defgeneric), creating methods for it (using defmethod), and calling it.

The CLOS programmer interface can be divided into two separate levels. The macros defclass, defmethod, and defgeneric are in the "macro level," which has a convenient syntax and enables you to deal with names of objects. The macro level is implemented in terms of the "functional level," which deals with objects and not with names. Most application programs can be written entirely in terms of the macro level. The functional level offers greater flexibility, such as supporting anonymous classes and generic functions.

7.4 MAPPING BETWEEN NAMES AND OBJECTS

This section describes the relationships between the names of CLOS elements and the LISP objects that represent them.

Classes

When you use defclass, the returned value is a class object. That class object has a name, which is a symbol. Actually, there are two associations between the name of the class and the class object. The defclass macro sets up both of these associations automatically.

One association is maintained by the class object itself. You can query a class object for its name by using class-name and use (setf class-name) to change that association:

(class-name *class-object*)
(setf (class-name *class-object*) *symbol*)

The other association is maintained by a symbol. You can query a symbol for the class with that name by using find-class and use (setf find-class) to change that association:

(find-class *symbol*)
(setf (find-class *symbol*) *class-object*)

You use class-name to ask "What is the name of this class object?" and you use find-class to ask "What is the class object with this name?"

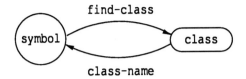

Figure 7.1 Links between a class and its name.

Figure 7.1 shows that these two associations are independent. Changing the class associated with a name (maintained by the symbol) does not affect the name associated with a class (maintained by the class object). Therefore, the two associations can become out of synch with each other.

Generic Functions

Generic functions are named just as ordinary functions are named. A generic function object is stored in the function cell of a symbol; that symbol is the name of the generic function. You can query a symbol for the generic function associated with it by using symbol-function, and use (setf symbol-function) to change that association.

Since generic and ordinary functions are named in the same way, the COMMON LISP technique of using packages to keep related functions and symbols together is just as useful for generic functions as it is for ordinary functions. Also, one symbol cannot name both an ordinary and a generic function.

In LISP, functions need not have names; you can use lambda to define an anonymous function. CLOS does not require that generic functions have names. To create an anonymous generic function, you can use the generic-function macro. It has the same syntax as defgeneric, except there is no argument for the name of the generic function.

Methods

Methods do not have names. A method is identified by the generic function it implements, its parameter specializers, and its qualifiers. Rarely would you need to access a method directly. Usually, you simply define methods, and they are called automatically by the generic dispatch procedure. One situation in which you need to access a method occurs when you want to use remove-method to break the association between a generic function and a method. We give an example of this in "Removing Generic Functions and Methods," page 136.

Parameter Specializers

CLOS distinguishes between the names of parameter specializers and the objects that represent them. Only parameter specializer names appear in the `defmethod` lambda-list, whereas operators in the functional level use parameter specializer objects.

Name	Corresponding Object
a class name	the class object of that name, which is obtained by `find-class`
(`eql` *form*)	(`eql` *object*), where *object* is the result of evaluating *form*

7.5 REMOVING GENERIC FUNCTIONS AND METHODS

This section describes how to "remove" the definition of a generic function or method, in the sense of making sure that it is never called.

Generic Functions

You can remove a generic function by breaking the association between the name and the object. Just as for ordinary functions, you can do this by using `fmakunbound`.

Methods

You can remove a method by breaking the association between the method object and the generic function. Although CLOS does not provide a convenient macro for doing this, you can use `remove-method` and `find-method`, two operators in the CLOS functional level. As mentioned earlier, the functional level deals in objects, not names. To use these operators, we must access a generic function object, a method object, and parameter specializer objects. The syntax of `remove-method` is

(`remove-method` *generic-function-object method-object*)

To access the generic function object, use `symbol-function` of the name of the generic function. To access the method object, use the `find-method` generic function. The syntax of `find-method` is

```
(find-method generic-function-object
             ({method-qualifier}*)
             ({parameter-specializer-objects}*))
```

The list of parameter specializer objects must have as many elements as there are required parameters. An unspecialized required parameter has the class named t as its parameter specializer.

Here, we show an example of removing a method. The parameter specializer names are class names, so we access the parameter specializer objects by using find-class.

```
;;; The method to remove
(defmethod restore-product :before (sw (os genera))
  body)

;;; Removing the method
(let* ((generic-function (symbol-function 'restore-product))
       (method (find-method generic-function
                            '(:before)
                            (list (find-class 't)
                                  (find-class 'genera)))))
  (remove-method generic-function method))
```

8

Redefining CLOS Elements

To redefine an element of CLOS is to evaluate a new defining form (such as a `defmethod` form) when that element (the method) already exists. In general, CLOS replaces the old definition with the new.

The capability of redefining classes and methods is crucial to software development. It allows you to continue to refine your design of a running program even after you have created instances; when a class is redefined, any existing instances are updated to the new definition. Often, the most challenging part of designing an object-oriented program is choosing the right modularity. Sometimes, when you begin writing methods, you think of a better organization of classes that would yield more modular code. CLOS supports a flexible means of redefining classes and methods, so you have the freedom to modify your original design, including the organization of classes.

In this chapter, we give an example of redefining a class, updating instances to the new class definition, and redefining affected methods. The first goal of this example is to illustrate the mechanics of redefining CLOS elements. The second goal is to give some guidelines on designing a program in which most of the elements are independent of one another; in such a program, you can redefine one element without affecting most of the other elements.

8.1 REDEFINING CLASSES

If you evaluate a defclass form and a class of that name already exists, the new class definition replaces the old. You can redefine a class to change any aspect of it, including its slots, its superclasses, its accessor methods, and any defclass options.

What Is Affected by the Redefinition

Note that changing a class definition affects all subclasses of the class, because they inherit structure from the class. Since a class controls the structure of its instances, all instances of the class and subclasses are also affected. In addition, since defclass options define methods for readers and writers, these methods might also be affected by redefining a class. When you redefine a class, CLOS automatically propagates the changes to everything that is affected, including subclasses, instances of the class and of subclasses, and methods for accessors.

What Happens to Accessor Methods

Any accessor method that was created by the old class definition (by means of the :accessor, :reader, or :writer slot options), but is not requested by the new class definition, is removed from the generic function.

Automatic Updating of Instances

When you redefine a class such that the structure of the instances changes (which happens when you add or delete slots, for example), all instances of the class and its subclasses must be updated to the new structure. CLOS updates the instances automatically.

CLOS specifies that the updating of each instance happens at some time before any slot of that instance is accessed for reading or writing. Although you cannot assume the updating of instances happens immediately upon evaluating the new class definition, the effect is semantically the same; you are safeguarded from ever accessing an obsolete instance.

CLOS updates instances as they are needed, instead of all at once. Thus, CLOS does not need to keep track of all instances of a class and any unreferenced instances can be garbage collected.

What Happens to the Slots of Existing Instances

When you redefine a class, the slots specified in the new definition might be different from the slots of the old definition. There are three common cases:

- When the same slot is specified in both definitions, the value of the slot is preserved.

- When a slot is specified by the new definition, but was not specified by the old, the slot is added to instances and initialized according to the :initform option.

- When a slot specified by the old definition is not specified by the new, the slot is deleted from the instance and any value is discarded. However, the values of deleted slots are not immediately discarded; you can access them by writing a method to customize the updating.

We summarize this information in Table 8.1, which also shows what happens when the allocation type of a slot is changed from local to shared, or from shared to local. The entries in Table 8.1 have the following meanings:

preserved   The value of the slot is the same before and after the instance is updated. If the slot was previously unbound, it is still unbound after the updating.

initialized   The slot receives the value of the :initform of the slot, if one is specified by the class or inherited from superclasses. If there is no :initform, the value of the slot is unbound.

discarded   The slot is deleted from instances and its value is lost.

	Shared (New)	Local (New)	None (New)
shared (old)	preserved	preserved	discarded
local (old)	initialized	preserved	discarded
none (old)	initialized	initialized	no action

Table 8.1 Effects on slots when a class is redefined.

Customizing the Updating

CLOS enables you to specify other actions to be taken when an instance is updated to conform to the new definition of the class. To do so, you can provide a method for `update-instance-for-redefined-class` to do further work in updating instances. The body of the method can access the values of discarded slots, which you can use to initialize other slots.

When you redefine a class, CLOS updates the structure of the class and the subclasses (if necessary) and removes or adds accessor methods (if necessary). CLOS updates the structure of each instance (at an implementation-dependent time prior to the next access of a slot of the instance), by adding new slots and deleting obsolete slots. Finally, CLOS calls the `update-instance-for-redefined-class` generic function. The default primary method for `update-instance-for-redefined-class` initializes slots in the way described previously.

In most cases, users should provide before- or after-methods for `update-instance-for-redefined-class`, not primary methods. A primary method would override the default method that initializes new slots, and would prevent the usual initialization from happening. If you initialize a slot in a before-method, the default primary method does not fill the slot with its initform.

You can customize `update-instance-for-redefined-class` to store values in the new slots based on values of slots being discarded. As a simple example, to rename a slot you can write a method to store the value of the discarded slot into the new slot.

The `update-instance-for-redefined-class` generic function has four required arguments and one &rest argument:

instance	The instance, which has been updated to the new structure
added-slots	A list of the names of the added slots
discarded-slots	A list of the names of the discarded slots
property-list	A list containing alternating names and values of the discarded slots (not including any discarded slots that were unbound), and any slots specified as local in the old definition and shared in the new definition
&rest *initargs*	The &rest argument is rarely used; we discuss it in "Performing Initialization by Initargs," page 168

The most useful argument is the *property-list*, which gives you a way to access the values of discarded slots. For an example of redefining a class and defining a method for `update-instance-for-redefined-class`, see "Example of Redefining CLOS Elements," page 144.

8.2 REDEFINING METHODS AND GENERIC FUNCTIONS

Methods

If you evaluate a `defmethod` form, and a method already exists for the same generic function, with the same parameter specializers and the same qualifiers, the new method definition replaces the old.

Any future calls to the generic function will see the new definition of the method. If the method is redefined *during* the execution of the generic function itself, the effects are not predictable. Many CLOS implementations optimize portions of the generic dispatch, so it is possible that the new method definition will not be used for this generic function call.

Generic Functions

If you evaluate a `defgeneric` form and a generic function already exists by that name, `defgeneric` redefines the existing generic function. An error is signaled if any methods for the generic function are not congruent with the lambda-list specified by the `defgeneric`. When you redefine a generic function, the new definition of the generic function replaces the old definition.

A `defgeneric` form can define methods, by including the `:method` option. The `:method` option to `defgeneric` has the same effect as using `defmethod` to define a method for that generic function. Sometimes, it is useful to define methods in the `defgeneric` form itself, especially for default methods. This is a way to highlight the default behavior. For examples of using that syntax, see "Defining Directional Streams," page 180.

If you redefine a generic function and the new `defgeneric` form uses the `:method` option, two things can happen. If that method already exists (a method for the same generic function with the same parameter specializers and the same qualifiers), it is replaced by the method defined in the `:method` option. If that method does not already exist, it is created. Redefining a generic function might add methods to the generic function and might replace methods, but it never removes methods: If the previous `defgeneric` defined a method with the `:method` option, but the current `defgeneric` does not define that method, the method object continues to exist in LISP.

You cannot use `defgeneric` to redefine an ordinary LISP function, macro, or special form. An error is signaled if you evaluate a `defgeneric` form and the first argument is the name of an ordinary function, macro, or special form. In contrast, you can use `defun` to redefine a generic function. If you define an ordinary LISP function, macro, or special form with the same name as an existing generic function, that name is no longer associated with the generic function.

8.3 EXAMPLE OF REDEFINING CLOS ELEMENTS

The purpose of this example is to show how easily you can redefine portions of a CLOS program, even after instances have been created and clients are using the program.

First, we define two protocols for dealing with triangles, one external (intended for clients) and one internal (to be used within the implementation of this program). We then define the implementation of both protocols, including the class for representing triangles and a set of methods.

Later, we decide to change the internal representation of triangles. We can do this without altering the external protocol at all. However, the change requires only that we redefine some of the methods for the internal protocol and provide a method for updating any existing triangles to the new representation.

The External Triangle Protocol

The interface that we advertise to clients consists of the following operations:

`make-triangle` *side-a side-b side-c*
> Returns a new triangle; each argument is the length of one side of the triangle

`area` *triangle*
> Returns the area of the triangle

`dimensions` *triangle*
> Returns a list of the lengths of the three sides of the triangle

angles *triangle*
  Returns a list of the three angles of the triangle

The Internal Triangle Protocol

The following six operations are useful within the implementation, because they are all needed for supporting the external protocol. Clients are not expected to use these operations.

<table>
<tr><td>side-a triangle</td><td>angle-A triangle</td></tr>
<tr><td>side-b triangle</td><td>angle-B triangle</td></tr>
<tr><td>side-c triangle</td><td>angle-C triangle</td></tr>
</table>

Each of these operations returns one aspect of the triangle: either the length of one side, or the measurement of one angle. Note that angle-A is the angle opposite side-a. Figure 8.1 shows how the angles and sides are related to one another.

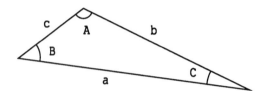

Figure 8.1 Angles and sides of a triangle.

The Initial Implementation

First, we implement the triangle class. The internal representation of triangles is straightforward; we store the length of each side in a slot. By using the :reader option, we can conveniently provide methods for side-a, side-b, and side-c.

```
(defclass shape () ()
  (:documentation "The foundation of all shapes."))

(defclass triangle (shape)
        ((a :reader side-a :initarg :side-a)
         (b :reader side-b :initarg :side-b)
         (c :reader side-c :initarg :side-c)))
```

Next, we provide the constructor, make-triangle. This constructor co-
erces each side length into the type float prior to making the instance,
to ensure that all mathematical operations on sides use floating-point
arithmetic.

```
(defun make-triangle (a b c)
  ;; All sides should be represented as floats
  (make-instance 'triangle :side-a (coerce a 'float)
                          :side-b (coerce b 'float)
                          :side-c (coerce c 'float)))
```

The function three-sides-to-angle will be useful in the bodies of the
methods that return the angles of the triangle.

```
;;; Return the angle A between adjacent sides b and c
;;; and opposite side a, given all sides of a triangle
;;; Law of Cosines:   a^2 = b^2 + c^2 - 2bc(cos A)
(defun three-sides-to-angle (a b c)
  (acos (/ (- (+ (expt b 2)
                 (expt c 2))
              (expt a 2))
           (* 2 b c))))
```

Next, we define the methods for returning the individual angles of a
triangle:

```
(defmethod angle-A ((tri triangle))
  (three-sides-to-angle
    (side-a tri) (side-b tri) (side-c tri)))

(defmethod angle-B ((tri triangle))
  (three-sides-to-angle
    (side-b tri) (side-c tri) (side-a tri)))

(defmethod angle-C ((tri triangle))
  (three-sides-to-angle
    (side-c tri) (side-a tri) (side-b tri)))
```

We choose to define explicitly the generic functions for the operations
that are part of the external protocol. The defgeneric forms indicate
that these three operations are intended to work on any shape:

```
(defgeneric dimensions (shape)
  (:documentation "Returns list of side lengths."))
```

```
(defgeneric angles (shape)
  (:documentation "Returns list of angles."))

(defgeneric area (shape)
  (:documentation "Returns area of the shape."))
```

The three external operations that deal with existing triangles can be defined in terms of the internal operations, without depending on any knowledge of how those internal operations are implemented.

```
(defmethod dimensions ((tri triangle))
  (list (side-a tri)
        (side-b tri)
        (side-c tri)))

(defmethod angles ((tri triangle))
  (list (angle-A tri)
        (angle-B tri)
        (angle-C tri)))

;;; Return the area of a triangle
;;; Algorithm is: area = ab(sin C)/2
(defmethod area ((tri triangle))
  (* (side-a tri) (side-b tri)
     (sin (angle-C tri))
     .5))
```

Changing the Representation of Triangles

Now we decide to change the internal representation of triangles. We want to redefine the `triangle` class to store two sides and the angle between them, instead of storing three sides.

For a real program, one possible motivation for changing the internal representation would be to increase the efficiency of an operation. In this case, the `angle-C` operation probably will be faster when the method simply reads the value of a slot instead of doing the somewhat expensive calculation of computing the angle from the three sides. On the other hand, `side-c` will be slower. This is a tradeoff based on how the program is used.

The following class definition can replace the previous class definition. At this point, we write the `defclass` form, but we do not evaluate it immediately. Prior to redefining the class, we must ensure that any existing instances will be updated properly.

```
(defclass triangle (shape)
     ((a :reader side-a :initarg :side-a)
      (b :reader side-b :initarg :side-b)
      (angle-C :reader angle-C :initarg :angle-C)))
```

Note that this class definition creates a method for the reader generic function, angle-C. In fact, this method will replace the existing method for the generic function angle-C. (We should also remove the previous definition of the angle-C method from the source.) This is exactly what we want; when the new class definition is evaluated, the angle-C generic function will return the value of the angle-C slot, instead of calculating the angle from the three sides of the triangle.

To update the instances, we provide a method for update-instance-for-redefined-class. We choose to supply an after-method, so as not to override the system-supplied default method. This is a safe practice, even though in this case none of the slots use the :initform slot option, and thus do not need to be initialized in this way. Possibly the class triangle has a subclass with slots that do need to be initialized from their initforms. Unless we have an explicit reason for preventing the system-supplied method from occurring, it is best to allow it to run.

The values of the slots a and b are preserved, since these are local slots that are defined in both the previous and the new classes. Before this method is called, the slot c will be deleted from the instance and the slot angle-C will be added. This method will use the value of the discarded slot c to calculate the value of the new slot angle-C, and will store the value in the slot.

Keep in mind that a class can be redefined more than once. We might later decide that yet another representation of triangles is preferable. Since instances are not necessarily updated immediately upon redefinition, some existing instances might be several formats behind the current format. This method attempts to be safe in the face of multiple class redefinitions. Before doing anything else, this method checks that the instance is being updated in the expected way; that is, that slot c is being discarded and slot angle-C is being added. If both of these conditions are met, the method computes the appropriate value for the slot angle-C and stores it in the slot.

```
;;; Here we delete slot c and add angle-C
;;; We need to initialize the new slot angle-C
(defmethod update-instance-for-redefined-class :after
            ((instance triangle)
             added-slots discarded-slots
             plist &rest initargs)
  (declare (ignore initargs))
  ;; Identify this particular redefinition
  (if (and (member 'c discarded-slots)
           (member 'angle-C added-slots))
      (setf (slot-value instance 'angle-C)
            (three-sides-to-angle
              (getf plist 'c)
              (side-a instance)
              (side-b instance)))))
```

It is crucial to evaluate the method for `update-instance-for-redefined-class` before evaluating the new class definition. Otherwise, in the interval after redefining the class and before evaluating the method for `update-instance-for-redefined-class`, it is possible for instances to be updated to the new definition. An instance is updated sometime before any of its slots are accessed. If an instance is updated before the method is defined, only the slots `a` and `b` will have values. There will be no way of calculating the `angle-C` slot, because the value of the deleted slot `c` will have been discarded.

The methods for `side-a` and `side-b` are unchanged; they continue to work as before. However, the method for `side-c` (which was a reader method generated by the previous class definition) will be removed from LISP when the new class definition is evaluated. Therefore, we need to write a new method for `side-c`. The method calculates the third side of a triangle, based on two sides and the angle between them.

```
(defmethod side-c ((tri triangle))
  (third-side (side-a tri)
              (side-b tri)
              (angle-C tri)))
```

```
;;; Algorithm is: c^2 = a^2 + b^2 - 2ab(cos C)
(defun third-side (a b angle-C)
  (sqrt (- (+ (expt a 2)
              (expt b 2))
           (* 2 a b (cos angle-C)))))
```

We also need to revise our constructor function, because it calls make-instance with the initarg :side-c, which is no longer a valid initarg. It is an easy matter to write a new constructor that takes the same arguments, but fills different slots using that information. This constructor uses the c argument to calculate the appropriate value for the angle-C slot.

```
(defun make-triangle (a b c)
  (let* ((float-a (coerce a 'float))
         (float-b (coerce b 'float))
         (float-c (coerce c 'float))
         (angle-C (three-sides-to-angle
                       float-c float-a float-b)))
    (make-instance 'triangle :side-a float-a
                             :side-b float-b
                             :angle-C angle-C)))
```

Often a constructor needs to be redefined when the class itself is redefined. Constructors are closely tied to the structure of the class, because they usually take arguments and use them to fill slots.

What Changed, and What Stayed the Same

It is essential that, no matter what changes occur in the internals of the program, the documented external protocol remains the same. This allows any client code to continue to work. Here we also endeavored to keep the documented internal protocol the same, which minimized the amount of internal code that needed to be changed.

What Changed	What Stayed the Same
Definition of the triangle class Implementation of side-c, angle-C, and make-triangle	User's perception of triangles Documented external protocol Documented internal protocol Implementation of side-a, side-b, angle-A, angle-B, area, dimensions, and angles

Since the constructor takes the three sides as arguments, we are encouraging the users to think of triangles as being represented by the three sides. The new internal representation of triangles does not match this perception, but since the external protocol remains the same, we are not requiring users to change their mental model of triangles. Similarly, our documentation of the external protocol intentionally did not state that `side-c` was previously implemented as a reader. The documentation of the external protocol should never expose the internals, such as mentioning that a generic function is implemented as an accessor.

We were "lucky" that a great deal of the implementation of the program continued to work when the representation of triangles changed. Actually, this is not luck at all, but rather is a direct result of documenting and adhering to an internal protocol.

First, consider the operations `area`, `dimensions`, and `angles`. These external operations are all implemented in terms of the internal protocol, which we continued to support after redefining the class. The internal protocol guarantees that those three operations remain valid.

Next, consider the internal operations themselves. Each one fulfills a specific task, returning one angle or side. This modularity of design implies that a method needs to be rewritten only if it depends on some aspect of the class definition that has been changed. For example, since the slots `a` and `b` remain the same, the methods for `side-a` and `side-b` continue to be valid.

Another reason that most methods for the internal operations remain valid is that those methods depend on the internal protocol, and not on the internal structure of the class. Except for the accessors (which necessarily depend on the slots), none of the methods use knowledge of the internal details of the class. For example, to get the length of `side-c`, the methods called the generic function `side-c`. An equivalent alternative to calling `side-c` is to use `with-accessors`. In contrast, any code that uses `with-slots` has a built-in dependency on the internal representation of the class; that code would need to be rewritten if the class were redefined to delete the slot.

8.4 CHANGING THE CLASS OF AN INSTANCE

You can change the class of an existing instance by calling `change-class`. We use the term "previous class" to mean the class of the instance before it is changed, and "target class" to mean the class of the instance after it is changed. CLOS updates the instance to the structure of the target class, which might involve deleting or adding slots.

What Happens to the Slots of the Instance

When an instance is changed to a different class, there is no effect on the values of any shared slots. The instance, however, will lose access to any shared slots of the previous class. If the target class defines another slot of the same name (whether shared or local), the instance will access that slot instead. (If the previous and target classes access the same shared slot because one of the classes inherits it from the other, the instance will continue to access that slot.)

Table 8.2 indicates what happens to the values of slots. "Preserved," "initialized," and "discarded" have the meanings described in "Redefining Classes," page 140. We introduce two more terms:

inaccessible   The shared slot of the previous class is not accessible to the instance after its class has been changed to the target class.

replaced   For any shared slot of the target class, the instance is updated to access that shared slot. If the previous class defined a slot of the same name, whether local or shared, the updated instance no longer accesses that slot. Thus, we say the value of the slot is "replaced" by the value of a shared slot of the target class.

	Shared (Target)	Local (Target)	None (Target)
shared (previous)	replaced	preserved	inaccessible
local (previous)	replaced	preserved	discarded
none (previous)	replaced	initialized	no action

Table 8.2 Effects on slots when the class of an instance is changed.

Customizing the Updating

CLOS enables you to specify other actions to be taken when an instance is updated to conform to the definition of a different class. You can provide methods for update-instance-for-different-class to do further work in updating the instance.

When you call change-class, CLOS updates the structure of the instance and then calls the generic function update-instance-for-different-class. The default primary method initializes any new local slots, according to the :initform of the target class.

Note that, if you define a primary method for update-instance-for-different-class, it will override the default method, which initializes new local slots. In most cases, it is preferable to let that behavior occur and to specialize update-instance-for-different-class by writing before- or after-methods. If you initialize a slot in a before-method, the default primary method does not fill the slot with its initform.

When CLOS calls update-instance-for-different-class, the first argument, *previous*, is a copy of the instance before it was updated. The second argument, *target*, is the updated instance. The *target* and *previous* arguments are not eq. You can access the values of all slots in the previous instance by using accessors or slot-value on the *previous* argument; you can also use other functions or generic functions on the *previous* argument.

9

Creating and Initializing Instances

Client programs usually use constructors to make instances. Constructors call `make-instance`, which creates, initializes, and returns a new instance. CLOS enables you to control many aspects of the initialization, ranging from supplying a default value for a slot to customizing the initialization by writing a method. This chapter begins by describing the arguments to `make-instance` and summarizing the steps CLOS performs when `make-instance` is called. It then shows how to use the techniques for controlling initialization.

9.1 ARGUMENTS TO MAKE-INSTANCE

The syntax of `make-instance` is

> `make-instance` *class* &rest *initargs*

The first argument is the class, which can be either the name of the class or the class object itself. This gives you a clue that `make-instance` straddles the fence between the macro level and the functional level. In fact, `make-instance` is a powerful tool used by both applications programmers and metaobject programmers; we describe only those techniques intended for applications programmers.

The &rest argument consists of *initargs*, which is short for *initialization arguments*. An initarg controls some aspect of initialization; it might fill a slot, or be used by an initialization method, or both.

Each initarg consists of an initarg name followed by a value. An initarg name can be any symbol, not necessarily a keyword. The format of the &rest argument is the same as the format of keyword arguments that are processed as &key parameters.

9.2 SUMMARY OF WHAT MAKE-INSTANCE DOES

When you call make-instance, CLOS performs the following steps:

1. Combines the initargs you supply to make-instance with the default values for any initargs you do not explicitly supply. The result is a *defaulted initarg list*.

2. Ensures that all initarg names in the defaulted initarg list are valid, and signals an error if they are not. If :allow-other-keys is provided as true in the call to make-instance, all initarg names are valid.

3. Allocates storage for the instance and creates an instance whose slots are all unbound.

4. Applies the initialize-instance generic function to the newly created instance and the defaulted initarg list. The default primary method for initialize-instance does the following:

    a. Initializes slots according to the defaulted initarg list

    b. Initializes any slots that have :initforms and are still unbound

    The primary method for initialize-instance does this work by calling shared-initialize, which we discuss in "A Procedural Definition: Initialization," page 165.

5. Returns the initialized instance.

9.3 CONTROLLING INITIALIZATION WITH DEFCLASS OPTIONS

In this example, we define some classes to represent windows. These class definitions use techniques for initializing windows. The basic class `window` is intended to be the foundation of all windows. The `defclass` form uses two slot options that pertain to initialization—the `:initarg` and `:initform` options.

```
(defclass window ()
      ((x :initarg :x-position :accessor x-position)
       (y :initarg :y-position :accessor y-position)
       (height :initarg :height :accessor window-height)
       (width :initarg :width :accessor window-width)
       (exposed-p :initform nil :accessor exposed-p))
   (:documentation "Foundation of all windows."))
```

Using the :initarg slot option

In the `window` class definition, four slots (`x`, `y`, `height`, and `width`) use the `:initarg` option. This declares four symbols as valid initarg names for the class `window`. For example, the symbol `:x-position` is an initarg name. If you give it to `make-instance` followed by a value, that value will be stored in the `x` slot. Similarly, the symbol `:height` is an initarg that can be used to initialize the slot named `height`.

```
(make-instance 'window :x-position 0
                       :y-position 0
                       :height 200
                       :width 75)
```

Note that the slot named `exposed-p` does not use the `:initarg` option. Thus, you cannot initialize that slot by giving an argument to make-instance. The `exposed-p` slot is not intended to be initialized by the user.

Using the :initform slot option

The slot named `exposed-p` uses the `:initform` slot option to associate a default initial value with the slot. The value is `nil`. The semantics of this slot are simple: When you first create a window, it is not exposed. We intentionally do not offer an initarg, because we want all newly created windows to be deexposed; this approach causes the slot to be initialized automatically to its initform (which is `nil`) and effectively prevents users from initializing the `exposed-p` slot.

Using the :default-initargs class option

Sometimes, it is useful for a class to provide a default value for an initarg. The :default-initargs class option does this. It is used mostly for remote defaulting; that is, for providing a default value for an inherited initarg.

If an initarg is provided in the call to make-instance, it overrides the default initarg. But if an initarg is omitted, the value of the the default initarg is used.

We shall use :default-initargs when defining a class that is commonly used in the window program. A full-screen window is a window that covers the entire screen. The height and width of such a window are obtained from variables that store the screen's dimensions. A full-screen window is normally positioned at the origin, so we also give defaults for :x-position and :y-position.

```
(defclass full-screen-window (window) ()
  (:default-initargs
    :x-position *screen-origin-x*
    :y-position *screen-origin-y*
    :height *screen-height*
    :width *screen-width*))
```

This class can be used alone or as a building block for other classes. It has the same slots as does window, but it offers defaults for four initargs as a convenience for clients that need to make full-screen windows.

Two Kinds of Defaults

It is important to keep in mind the difference between :default-initargs and :initform. The :default-initargs option gives a default value to an initarg, and the :initform option gives a default value to a slot.

If you intend to allow users to initialize a slot, then you should

- Use :initarg to declare a symbol for initializing the slot
- Use :default-initargs, if you want to give that initarg a default value

If you do not intend to allow users to initialize a slot, then you should

- Not use the :initarg option

- Use :initform, if you want to give the slot a default initial value

These two options come into conflict if they are used together. Consider what happens when a slot has a default value via :initform and an initarg via :initarg, which itself has a default value via :default-initargs. The default given in the :default-initargs effectively overrides the default given by :initform.

For both of these options, the default value form is evaluated every time it is used. The value of an :initform is evaluated each time it is used to initialize a slot. The value of an initarg in :default-initargs is evaluated each time make-instance is called and that initarg is not given as an argument to make-instance.

9.4 CONTROLLING INITIALIZATION WITH METHODS

When make-instance is called, it creates an instance and calls the initialize-instance generic function to initialize the new instance. CLOS supplies a default primary method for initialize-instance, which fills the slots with values according to their initargs and initforms. You can customize the initialization of instances by writing a method for initialize-instance to do additional work.

Defining After-Methods for initialize-instance

A window system probably needs to keep track of all windows. Here we add the new window to the data structure that keeps track of the deexposed windows.

```
(defmethod initialize-instance :after ((w window) &key)
  (push w *deexposed-windows*))
```

Usually you should define after-methods for initialize-instance (as we do here) instead of primary methods. A primary method would override the default primary method and prevent the usual slot initialization from occurring.

Since methods for initialize-instance receive all the defaulted initargs as arguments, methods for initialize-instance should use &key in their lambda-lists. The result of using &key here is that the method allows keywords without specifying that it uses any keyword arguments. For more details on method lambda-lists, see "Congruent Lambda-Lists," page 132.

The Default Method for initialize-instance

make-instance calls initialize-instance with the instance and the defaulted initarg list. With these arguments, the default method for initialize-instance fills the slots with values, as follows:

Step 1   If you provide a slot-filling initarg to make-instance, then its value is stored in the associated slot. (A slot-filling initarg is specified by the :initarg slot option.)

Step 2   If the slot is not filled by Step 1, and the initarg has a default value form, then that form is evaluated and the result is stored in the slot. (A default for an initarg is specified by the :default-initargs class option.)

Step 3   If the slot is not filled by Step 2, and the slot has a default initial value form, then that form is evaluated and the result is stored in the slot. (A default for a slot is specified by the :initform slot option.)

Step 4   If the slot is not filled by Step 3, then the slot remains unbound.

The default method for initialize-instance does this initialization work by calling shared-initialize, a generic function that is called in other contexts as well as in creating new instances. We describe shared-initialize in detail in "Isolating Work Shared Among Procedures," page 167.

9.5 INITIALIZATION ARGUMENTS

This section describes initargs in more detail, focusing on how they are used to initialize new instances. Initargs are used in other contexts as well; see "Performing Initialization by Initargs," page 168.

Validity of Initarg Names

An initarg name must be declared as valid for a given class before it is used in a call to make-instance. There are two ways to declare that an initarg name is valid:

:initarg slot option

> Declares a symbol as a valid initarg name and specifies that the value of the initarg should be stored in the slot. Such a symbol is called a slot-filling initarg. The :initarg slot option is inherited by union: all initarg names declared by the class or any of its superclasses are valid for the class.

initialize-instance methods

> Declare all &key parameter names in the lambda-list as valid initarg names for the class. (Methods for other generic functions also declare &key parameters as valid initarg names. See "Declaring Initarg Names as Valid," page 170.)

In addition, the initarg name :allow-other-keys is valid for all classes. Its default value is nil, which means that CLOS checks the validity of all initargs and signals an error if an invalid initarg name is detected. If you call make-instance and give :allow-other-keys followed by a non-nil value, this error checking is disabled.

If the lambda-list of an initialization method uses &allow-other-keys, all possible symbols are declared as valid initargs. In other words, &allow-other-keys in an initialization method disables the error checking of initarg names.

Inheritance of Default Initargs

The :default-initargs class option associates a default value with an initarg. The set of default initargs is inherited by union, but the default value of any one initarg is inherited by shadowing. In other words,

Union   The set of default initargs of a class is the union of all default initargs provided by the classes in its class precedence list

Shadowing   The default value for any one initarg comes from the most specific class that provided a default value for it

Separation of Initarg and Slot Names

When you use the `:initarg` slot option, the name of the initarg is independent of the name of the slot. This independence allows for a level of
abstraction; clients cannot assume that an initarg maps directly into a
slot of the same name. In fact, some initargs might not map into a slot
at all, and some slots might be filled with values that are calculated on
the basis of several initargs.

For example, the `triangle` class might accept three initargs, one for
the length of each side. However, the class might be implemented to
store the length of two sides and the angle between them, which can be
calculated from the three initargs. Thus, invisibly to the client, the third
side would be used to calculate the opposing angle, and then would be
discarded.

The following example uses this approach. Notice that the initialization method declares `:side-a`, `:side-b`, and `:side-c` as valid initarg
names, whereas the `defclass` form does not declare any initarg names.
We define the constructor `make-triangle` to make an abstract interface
for creating triangles and to make all sides be required arguments. All
the initialization work is done in the method for `initialize-instance`.

```
(defclass triangle (shape)
      ((a :reader side-a)
       (b :reader side-b)
       (angle-C :reader angle-C)))


;;; Do all initialization in this method
(defmethod initialize-instance :after
            ((tri triangle) &key side-a side-b side-c)
   (let* ((float-a (coerce a 'float))
          (float-b (coerce b 'float))
          (float-c (coerce c 'float))
          (float-angle-C (three-sides-to-angle
                               float-c float-a float-b)))
     (with-slots (a b angle-C) tri
       (setf a float-a)
       (setf b float-b)
       (setf angle-C float-angle-C))))
```

```
;;; Define the constructor
(defun make-triangle (side-a side-b side-c)
  (make-instance 'triangle :side-a side-a
                           :side-b side-b
                           :side-c side-c))
```

9.6 CONSTRUCTORS

We recommend using constructors as the external interface for creating instances, because constructors add a valuable level of abstraction between the client and the implementation. Consider triangles: The name of the constructor, make-triangle, implies "making a triangle," which is a higher-level concept than is "making an instance of the triangle class."

Another advantage of constructors is that they can use the full power of COMMON LISP argument-processing. The make-instance syntax is extremely limited: Following the first argument (the class) is an &rest parameter consisting of initargs. In many cases, the semantics of a class can be better expressed with required arguments, optional arguments, and so on. With triangles, for example, the &rest argument to make-instance fails to imply that all three initargs—the sides—are required to make a triangle. The constructor, however, can make the three sides be required arguments; the syntax of the constructor accurately reflects the semantics of triangles.

Perhaps most important, constructors conceal the implementation of objects, which frees you to change the implementation without disturbing client programs. If you advertise constructors as the external interface, you can later change to a defstruct representation of the object or change the name or initargs of the class, without invalidating client programs. Constructors can also select one of several classes, based on its arguments. If you advertise make-instance as the external interface, you cannot make these changes within the implementation.

10

A Procedural Definition: Initialization

In this chapter, we discuss the technique of designing a "procedural definition" of a high-level task; this entails breaking down the task into separate generic functions, each of which is responsible for a clearly defined portion of the task. Usually, there is a default behavior for the generic functions. Programmers use these generic functions as entry points; they can control portions of the task by specializing one or more of the generic functions.

Some programs have several related tasks. The procedural definitions of the tasks can overlap, to share code. Two or three tasks might be defined to call a single generic function. This technique can lead to modular programs; it requires a careful design in which the shared work can be shared, while the separate work can be kept separate. We examine one example in detail: the CLOS procedural definition of initialization.

10.1 EXAMPLES OF PROCEDURAL DEFINITIONS

We used the technique of a procedural definition in "The Implementation of install," page 80. As shown in Fig. 10.1, the installation task is divided into four generic functions, each of which performs a single aspect of the installation.

Installation Task

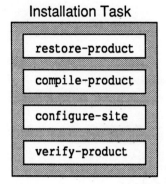

Figure 10.1 Procedural definition of the installation task.

Later, in "A Procedural Definition for Creating Streams," page 207, we design a procedural definition for choosing the correct class of stream to create, and for creating the stream by giving the appropriate arguments to `make-instance`.

CLOS itself uses the technique of procedural definitions. We have already seen that `make-instance` has a procedural definition: it always calls `initialize-instance`. Class redefinition is another example; it always calls `update-instance-for-redefined-class`. Similarly, `change-class` always calls `update-instance-for-different-class`. The generic functions `initialize-instance`, `update-instance-for-redefined-class`, and `update-instance-for-different-class` are defined intentionally as entry points—generic functions that can be specialized with methods.

Certain error situations also have procedural definitions: generic functions that are called when errors are encountered. The default method signals an error, but you can specialize the generic function to do something different. The generic functions include the following:

`slot-unbound`
> Called when an attempt is made to read an unbound slot

`slot-missing`
> Called when an attempt is made to access a slot of an instance, but there is no slot by that name accessible to the instance

`no-applicable-method`
> Called when a generic function is called and there is no applicable method for it

no-next-method

>Called when call-next-method is used and there is no "next method"

10.2 ISOLATING WORK SHARED AMONG PROCEDURES

CLOS initializes instances in several contexts: when an instance is first created with make-instance, when an instance is being updated because its class was redefined, and when you use change-class to change the class of an instance. In addition, the function reinitialize-instance (rarely used in application programs, but used within the implementation of CLOS itself, in the metaobject protocol) performs initialization of an instance based on initargs.

In each of these tasks, the initialization work is similar but not identical. In an object-oriented design, the goal is to isolate the work that can be shared, define it once, and use it everywhere it is needed. In this section, we describe how CLOS defines these related procedures in an object-oriented way. You can use this approach when designing your own programs. The four related initialization procedures are somewhat complicated, and most application programs do not require this much complexity; still, the example provides a good illustration of procedural definitions.

The first step is to identify what the procedures have in common. Here we focus on the initialization work done in each task:

initialize-instance

>Performs initialization according to initargs; then, for any slots that are still unbound, fills those slots with the values of their initforms

reinitialize-instance

>Performs initialization according to initargs

update-instance-for-redefined-class

>Performs initialization according to initargs; then, for any added local slots that are still unbound, fills those slots with the values of their initforms

update-instance-for-different-class

>Performs initialization according to initargs; then, for any added local slots that are still unbound, fills those slots with the values of their initforms

We have identified two phases of initialization: performing initialization according to initargs, and then filling some unbound slots with the values of their initforms. CLOS arranges for both phases to be done by one generic function, `shared-initialize`, which is called by all four generic functions mentioned. The four functions have slightly different requirements; these differences are managed by providing arguments to `shared-initialize`. The syntax of `shared-initialize` is

> (shared-initialize *instance slots-for-initform* &rest *initargs*)

10.3 FILLING UNBOUND SLOTS WITH INITFORMS

For the two updating functions, the phase of filling unbound slots with initforms is done for the added local slots. For `initialize-instance`, this phase is done for all slots; for `reinitialize-instance` it is not done for any slots.

The generic function `shared-initialize` takes a required argument called *slots-for-initform*, indicating which slots to fill with their initforms. This argument is a list of names of slots, or t to indicate all slots, or nil to indicate no slots. The following table shows how the callers (default methods for the four generic functions) provide the *slots-for-initform* argument:

Caller of shared-initialize	Value of slots-for-initform
initialize-instance	t
reinitialize-instance	nil
update-instance-for-redefined-class	added local slots
update-instance-for-different-class	added local slots

10.4 PERFORMING INITIALIZATION BY INITARGS

As described in "Controlling Initialization with Methods," page 159, `initialize-instance` performs initialization according to initargs. If a slot-filling initarg is given in the call to `initialize-instance`, the slot is filled with that value, even if the slot already has a value. Initargs can also be used by user-defined initialization methods that do extra work required by the application program.

In most cases, there is no need for updating functions to use initialization arguments. Sometimes, however, an application program needs a method for a special purpose, and that method needs some arguments as input. For example, a method for `update-instance-for-redefined-class` might need an argument in addition to the four required arguments; the same could be true for a method for `update-instance-for-different-class`.

Initargs can be useful in all initialization tasks, so this is another piece of work that can be shared. Thus, `shared-initialize` accepts an `&rest` argument consisting of initargs. Each caller of `shared-initialize` chooses whether or not to supply initargs.

The user can provide initargs directly to `make-instance`; these initargs are passed to `initialize-instance`, and then are passed to `shared-initialize`. When redefining a class or changing the class of an instance, however, the user cannot provide initargs. So how are initargs useful in these updating procedures? You can define an around-method for `update-instance-for-redefined-class` or `update-instance-for-different-class`. The around-method computes initargs and passes them on in a call to `call-next-method`; the default method is invoked with those initargs, and it passes them on to `shared-initialize`. Thus, around-methods are the entry point that allows the updating functions to use initargs.

10.5 SPECIALIZING A PORTION OF THE PROCEDURE

A procedural definition enables users to specialize one or more aspects of the procedure as a whole. The initialization scheme recognizes that some work is appropriate to one task only (such as class redefinition), whereas other work is appropriate to all initialization tasks. The procedural definition both separates the four initialization tasks from one another, and combines them via the call to `shared-initialize`.

Specializing this Generic Function	Affects
`initialize-instance`	instance creation
`reinitialize-instance`	instance reinitialization
`update-instance-for-redefined-class`	class redefinition
`update-instance-for-different-class`	class change
`shared-initialize`	instance creation, instance reinitialization, class redefinition, and class change

Each of the five initialization functions has a default primary method. For example, the default method for `update-instance-for-different-class` calls `initialize-instance` with the appropriate arguments. In turn, the default method for `initialize-instance` performs initialization according to initargs and initforms, based on its arguments. Typically, programmers specialize these generic functions by providing after-methods, not primary methods.

10.6 DECLARING INITARG NAMES AS VALID

All five initialization functions accept initargs. As mentioned in "Initialization Arguments," page 160, initarg names must be declared as valid. If a generic function is called with an unrecognized initarg name, an error is signaled.

The `:initarg` slot option declares initarg names as valid for all five initialization functions. Defining initialization methods that use &key parameters declares the parameter names as valid initarg names. For each call to an initialization generic function, the set of valid initarg names depends on the appropriate applicable initialization methods:

Task Performed	Initialization Methods that Declare Initarg Names as Valid
Instance creation	`make-instance,` `initialize-instance,` `shared-initialize`
Instance reinitialization	`reinitialize-instance,` `shared-initialize`
Class change	`update-instance-for-different-class,` `shared-initialize`
Class redefinition	`update-instance-for-redefined-class,` `shared-initialize`

11

Developing an Advanced CLOS Program: Streams

This chapter illustrates an object-oriented foundation for implementing COMMON LISP streams, whose behavior is specified in Steele's *Common LISP: The Language*. Streams fit naturally into the object-oriented model. The many varieties of related streams can be modeled with multiple inheritance.

This example is considerably more challenging than the other examples in this book. Our goal is to demonstrate how to attack a good-sized problem by using CLOS techniques to break up the problem into manageable modules. The design of the stream foundation specifies the responsibility of each module. The implementation consists of the modules themselves, which are classes, generic functions, and methods. The design is the challenging part—but if it is done right, the implementation should be relatively straightforward. (You will notice that the implementation of one of the modules—disk streams—is actually quite complex, but the complexity is due to the handling of the disk device itself, which would be necessary regardless of the design of streams.)

We start by summarizing what COMMON LISP streams are, and how they are created and used. We then describe our overall design and show the portions of the implementation that illustrate CLOS and the object-oriented style. This example develops a foundation for streams and illustrates how a handful of the familiar COMMON LISP stream functions can be written to use that foundation. For example, we show how read-char, write-char, read-byte, and write-byte can be written using this foundation, but we omit the definitions of other functions, such as read-line and write-line.

The external interface is specified by *Common LISP: The Language*, in the following chapters and sections:

Chapter 21	Streams
Section 22.2	Input Functions
Section 22.3	Output Functions
Section 23.2	Opening and Closing Files

This example is not intended to be an actual implementation of streams; that is a topic that could fill an entire book. For the most part, we ignore efficiency considerations. Streams need to access devices for I/O, so we assume (and document) a set of low-level primitives for tape and disk I/O that we call in the methods. These primitives are simplified versions of what might exist in a real I/O system. We do not include LISP code to implement these primitives, because it would be device-dependent, long and complex, and probably not relevant to object-oriented programming.

The value of this example lies in the techniques of decomposing a substantial problem into separate components of functionality, and of specifying a protocol for communication among these components. The details of the method bodies are less important than the overall modularity. As you read, we encourage you to focus on how the pieces fit together, instead of getting bogged down in the details of any one piece.

11.1 OVERVIEW OF STREAMS

The first step in designing and developing an object-oriented program is to understand the problem you are trying to solve. We start by describing all the types of objects we need to model and the operations on the objects. With this information we will be able to design an organization of classes.

COMMON LISP streams are used to transmit data from a source to a destination. For example, when you are using a text editor, and you give the editor command to save the contents of a buffer to a file, a stream is used to transmit the data.

Types of Streams

There are different types of streams, which are used for different purposes. The following stream types are related to the direction of data flow:

input stream	Brings data from an outside source into LISP. An example is the stream to which *standard-input* is bound.
output stream	Sends data from LISP to an outside destination. An example is the stream to which *standard-output* is bound.
bidirectional stream	Transmits data in both the input and output directions. An example is the stream to which *query-io* is bound.

The following stream types are related to the type of the data being transmitted, which is the element type of the stream:

character stream	Transmits characters
byte stream	Transmits binary bytes of data, where a "byte" is an integer with a specified number of bits

Streams have two ends; they connect two things. One end is connected to LISP, and the other end is connected to some sort of device. An input stream brings data from the device into LISP, whereas an output stream sends data from LISP to the device.

The device might be a disk, magnetic tape, network, terminal, or some other kind of device. In this example, we support disk and magnetic-tape devices. The following stream types are related to the device connected to the stream:

disk stream	Transmits data to and from a disk device
tape stream	Transmits data to and from a magnetic tape device

When you use a stream, that stream has three aspects: a direction, an element type, and a device type. For example, when saving the contents of an editor buffer to a disk file, you are using a stream that is at once a character stream, an output stream, and a disk stream.

COMMON LISP defines the notion of directional streams; the predicates input-stream-p, output-stream-p, and bidirectional-stream-p are used to determine the direction of a stream. COMMON LISP also defines the notion of element type streams by providing the stream-element-type function to query a stream for its element type. Device streams are not a COMMON LISP concept; they belong to the design of our stream foundation.

The Stream's Type Determines Its Operations

The type of a stream determines which operations can be performed on that stream. An output stream supports operations such as force-output and finish-output. A character input stream supports read-char; a character output stream supports write-char. A character bidirectional stream supports both the character input and output operations. Similarly, a byte input stream supports read-byte; a byte output stream supports write-byte; and a byte bidirectional stream supports both read-byte and write-byte.

The device type of a stream also controls the operations that can be performed on the stream. In this example, the magnetic-tape device supports sequential access, and the disk device supports both sequential and random access. Because we have greater control in using the disk device, the disk streams have greater capabilities than do the tape streams, which are limited to sequential operations.

Creating and Using Streams

One way to create a stream is to open a file. The function open returns a stream connected to the specified file. The arguments to open control the type of the stream. For example, to create a character output stream (for the purpose of transmitting characters to a file), you could evaluate this form, with an appropriate *filename* argument:

```
(open filename :direction :output :element-type 'character)
```

The device type of the file stream is extracted from the *filename* argument. If the filename indicates a disk device, the stream will be a disk stream. When you are finished using the file, you can close the stream. No input or output operations are permitted on a closed stream.

```
(close filename)
```

When you use open, you are creating a file stream. A file stream supports operations on files such as deleting and renaming. Our stream foundation provides the lower-level support for file streams; file streams could be built on this foundation.

11.2 DESIGN OF OUR STREAM FOUNDATION

We have the following design goals:

- To organize a set of stream classes in a way that accurately reflects the relationships among the different kinds of streams.
- To extract common behavior into distinct modules that can be used in several contexts. In other words, we will define a set of classes, each of which has methods that support a well-defined aspect of stream behavior. We want to share code that is common among several classes, to avoid duplication of code, and to make the program as a whole smaller, simpler, and easier to maintain.
- To plan for extensions to our foundation. We will define an internal protocol, use it within our implementation, and document it for other programmers to use.

Organization of Stream Classes

To meet the stated goals, we define these groups of classes:

- The foundation of all streams: stream
- Directional streams, including input-stream, output-stream, bidirectional-stream
- Element type streams, including character-stream, byte-stream
- Device streams, including disk-stream, tape-stream

Our design effectively defines a stream as "an object built on the stream class." Thus, clients can find out whether an object is a stream by using typep, as well as by using streamp. The following two forms are equivalent:

```
(typep object 'stream)
(streamp object)
```

Each of these classes is a building block equipped to handle only one aspect of the stream. A complete stream consists of building blocks that specify the direction, the element type, and the device. One example of a complete stream is `character-disk-input-stream`: This class inherits from `character-stream`, `disk-stream`, `input-stream`, and `stream`.

The device streams manipulate elements of data without knowing whether the elements are characters or bytes. Each element type stream manipulates data with knowledge of the datatype, but without knowledge of the various devices. We want to isolate the device-specific operations within the realm of the device streams, and to isolate all datatype-specific operations within the element type streams.

This design makes it easy for clients to extend our stream program. To add support for a new element type, the client needs to provide methods for only the generic functions that are specific to the element type of the stream. The new element type stream immediately works with all types of devices supporting the internal protocol. Similarly, introducing a new device requires adding methods for the device-specific generic functions, and the new device will immediately work with all types of elements.

There are three basic directional types of streams, each of which is built on `stream`: `input-stream`, `output-stream`, and `bidirectional-stream`. As shown in Fig. 11.1, `bidirectional-stream` is built on both `input-stream` and `output-stream`.

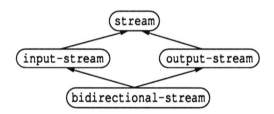

Figure 11.1 Directional stream classes.

This pattern is reflected in the other groups of classes. Figure 11.2 shows the organization of character classes.

Although not shown in these figures, each of the character stream classes is built on a directional stream class. That is, `character-stream` is built on `stream`, `character-input-stream` is built on `input-stream`, and so on.

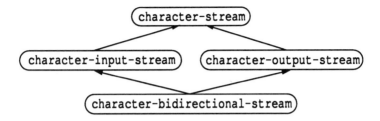

Figure 11.2 Character stream classes.

The device stream classes follow the same pattern. For example, we will define the following classes for the disk device: disk-stream, disk-input-stream, disk-output-stream, and disk-bidirectional-stream.

External Stream Protocol

The external protocol of streams is specified in *Common LISP: The Language*. In this example, we implement the following subset of the COMMON LISP stream operations:

Stream Type	Operations
all streams	input-stream-p, output-stream-p, close, stream-element-type
output	force-output, finish-output
byte input	read-byte
byte output	write-byte
byte bidirectional	read-byte, write-byte
character input	read-char
character output	write-char
character bidirectional	read-char, write-char
disk	set-position

The function set-position is an extension to COMMON LISP for disk streams. We document the contract of set-position here:

set-position *stream new-position* &optional *eof-error-p eof-value*
          Sets the current position to the desired element position.

The element position is the element number in the file, where the first element is number 0, the next is 1, and so on. If the *new-position* is beyond the end of file, *eof-error-p* and *eof-value* define whether an error or a value is returned; otherwise, the new position is returned.

We discuss how streams are created and opened later, in "A Procedural Definition for Creating Streams," page 207.

Internal Stream Protocol

Our purpose in defining an internal protocol is to codify the communication among the different stream classes. This makes it possible for each class to implement a well-defined aspect of the internal protocol and depend on the other classes to implement their aspects. The internal stream protocol consists of the following operations:

`bytes-per-element` *stream*

> Supported by all element type streams. Returns the number of eight-bit bytes required to store one element of this datatype. This must be a positive integer.

`storage-unit-size` *stream*

> Supported by all device streams. Returns the size of a unit normally read or written by this device, expressed in eight-bit bytes. For a disk stream, this is the size of a disk sector. For a tape stream, this is the size of a tape record.

`make-element-array` *stream*

> Supported by all streams. Creates an array to serve as a buffer for input or output. The size of the array is appropriate for the device (note that the low-level device primitives read and write in fixed-size blocks), and for the element type appropriate to the stream. This can be implemented in terms of `storage-unit-size`, `stream-element-type`, and `bytes-per-element`.

`ensure-open-stream` *stream*

> Supported by all streams. Checks whether a stream is open before allowing access to it. Signals an error if an attempt is made to access a stream that is closed.

`read-next-element` *input-stream*

> Supported by all device input streams. Uses low-level de-

vice primitives to read one element of data. Returns a second value, which is t if the end of file was reached, else nil.

write-next-element *output-stream*
> Supported by all device output streams. Uses low-level device primitives to write one element of data.

force-output-internal *output-stream*
> Supported by all output streams. Does the work of force-output.

finish-output-internal *output-stream*
> Supported by all output streams. Does the work of finish-output.

11.3 EXPERIMENTING WITH THE STREAM EXAMPLE

If you intend to try out the code in this example, keep in mind that we redefine several important COMMON LISP functions that operate on streams. You can define a package for the purpose of testing this example and specify that certain COMMON LISP symbols should be shadowed. This enables you to retain the previous definitions of the stream functions, which is necessary for keeping your LISP usable. (If COMMON LISP specified that the stream functions were generic, there would be no need to shadow the existing definitions; you could simply add methods to the existing generic functions.)

```
(setq *clos-streams-package*
      (make-package 'clos-streams :nicknames '("cs")
                    :use 'lisp))

(shadow '(input-stream-p output-stream-p
          force-output finish-output
          close stream-element-type
          read-char write-char
          read-byte write-byte)
        'clos-streams)
```

You will notice that we declare the returned values of generic functions in several defgeneric forms. This is a convenient way to document part of the contract of the generic function—the expected returned values. Although COMMON LISP does not specify values as a recognized declaration specifier, we can make it one by proclaiming values as a declaration as follows:

```
(proclaim '(declaration values))
```

If we neglected to proclaim `values` as a declaration, the compiler would probably give a warning that the declaration was unsupported.

11.4 DIRECTIONAL STREAMS

Here we define the classes `stream`, `input-stream`, `output-stream`, and `bidirectional-stream`. We also define the methods that each of these classes supplies. Then, we mention aspects of this code that are of particular interest.

The style of this program groups methods and generic functions according to the class definitions. For example, under the `stream` class definition, you will find definitions for the generic functions that are supported by all streams. All methods supplied by a class are located under the class definition. We also separate the external interface from the internal interface with comments in the code.

This style fits this particular example well; another program might benefit from a different style. A program that depends heavily on multi-methods could not group methods this way, because a multi-method is attached to more than one class. One alternative would be to group the classes, methods, and generic functions together according to the protocols they support.

Defining Directional Streams

```
;;;; THE CLASS STREAM

;;; This basic class must be included in all streams.
(defclass stream ()
      ((state :initform 'open :accessor stream-state))
   (:documentation "Foundation of all streams."))

;;;; EXTERNAL PROTOCOL SUPPORTED BY ALL STREAMS

;;; Page 332 in Common LISP: The Language
(defgeneric input-stream-p (stream)
   ;; Input streams should override this default method.
   (:method ((stream stream)) nil))
```

```
;;; Page 332 in Common LISP: The Language
(defgeneric output-stream-p (stream)
  ;; Output streams should override this default method.
  (:method ((stream stream)) nil))

;;; Page 332 in Common LISP: The Language
(defgeneric close (stream &key abort)
  (:documentation "Prevents further I/O operations on stream")
  (:method ((stream stream) &key abort)
    (declare (ignore abort))
    (setf (stream-state stream) 'closed)))

;;; Page 332 in Common LISP: The Language
;;; Must be implemented by the element type streams.
(defgeneric stream-element-type (stream)
  (:documentation "Returns the type of elements of stream"))

;;;; INTERNAL PROTOCOL SUPPORTED BY ALL STREAMS

(defun ensure-open-stream (stream)
  "Prevents access to a stream if it is not open."
  (let ((state (stream-state stream)))
    (unless (eq state 'open)
      (error "Attempt to use stream ~A which is ~A"
             stream state))))

;;; bytes-per-element must be implemented by element type streams.
(defgeneric bytes-per-element (stream)
  (declare (values n-bytes))
  (:documentation "Returns length of one element, in 8-bit bytes."))

;;; storage-unit-size must be implemented by device streams.
(defgeneric storage-unit-size (stream)
  (declare (values n-bytes))
  (:documentation "Returns size of i/o buffer, in 8-bit bytes."))

(defun make-element-array (stream)
  "Returns array of correct size and element type for stream."
  (make-array (/ (storage-unit-size stream)
                 (bytes-per-element stream))
              :element-type (stream-element-type stream)))
```

```
;;;; THE CLASS INPUT-STREAM AND ITS METHODS

;;; This basic class must be included in all input streams.
(defclass input-stream (stream) ()
  (:documentation "Foundation of all input streams."))

;;; Override the default primary method to return true.
(defmethod input-stream-p ((stream input-stream))
  t)

;;;; INTERNAL PROTOCOL SUPPORTED BY ALL INPUT STREAMS

;;; Make sure the stream is open before any input is allowed.
(defgeneric read-next-element (input-stream)
  (declare (values element eof-p))
  (:method :before ((stream input-stream))
    ;; This method ensures that stream is open before
    ;; reading; it is inherited by all element type input
    ;; streams, so it saves each of those methods from
    ;; duplicating this code.
    (ensure-open-stream stream)))

;;; This default method on stream is overridden by input
;;; streams.  It is defined simply to give a comprehensible
;;; error message when this situation occurs, and to make it
;;; unnecessary for all external functions to check the
;;; stream argument type.
(defmethod read-next-element ((stream stream))
  (error "Cannot get input from stream ~A of type ~A."
         stream (type-of stream)))

;;;; THE CLASS OUTPUT-STREAM AND ITS METHODS

;;; This basic class must be included in all output streams.
(defclass output-stream (stream) ()
  (:documentation "Foundation of all output streams."))

;;; Override the default primary method to return true.
(defmethod output-stream-p ((stream output-stream))
  t)

;;;; EXTERNAL PROTOCOL SUPPORTED BY ALL OUTPUT STREAMS
```

```
;;; Although COMMON LISP implies that force-output
;;; and finish-output are supported by character
;;; streams only, they should apply to all output
;;; output streams, which is how we do it below.

;;; Also, since COMMON LISP specifies that the stream
;;; argument of force-output and finish-output is
;;; optional, we can't implement these operations
;;; directly as generic functions.
;;; Therefore, we define force-output-internal and
;;; finish-output-internal as generic functions, both of
;;; which belong to the internal protocol.

;;; Standardize stream variable if t or nil was given
(defmacro standardize-output-stream-var (stream)
  '(setf ,stream (cond ((eq ,stream t) *terminal-io*)
                       ((null ,stream) *standard-output*)
                       (t ,stream)))))

;;; Page 384 in Common LISP: The Language
(defun force-output (&optional (stream *standard-output*))
  (standardize-output-stream-var stream)
  (force-output-internal stream))

;;; Page 384 in Common LISP: The Language
(defun finish-output (&optional (stream *standard-output*))
  (standardize-output-stream-var stream)
  (finish-output-internal stream))

;;;; INTERNAL PROTOCOL SUPPORTED BY ALL OUTPUT STREAMS

(defgeneric force-output-internal (output-stream)
  (:method :before ((stream output-stream))
   ;; The stream must be open, else generate an error.
   (ensure-open-stream stream)))

(defgeneric finish-output-internal (output-stream)
  (:method :before ((stream output-stream))
   ;; The stream must be open, else generate an error.
   (ensure-open-stream stream)))
```

```
(defgeneric write-next-element (output-stream element)
  (:method :before ((stream output-stream) element)
    (declare (ignore element))
    ;; Default method ensures that stream is open before
    ;; writing.  This method is inherited by all element type
    ;; output streams, and thus it saves each of those
    ;; methods from duplicating this code.
    (ensure-open-stream stream)))

;;; This default method on stream is overridden by output streams.
;;; It is defined simply to give a comprehensible error message
;;; when this situation occurs, and to make it unnecessary for
;;; all user-interface functions to check the stream argument type.
(defmethod write-next-element ((stream stream) element)
  (declare (ignore element))
  (error "Cannot do output to stream ~A of type ~A."
         stream (type-of stream)))

;;; THE CLASS BIDIRECTIONAL-STREAM

;;; This class inherits all needed methods, and supplies none
;;; of its own.
(defclass bidirectional-stream
    (input-stream output-stream)
    ()
  (:documentation "A combined input and output stream."))
```

Highlights of Directional Streams

The relationships among directional streams are defined here. All streams are built on the class stream. Input streams are built on input-stream, and output streams are built on output-stream.

The COMMON LISP type predicates on streams are defined here, including input-stream-p and output-stream-p. The inheritance of these methods works neatly and effectively.

- The class stream provides default methods for input-stream-p and output-stream-p, which return nil.

- The class input-stream provides a method for input-stream-p that overrides the default method and returns t. However, the class input-stream inherits the default method for output-stream-p.

- The class `output-stream` provides a method for `output-stream-p` that overrides the default method and returns t. However, the class `output-stream` inherits the default method for `input-stream-p`.

- The class `bidirectional-stream` inherits all these methods from its superclasses `input-stream`, `output-stream`, and `stream`. The method for `input-stream-p` supplied by class `input-stream` overrides the method supplied by the class `stream`; therefore, a bidirectional stream is defined to be an input stream. Similarly, a bidirectional stream is defined to be an output stream.

Sometimes it is not possible to implement a function as a generic function. For example, COMMON LISP specifies that the stream argument to `force-output` is optional. In CLOS, methods cannot specialize on optional arguments. Since we want the stream argument to select methods, we define `force-output` as an ordinary function, which processes its arguments and then calls `force-output-internal` to do its work. We define `force-output-internal` as a generic function whose stream argument is required. We do the same for `finish-output`.

We implemented `ensure-open-stream` and `make-element-array` as ordinary LISP functions. We do not anticipate that different types of streams will need specialized behavior for these operations. The stream protocol can be implemented in terms of both ordinary and generic functions.

11.5 TAPE STREAMS

For the purpose of this example, we assume an extremely simple tape system. Tape streams do not support all the capabilities of disk streams because the tape device supports sequential access, not random access. Note that tape streams do not support `set-position` or the appending of data. We also do not provide a bidirectional tape stream.

Low-Level Tape Interface

Here we specify the interface to an imaginary operating system for streams to magnetic-tape units. We document these primitives, but do not include LISP code that implements them. We assume that these primitives exist, and we call them in the methods for tape streams.

To keep the example simple, tape records are all fixed size, except for the last record, which usually is incomplete (it does not contain a full tape record of data), and thus smaller. This tape system supports only one contiguous amount of data, starting at the beginning of the tape and going to an EOF (end of file) mark.

`open-tape-unit` *tape-unit-number*
> Returns a "tape-handle" identifying the tape unit.

`close-tape-unit` *tape-handle*
> Closes the tape unit and deallocates the tape-handle.

`read-record` *tape-handle array element-type*
> Reads the next tape record into the array. Returns two values, named eof and eof-position. The first value (eof) is nil if the array contains a complete record, or t if the array contains an incomplete record; in this case, the second value is a number marking the position of the EOF.

`write-record` *tape-handle array element-type* `&optional` (*size* `*tape-record-byte-size*`)
> Writes the contents of the array into the next tape record. The size argument is used for writing the last record, which is usually incomplete, and thus smaller than `*tape-record-byte-size*`. `write-record` does not write any elements of the array past the given size.

`write-eof-mark` *tape-handle*
> Writes an EOF mark on the tape.

`rewind` *tape-handle*
> Rewinds the tape unit to the beginning of the tape.

Defining Tape Streams

```
;;;; THE CLASS TAPE-STREAM AND ITS METHODS

(defclass tape-stream
     (stream)
     ((unit :accessor tape-unit
             :initform 0
             :initarg :unit)
      (tape-handle :initform nil :accessor tape-handle)
      (tape-record-size :allocation :class
                        :initform *tape-record-byte-size*
                        :reader storage-unit-size)
      (element-buffer :accessor element-buffer)
      (buffer-index :accessor buffer-index))
   (:documentation "A stream for accessing a tape device."))
```

```
(defmethod initialize-instance :after
           ((stream tape-stream) &key)
   (with-accessors ((tape-handle tape-handle)
                    (unit tape-unit)
                    (element-buffer element-buffer))
                 stream
     (setf tape-handle (open-tape-unit unit))
     (setf element-buffer (make-element-array stream)))))

;;; Close the tape unit and clear the tape-handle.
(defmethod close ((stream tape-stream) &key abort)
   (declare (ignore abort))
   (with-accessors ((tape-handle tape-handle))
                 stream
     (when tape-handle
       (close-tape-unit tape-handle)
       (setf tape-handle nil)))))

;;;; THE CLASS TAPE-INPUT-STREAM AND ITS METHODS

(defclass tape-input-stream
      (tape-stream input-stream)
      ;; position in buffer of EOF
      ;; or nil if EOF has not been reached
      ((eof-offset :initform nil
                   :accessor eof-offset)
       ;; provide a default value for this inherited slot
       (buffer-index :initform nil))
   (:documentation "A stream for getting input from a tape device."))

(defmethod read-next-element ((stream tape-input-stream))
   (with-accessors ((element-buffer element-buffer)
                    (buffer-index buffer-index)
                    (tape-handle tape-handle)
                    (eof-offset eof-offset))
                 stream
     ;; Make sure the input buffer contains the desired data
     (unless (and buffer-index
                  (< buffer-index (length element-buffer)))
       ;; The current buffer does not contain the desired element.
       ;; Read the next record.
       (multiple-value-bind (eof byte-offset)
```

```
                  (read-record tape-handle element-buffer
                               (stream-element-type stream))
            (if eof (setf eof-offset
                          (/ byte-offset (bytes-per-element stream))))
            (setf buffer-index 0)))
       ;; Return nil t if EOF is reached
      (if (and eof-offset (>= buffer-index eof-offset))
          (values nil t)
          ;; Otherwise return data element and update buffer index
          (prog1 (aref element-buffer buffer-index)
                 (incf buffer-index)))))))

;;;; THE CLASS TAPE-OUTPUT-STREAM AND ITS METHODS

(defclass tape-output-stream
     (tape-stream output-stream)
     ((buffer-index :initform 0))
   (:documentation "A stream for writing output to a tape device."))

(defmethod write-next-element ((stream tape-output-stream) element)
  (with-accessors ((element-buffer element-buffer)
                   (buffer-index buffer-index)
                   (tape-handle tape-handle))
                  stream
    (unless (< buffer-index (length element-buffer))
      ;; index is past the end of the buffer, so we
      ;; need to write out the buffer and update index
      (write-record tape-handle element-buffer
                    (stream-element-type stream))
      (setf buffer-index 0))
    (setf (aref element-buffer buffer-index) element)
    (incf buffer-index)))

;;; For close :abort, rewind tape immediately and write EOF.
;;; For normal close, write out remaining buffered data (if
;;; necessary) and then write EOF.
(defmethod close :before ((stream tape-output-stream)
                          &key abort)
  (with-accessors ((tape-handle tape-handle))
                  stream
    (if abort
        (rewind tape-handle)
```

```
;; No need to write buffer out if there is no buffer-index
;; because that implies that no writing has begun
(unless (zerop buffer-index)
   (write-record tape-handle element-buffer
                 (stream-element-type stream)
                 ;; include the size argument
                 (* buffer-index
                    (bytes-per-element stream)))))))
(write-eof-mark tape-handle)))


;;; Neither force-output-internal nor finish-output-internal
;;; should write an incomplete tape record to the tape device,
;;; because it would then be impossible to continue to do
;;; output at the correct tape position.  Therefore the two
;;; methods below don't do anything.

(defmethod force-output-internal ((stream tape-output-stream))
   nil)                      ;nil is the documented returned value.

(defmethod finish-output-internal ((stream tape-output-stream))
   nil)                      ;nil is the documented returned value.
```

Highlights of Tape Streams

The purpose of tape streams is to isolate all knowledge of the magnetic-tape device. The only part of our program that uses the tape primitives is the tape streams. An equally important aspect of tape streams is that they access the magnetic-tape device for input and or output, without any knowledge of the type of elements being read or written. Tape streams manipulate data without knowing whether the data consist of characters, bytes, or other types of data.

This modularity is the keystone of our design. The modularity depends on a strict delineation of responsibility. Tape stream classes are responsible for accessing the magnetic-tape device, and they must rely on the element type stream classes to handle any work that is specific to the element type of the data.

The primitives in our tape interface do not support set-position. The tape device reads from beginning to end, or writes from beginning to end, and cannot change its notion of current position, other than to rewind all the way to the beginning of the tape. This limitation has two effects on tape streams:

- Tape streams do not supply a method for `set-position`. If a client tries to set the position of a tape stream, the "no applicable method" error is signaled.

- Since we cannot set the position, it is not possible to implement `force-output-internal` or `finish-output-internal`. If we were to write an incomplete tape record to the tape device, we could no longer continue to do output at the correct tape position. However, even though we cannot implement these generic functions, it is essential that we define methods for them. When called, the methods simply return `nil`. The existence of these methods enables clients to use `force-output` and `finish-output` on all output streams. If the device can force or finish the output it does so; if it cannot, no error is signaled.

This behavior is consistent with our defined external protocol. All output streams must support `force-output` and `finish-output`, although the actual details of what happens depend on the device. It is part of the contract of these two functions that no error should be signaled, even if the device cannot support the functions. This is unusual; typically, it is appropriate to allow the "no applicable method" error to be signaled when the generic function is not implemented for the set of arguments.

11.6 DISK STREAMS

Disk streams need to have direct access to the disk. For the purpose of this example, we assume a simple interface to an imaginary operating system for streams to disk files. In a real implementation, this layer would be the very lowest file-system support.

Low-Level Disk Interface

We assume a simple operating system that supports random-access files with fixed-size blocks (corresponding to a disk sector). The interface assumes that the file already exists, or else `open-disk-file` will create it. `disk-write` creates the block if it does not already exist. We assume the following primitives for accessing the disk:

`open-disk-file` *file-name-string*

> Returns a "file-handle" for identifying the file and opens the file for random block-oriented access.

`byte-length` *file-handle*
> Returns the length of the file in bytes.

(`setf byte-length`) *n-bytes file-handle*
> Sets the length of a file in bytes. Called with the `setf` syntax as follows:
>
> (`setf` (`byte-length` *file-handle*) *n-bytes*)

`close-disk-file` *file-handle*
> Closes the file and deallocates the file-handle.

`disk-read` *file-handle array block-number element-type* `&key` (*wait* t)
> Reads the contents of the file's specified block into the array, automatically converting from the disk's internal data format into the element type. If *wait* is t, `disk-read` does not return until the disk operation finishes. Otherwise, `disk-read` returns immediately after requesting the operation, returning an identifier that can be passed to `disk-finished-p` to see whether the disk operation is finished. The contents of the array should not be accessed until the disk operation finishes. That is, if *wait* is nil, the array should not be accessed until `disk-finished-p` returns t.

`disk-write` *file-handle array block-number element-type* `&key` (*wait* t)
> Writes the contents of the array into the file's specified block, automatically converting from the element type into the disk's internal data format. If *wait* is t, `disk-write` does not return until the disk operation finishes. Otherwise, `disk-write` returns immediately after requesting the operation, returning an identifier that can be passed to `disk-finished-p` to see whether the disk operation is finished. The contents of the array should not be accessed until the disk operation finishes. That is, if *wait* is nil, the array should not be accessed until `disk-finished-p` returns t.

`disk-finished-p` *identifier*
> Returns t if the operation is finished. The *identifier* is the value returned by `disk-read` or `disk-write` if *wait* is nil.

Disk streams are considerably more complicated than tape streams. The `disk-write` primitive supports a *wait* keyword, which we will use for distinguishing between `force-output` and `finish-output`. COMMON LISP specifies that `force-output` should begin to write the buffered data, but should not wait for the writing to be finished. In contrast, `finish-output` writes the buffered data and does wait until the writing is finished. This distinction means that disk streams have some asynchronous activities, which requires us to keep in mind those situations for which we need to check whether a disk-write operation is in progress before proceeding.

Defining Disk Streams

```
;;;; THE DISK-STREAM CLASS

(defclass disk-stream
     ;; Disk streams are built on the basic class stream
     (stream)
     ;; Handle to file returned by OS
     ((file-handle :initform nil
                    :accessor file-handle)
      ;; Name of the file for the OS
      (pathname :initarg :pathname
                 :accessor disk-pathname)
      ;; Size of a disk sector, expressed in 8-bit bytes
      (disk-sector-size :allocation :class
                        :initform *disk-sector-byte-size*
                        :reader storage-unit-size)
      ;; Position of current element within file
      (element-number :initform 0
                       :accessor element-number)
      ;; Total number of elements in disk file
      (element-length :accessor element-length)
      ;; Element buffer, used for I/O
      (element-buffer :accessor element-buffer)
      ;; Index into element buffer or NIL if uninitialized
      (buffer-index :initform nil
                     :accessor buffer-index)
      ;; Disk block number of buffer.
      (block-number :initform 0
                     :accessor block-number))
   (:documentation "A stream for accessing a disk file."))

;;; This method does a lot of initialization, and some of
;;; it depends on happening in a certain order.   Hence an
;;; initialization method is preferable to initforms,
;;; whose execution order is not defined.
(defmethod initialize-instance :after
```

```
              ((stream disk-stream) &key)
    ;; we use with-accessors for convenient access to the slots
    (with-accessors ((file-handle file-handle)
                     (element-length element-length)
                     (pathname disk-pathname)
                     (element-buffer element-buffer))
                  stream
      (setf file-handle (open-disk-file (namestring pathname)))
      (setf element-buffer (make-element-array stream))
      (setf element-length (/ (byte-length file-handle)
                              (bytes-per-element stream))))))

;;;; EXTERNAL PROTOCOL SUPPORTED BY ALL DISK STREAMS

;;; set-position is an extension to COMMON LISP, which
;;; we include in the External Interface.   It allows
;;; greater control when accessing disk streams.

;;; This sets the current position to the desired element
;;; position.  If the element position is beyond the end
;;; of the file, eof-error-p and eof-value define whether
;;; an error or a value is returned. The element position
;;; is the element number in the file, where the first
;;; element is number 0, the next is 1, and so on.
(defgeneric set-position (disk-stream new-position
                          &optional eof-error-p eof-value)
  (:method ((stream disk-stream) new-position
            &optional eof-error-p eof-value)
    (with-accessors ((element-buffer element-buffer)
                     (buffer-index buffer-index)
                     (element-length element-length)
                     (file-handle file-handle)
                     (block-number block-number))
                  stream
      ;; Don't allow setting position past end of file
      (if (> new-position element-length)
          (if eof-error-p
              (error "End of file in ~A" stream)
              eof-value)
          ;; Here, new-position is OK
          (multiple-value-bind (block-no offset)
              (truncate new-position (length element-buffer))
```

```
                          ;; Unless current buffer is valid
                          (unless (and buffer-index
                                      ;; And contains the same block
                                      (= block-number block-no))
                            ;; Have to read in the desired block
                            (setf block-number block-no)
                            (disk-read file-handle element-buffer block-number
                                      (stream-element-type stream)))
                          (setf buffer-index offset)
                          (setf element-number new-position))))))

(defmethod close ((stream disk-stream) &key abort)
  (declare (ignore abort))
  (with-accessors ((file-handle file-handle))
                  stream
    ;; Checking and clearing the file-handle isn't essential
    ;; but is good practice in case CLOSE is called multiple
    ;; times, especially CLOSE then CLOSE :ABORT T
    (when file-handle
      (close-disk-file file-handle)
      (setf file-handle nil))))

;;;; THE CLASS DISK-INPUT-STREAM AND ITS METHODS

(defclass disk-input-stream (disk-stream input-stream) ()
  (:documentation "A stream for getting input from a disk."))

(defmethod read-next-element ((stream disk-input-stream))
  (with-accessors ((element-number element-number)
                   (element-length element-length)
                   (buffer-index buffer-index)
                   (element-buffer element-buffer)
                   (block-number block-number)
                   (file-handle file-handle))
                  stream
    (cond ((< element-number element-length)
           ;; Make sure the input buffer contains the desired data.
           (unless (and buffer-index
                       (< buffer-index (length element-buffer)))
             ;; Unless at beginning, advance to next block.
             (if buffer-index (incf block-number))
             (disk-read file-handle element-buffer block-number
```

```
                            (stream-element-type stream))
                 (setf buffer-index 0))
              ;; Update pointers and return data element.
              (incf element-number)
              (prog1 (aref element-buffer buffer-index)
                     (incf buffer-index)))
            (t ;; At EOF
             (values nil t)))))
```

;;;; THE CLASS DISK-OUTPUT-STREAM AND ITS METHODS

```
(defclass disk-output-stream
      (disk-stream output-stream)
      ;; disk-id is used to store the identifier returned
      ;; by disk-write, which we will use to find out if
      ;; the disk-write is still in progress.
      ((disk-id :initform nil
                :accessor disk-id))
  (:documentation "A stream for writing output to a disk."))
```

;;; This comes in useful when we need to ensure that
;;; there is no disk-write currently in progress.
```
(defmethod wait-for-disk ((stream disk-output-stream))
  (with-accessors ((disk-id disk-id))
                  stream
    (unless (null disk-id)
      ;; process-wait is not part of COMMON LISP, but we
      ;; defined it earlier, in "Locks and Processes"
      (process-wait "Disk wait" #'disk-finished-p disk-id)
      (setf disk-id nil))))
```

```
(defmethod write-next-element
          ((stream disk-output-stream) element)
  (with-accessors ((element-buffer element-buffer)
                   (buffer-index buffer-index)
                   (block-number block-number)
                   (element-number element-number)
                   (element-length element-length)
                   (file-handle file-handle))
                  stream
    ;; Ensure that no disk write is happening.
    (wait-for-disk stream)
```

```
            (unless (and buffer-index (< buffer-index
                                         (length element-buffer)))
              ;; Current buffer does not contain the desired element.
              (when buffer-index
                ;; Write out the old buffer and update the pointers.
                (disk-write file-handle element-buffer block-number
                            (stream-element-type stream))
                (incf block-number))
              ;; Need to read in next block in case we are
              ;; overwriting an existing file.
              (when (< element-number element-length)
                (disk-read file-handle element-buffer block-number
                           (stream-element-type stream)))
              (setf buffer-index 0))
            (setf (aref element-buffer buffer-index) element)
            (incf buffer-index)
            (incf element-number)
            ;; Update the EOF pointer as well, but defer the actual
            ;; setting of the EOF pointer on the disk until CLOSE (or
            ;; FINISH-OUTPUT) time to reduce overhead.  FINISH-OUTPUT
            ;; should be called anyway when dealing with files which
            ;; are being read by other processes.
            (when (>= element-number element-length)
              (setf element-length element-number))))

;;; The methods for force-output-internal and finish-output-internal
;;; check whether a force-output-internal is already in progress.
;;; If so, they don't do an additional, unnecessary disk-write.

(defmethod force-output-internal ((stream disk-output-stream))
  (with-accessors ((buffer-index buffer-index)
                   (file-handle file-handle)
                   (element-buffer element-buffer)
                   (disk-id disk-id)
                   (block-number block-number))
                  stream
    (unless disk-id
      ;; A force-output-internal is not already in
      ;; progress, so we start one.
      (when buffer-index
        ;; The current buffer contents are valid.  Write them
        ;; out.  Don't change any of the pointers in case
```

```
                ;; output is simply continued.
                (setf disk-id (disk-write file-handle element-buffer
                                          block-number
                                          (stream-element-type stream)
                                          :wait nil)))))
        nil)                ;; nil is the documented returned value.


(defmethod finish-output-internal ((stream disk-output-stream))
  (with-accessors ((file-handle file-handle)
                   (buffer-index buffer-index)
                   (element-length element-length)
                   (disk-id disk-id))
                  stream
      ;; Don't do anything if buffer is invalid
      (when buffer-index
        (unless disk-id
          ;; A force-output-internal is not already in
          ;; progress, so we start one.
          (force-output-internal stream))
        ;; Also, update the EOF pointer on the disk.  It's OK
        ;; if the operating system causes this to hang until
        ;; the disk is updated.  Note:  this could be optimized
        ;; to do this only if the value has changed.
        (setf (byte-length file-handle)
              (* element-length (bytes-per-element stream)))
        ;; And then wait for it to finish.
        (wait-for-disk stream))))

(defmethod set-position :before ((stream disk-output-stream)
                                 new-position
                                 &optional eof-error-p eof-value)
  (declare (ignore new-position eof-error-p eof-value))
  ;; Before a new disk block can be read in containing the
  ;; new position, we have to write out the old block if it
  ;; has been modified.  Note: this could be improved by
  ;; seeing whether the new-position argument is still in
  ;; the same buffer, and not doing finish-output-internal
  ;; in that case.
  (finish-output-internal stream))

;;; This needs to be done before the primary methods are
;;; called, to prepare the file to be closed by first sending
```

```
;;; out any buffered output.
(defmethod close :before ((stream disk-output-stream)
                          &key abort)
  (unless abort
    (finish-output-internal stream)))


;;;; THE CLASS DISK-BIDIRECTIONAL-STREAM

(defclass disk-bidirectional-stream
      (disk-input-stream disk-output-stream bidirectional-stream)
      ()
  (:documentation "A combined input and output disk stream."))

;;; Bidirectional streams do both reading and writing.
;;; Before reading, ensure that no disk-write is happening.
(defmethod read-next-element :before
          ((stream disk-bidirectional-stream))
  (wait-for-disk stream))
```

Highlights of Disk Streams

Disk streams are analogous to tape streams, in that they isolate all knowledge of the disk device. The disk streams are responsible for handling all work related to the disk, and they must do their job without depending on knowledge of the element type of the data.

However, the disk streams do need to provide the element type of the stream as an argument to disk-read and disk-write. To do so, the disk stream methods call the stream-element-type generic function. Each element type stream provides a method for stream-element-type. Thus, when disk stream methods need information about the element type, they use the documented internal protocol and rely on the element type classes handling the element type aspects of streams.

It is also worth noting that disk streams introduce one new function into the external protocol: set-position. Since the disk primitives support reading and writing random blocks, it is useful to bring that capability directly to the users of our stream program. Disk streams support set-position because to do so makes sense for a disk device; however, there is no requirement that all device streams must support set-position.

Disk streams are more complex than tape streams because of the asynchronous behavior of disk writing (supported by the :wait keyword to disk-write) and the set-position capability. It is valuable to identify the places in the code where we use `wait-for-disk`, because that gives us a framework for discussing the modularity of disk streams. The general guideline is that we must wait for the disk to finish writing before we modify the buffer of data. The buffer is modified by both `disk-read` and functions that write elements to the array.

- `wait-for-disk` is implemented by a method on `disk-output-stream` and by the slot `disk-id`, which is a slot of `disk-output-stream`. It is correct to associate the `wait-for-disk` behavior with disk output streams, because disk writing takes place in disk output streams only.

- An input-only disk stream would have no need to call `disk-write`, which means that an input-only stream never has to wait for the disk. No methods for `disk-input-stream` call `wait-for-disk`.

- In general, an output-only disk stream needs to wait for the disk before modifying the buffer. This happens in the method for `write-next-element`.

- The primary method for `set-position` is attached to the class `disk-stream`. This method calls `disk-read` without waiting for the disk because for input-only streams waiting is unnecessary and, in fact, is unsupported. However, output streams must wait for the disk before calling `disk-read`. We implement this waiting by providing a before-method for `set-position` for the class `disk-output-stream`. This method calls `finish-output`, which in turn calls `write-next-element`, which waits for the disk if necessary.

- A bidirectional disk stream needs to wait for the disk before calling `disk-read` or `disk-write`. Bidirectional streams inherit the waiting behavior already implemented by output streams, but there is no waiting behavior in input streams (because waiting is unnecessary for input-only streams). Therefore, we support the waiting behavior in a before-method for `read-next-element` for the class `disk-bidirectional-stream`.

11.7 CHARACTER STREAMS

Here we define our first element type streams; character streams do anything that is needed to handle the character element type. These streams are considerably simpler than the device type streams.

Defining Character Streams

```
;;;; THE CLASS CHARACTER-STREAM

(defclass character-stream
     (stream)
     ((bytes-per-element :allocation :class
                          :initform 1
                          :reader bytes-per-element)
      (element-type :allocation :class
                    :initform 'character
                    :reader stream-element-type))
   (:documentation "A stream for transmitting characters."))


;;;; EXTERNAL PROTOCOL SUPPORTED BY CHARACTER STREAMS

;;; Because COMMON LISP specifies that the stream argument to
;;; read-char and write-char is optional, we implement
;;; these operations as ordinary functions.   The "generic"
;;; aspect of read-char and write-char lies within the bodies
;;; of the functions, where they call the generic functions
;;; read-next-element and write-next-element.

;;; Standardize stream variable if t or nil was given.
;;; This is done for input streams on characters, but
;;; not on bytes, since the byte-stream operations do
;;; not default the stream argument; it is required.
(defmacro standardize-char-input-stream-var (stream)
  '(setf ,stream (cond ((eq ,stream t) *terminal-io*)
                       ((null ,stream) *standard-input*)
                       (t ,stream))))

;;; Page 379 in Common LISP: The Language
(defun read-char (&optional (input-stream *standard-input*)
                  eof-error-p eof-value recursive-p)
  (standardize-char-input-stream-var input-stream)
  (multiple-value-bind (element eof-p)
      (read-next-element input-stream)
    (cond (eof-p
           (if eof-error-p
               (if recursive-p
                   (error "End of file while reading from ~A"
```

```
                               input-stream)
                   (error "End of file in ~A" input-stream))
              eof-value))
      (t
       element)))))

;;; Page 384 in Common LISP: The Language
(defun write-char (character
                   &optional (output-stream *standard-output*))
  (standardize-output-stream-var output-stream)
  (write-next-element output-stream character))


;;;; THE DIRECTIONAL CHARACTER-STREAM CLASSES

(defclass character-input-stream
      (character-stream input-stream)
      ()
  (:documentation "A stream for getting character input."))

(defclass character-output-stream
      (character-stream output-stream)
      ()
  (:documentation "A stream for writing character output."))

(defclass character-bidirectional-stream
      (character-input-stream
       character-output-stream
       bidirectional-stream)
      ()
  (:documentation "A combined input and output character stream."))
```

Highlights of Character Streams

Character streams handle the character element type. The generic functions bytes-per-element and stream-element-type store information about the structure of character elements. Since both of these are constants, we chose to store them in class slots that have reader methods. Alternatively, we could have stored the information in defmethod forms, where the methods simply returned the constants.

The character-stream class assumes each character fits in a single byte. Some implementations support characters that require more than one byte of storage. Our model could be extended to include classes built on `character-stream`; such classes could provide a class slot named `bytes-per-element` to override the class slot defined by the `character-stream` class.

COMMON LISP specifies that character streams support the functions `read-char` and `write-char`. (COMMON LISP also specifies several other functions that manipulate character streams, but this example does not implement all of them.) The real benefits of our stream foundation become clear here: It is very easy to define `read-char` and `write-char` in terms of `read-next-element` and `write-next-element`. As we shall demonstrate in byte streams, it is equally easy to implement the byte input and output functions using the same foundation.

We define `character-input-stream`, `character-output-stream`, and `character-bidirectional-stream` to fill out the type organization. None of those classes supplies methods or slots of its own. By defining these classes, however, we enable clients to use `typep` to determine whether an object is of one of these stream types.

11.8 BYTE STREAMS

Here we define several kinds of byte streams, each intended to handle bytes of various sizes.

Defining Byte Streams

```
;;;; THE BYTE-STREAM CLASSES

(defclass byte-stream (stream) ()
  (:documentation "A stream for transmitting bytes of data."))

(defclass 8-bit-byte-stream
    (byte-stream)
    ((bytes-per-element :allocation :class
                        :initform 1
                        :reader bytes-per-element)
     (element-type :allocation :class
                   :initform '(unsigned-byte 8)
                   :reader stream-element-type))
  (:documentation "A stream for transmitting 8-bit bytes of data."))
```

```lisp
(defclass 32-bit-word-stream
     (byte-stream)
     ((bytes-per-element :allocation :class
                         :initform 4
                         :reader bytes-per-element)
      (element-type :allocation :class
                    :initform '(signed-byte 32)
                    :reader stream-element-type))
  (:documentation "A stream for transmitting 32-bit words of data."))

;;;; THE CLASS BYTE-INPUT-STREAM AND A METHOD

(defclass byte-input-stream (byte-stream input-stream) ())

;;; Page 382 in Common LISP: The Language
(defgeneric read-byte (byte-input-stream
                       &optional eof-error-p eof-value)
  (:method ((stream byte-input-stream)
            &optional eof-error-p eof-value)
   (multiple-value-bind (element eof-p)
       (read-next-element stream)
     (cond (eof-p
            (if eof-error-p
                (error "End of file while reading from ~A" stream)
                eof-value))
           (t
            element)))))

;;;; THE CLASS BYTE-OUTPUT-STREAM AND A METHOD

(defclass byte-output-stream (byte-stream output-stream) ())

;;; Page 385 in Common LISP: The Language
(defgeneric write-byte (output-stream byte)
  (:method ((stream byte-output-stream) byte)
   (write-next-element stream byte)))

;;;; THE OTHER BYTE-STREAM CLASSES

(defclass 8-bit-byte-input-stream
     (8-bit-byte-stream byte-input-stream)
     ())
```

```
(defclass 8-bit-byte-output-stream
     (8-bit-byte-stream byte-output-stream)
     ())

(defclass 8-bit-byte-bidirectional-stream
     (8-bit-byte-input-stream
      8-bit-byte-output-stream
      bidirectional-stream)
     ())

(defclass 32-bit-word-input-stream
     (32-bit-word-stream byte-input-stream)
     ())

(defclass 32-bit-word-output-stream
     (32-bit-word-stream byte-output-stream)
     ())

(defclass 32-bit-word-bidirectional-stream
     (32-bit-word-input-stream
      32-bit-word-output-stream
      bidirectional-stream)
     ())
```

Highlights of Byte Streams

Byte streams exhibit another good use of modularity. We have divided byte streams into two pieces: one piece supporting the directional aspect, the other piece supporting the structural aspect (the structure of the element type).

The directional aspect of byte streams includes the COMMON LISP functions read-byte and write-byte; that is, a byte input stream supports read-byte, whereas a byte output stream supports write-byte. The classes byte-input-stream and byte-output-stream support those functions with methods that call read-next-element and write-next-element. Thus, these two classes handle the directional aspect of byte streams.

The structural aspect of byte streams includes bytes-per-element and stream-element-type, which describe the structure of the element type. The classes 8-bit-byte-stream and 32-bit-word-stream support those generic functions with methods (reader methods that access the class slots where the information is stored). Thus, these two classes handle the structural aspect of byte streams.

We then define classes that are built on both a "directional aspect of the element type" stream and a "structural aspect of the element type" stream class. For example, the class `8-bit-byte-input-stream` inherits from `byte-input-stream` and `8-bit-byte-stream`.

11.9 INSTANTIABLE STREAMS

A usable stream needs three components: a directional class, a device class, and an element type class. We do not expect users to create an instance of any of the stream classes defined so far, because all these stream classes are incomplete. We now define the complete, usable streams, which we might call the "instantiable" streams. "Instantiable" indicates that we do expect clients to create instances of these streams.

Defining the Instantiable Streams

```
;;;; An instantiable stream needs three components, indicating
;;;; the element type, the direction, and the device type.

;;;; INSTANTIABLE CHARACTER DISK STREAMS

(defclass character-disk-input-stream
     (character-input-stream disk-input-stream)
     ())

(defclass character-disk-output-stream
     (character-output-stream disk-output-stream)
     ())

(defclass character-disk-bidirectional-stream
     (character-bidirectional-stream disk-bidirectional-stream)
     ())

;;;; INSTANTIABLE CHARACTER TAPE STREAMS

(defclass character-tape-input-stream
     (character-input-stream tape-input-stream)
     ())

(defclass character-tape-output-stream
     (character-output-stream tape-output-stream)
     ())
```

```
;;;; INSTANTIABLE 8-BIT-BYTE DISK STREAMS

(defclass 8-bit-byte-disk-input-stream
     (8-bit-byte-input-stream disk-input-stream)
     ())

(defclass 8-bit-byte-disk-output-stream
     (8-bit-byte-output-stream disk-output-stream)
     ())

(defclass 8-bit-byte-disk-bidirectional-stream
     (8-bit-byte-bidirectional-stream
      disk-bidirectional-stream)
     ())


;;;; INSTANTIABLE 8-BIT-BYTE TAPE STREAMS

(defclass 8-bit-byte-tape-input-stream
     (8-bit-byte-input-stream tape-input-stream)
     ())

(defclass 8-bit-byte-tape-output-stream
     (8-bit-byte-output-stream tape-output-stream)
     ())


;;;; INSTANTIABLE 32-BIT-WORD DISK STREAMS

(defclass 32-bit-word-disk-input-stream
     (32-bit-word-input-stream disk-input-stream)
     ())

(defclass 32-bit-word-disk-output-stream
     (32-bit-word-output-stream disk-output-stream)
     ())

(defclass 32-bit-word-disk-bidirectional-stream
     (32-bit-word-bidirectional-stream
      disk-bidirectional-stream)
     ())
```

```
;;;; INSTANTIABLE 32-BIT-WORD TAPE STREAMS

(defclass 32-bit-word-tape-input-stream
     (32-bit-word-input-stream tape-input-stream)
     ())

(defclass 32-bit-word-tape-output-stream
     (32-bit-word-output-stream tape-output-stream)
     ())
```

11.10 A PROCEDURAL DEFINITION FOR CREATING STREAMS

At this point, we have finished the foundation of streams, and have implemented several of the familiar COMMON LISP stream functions. However, we have ignored the question of how streams are created in the first place. We need to define an interface for creating streams. Since one of our goals was to make streams easily extensible, we should design this interface as an extensible protocol and document it; this protocol enables programmers to hook a new stream class into the existing mechanism and make the new class generally available.

Designing a Protocol for Creating Streams

The interface for creating streams will be used by open and other functions that need to create streams. The bulk of the work of creating a stream is done by make-stream, which we document as follows:

make-stream *device-type direction element-type name*

> Returns an opened stream of the correct type for the arguments. Calls select-stream-class to choose the class. Calls make-device-stream to choose the correct arguments to make-instance and to create the instance itself. *device-type* is a symbol, such as tape or disk. *direction* is the symbol input or output or bidirectional. *element-type* is a type specifier. *name* is a string: for a disk device it names a pathname; for a tape device, it names a unit number.

Since we document two functions that make-stream calls, we are designing a procedural definition for make-stream. We might envision the definition of make-stream as the following:

```
;;; Called by any function that needs to create a stream.
;;; make-stream creates, opens, and returns a stream.
(defun make-stream (device-type direction element-type name)
  (let* ((stream-class (select-stream-class
                          direction element-type device-type))
         (stream (make-device-stream device-type stream-class
                                       name)))
    (setf (stream-state stream) 'open)
    stream))
```

The two aspects of the make-stream procedure that we need to identify further are

- Selecting the stream class with select-stream-class
- Making an instance of the stream class with make-device-stream

We specify that make-stream calls select-stream-class to choose the appropriate class based on the desired direction, element type, and device. The association from sets of direction, element type, and device to the stream classes is set up by calling add-stream-class. In this design, both select-stream-class and add-stream-class are ordinary functions and are not intended to be specialized by programmers. Instead, we expect programmers to call add-stream-class for each instantiable class, to associate the stream class with the correct direction, element type, and device. We document select-stream-class and add-stream-class as follows:

add-stream-class *direction element-type device-type class*
> Sets up an association from the first three arguments to the class. This association is used by select-stream-class. *direction* is a keyword argument; *element-type* is a type specifier; and *device-type* is a symbol.

select-stream-class *direction element-type device-type*
> Returns the appropriate class for the arguments. The arguments are the same as the first three arguments to add-stream-class.

As far as the external protocol is concerned, the implementation of select-stream-class and add-stream-class is irrelevant. One possible way to implement these operations is with an association table, as follows:

```
;;; Maintains association used by select-stream-class.
(defvar *stream-selector* nil)

;;; Sets up association from first 3 args to the class.
(defun add-stream-class (direction element-type device-type class)
  (setq *stream-selector*
        (acons (list direction element-type device-type) class
               *stream-selector*)))

;;; Chooses the appropriate class based on its arguments.
;;; Signals an error if there is no matching stream.
(defun select-stream-class (direction element-type device-type)
  (let* ((entry (assoc (list direction element-type device-type)
                       *stream-selector*
                       :test #'compare-stream-lists))
         (class (cdr entry)))
    (if (null entry)
        (error "Cannot create a ~A ~A stream for device-type ~A."
               element-type direction device-type)
        class)))

;;; Returns t if the stream lists are equivalent.
;;; Used to compare plist keys in *stream-selector*.
(defun compare-stream-lists (list1 list2)
  (and (eql (first list1) (first list2))
       ;; compare the element-types
       (equal-typep (second list1) (second list2))
       (eql (third list1) (third list2))))

;;; Tests whether two type specifiers are equivalent.
(defun equal-typep (t1 t2)
  (and (subtypep t1 t2) (subtypep t2 t1)))
```

The keys in the association list are lists of direction, element type, and device type. We need to ensure that equivalent type specifiers choose the element type correctly: (mod 256) and (unsigned-byte 8) are equivalent and both should result in a stream whose element type is (unsigned-byte 8). We use equal-typep to compare type specifiers.

The job of make-device-stream is to call make-instance with the correct arguments for the device. We expect programmers to specialize make-device-stream for any new instantiable device type. In this example, we assume that the *device-type* argument is a symbol, such as disk or tape—so the methods must be individual methods that specialize on those symbols.

`make-device-stream` *device-type class name*

Creates and returns a stream; its main purpose is to provide the correct arguments to `make-instance` for the device class. This generic function is intended to be specialized for each device type. *device-type* is a symbol, such as `tape` or `disk`. *name* is a string: for a disk device it names a pathname; for a tape device, it names a unit number.

In summary, the protocol for hooking a new stream into the stream-creation mechanism consists of two tasks:

- `add-stream-class` must be called for new instantiable streams
- `make-device-stream` must be specialized for new device classes

Using the Protocol for Creating Streams

```
;;;; THE MAKE-DEVICE-STREAM GENERIC FUNCTION

(defgeneric make-device-stream (device-type class name)
  (:documentation "Create an instance with correct initargs."))

;;;; METHODS FOR MAKE-DEVICE-STREAM

(defmethod make-device-stream ((device-type (eql 'tape))
                               class name)
  (make-instance class :unit (parse-integer name)))

(defmethod make-device-stream ((device-type (eql 'disk))
                               class name)
  (make-instance class :pathname name))

;;;; ADDING CHARACTER DISK STREAMS

(add-stream-class :input 'character 'disk
                  (find-class 'character-disk-input-stream))

(add-stream-class :output 'character 'disk
                  (find-class 'character-disk-output-stream))

(add-stream-class :bidirectional 'character 'disk
                  (find-class 'character-disk-bidirectional-stream))
```

```
;;;; ADDING CHARACTER TAPE STREAMS

(add-stream-class :input 'character 'tape
                  (find-class 'character-tape-input-stream))

(add-stream-class :output 'character 'tape
                  (find-class 'character-tape-output-stream))

;;;; ADDING 8-BIT-BYTE DISK STREAMS

(add-stream-class :input '(unsigned-byte 8) 'disk
                  (find-class '8-bit-byte-disk-input-stream))

(add-stream-class :output '(unsigned-byte 8) 'disk
                  (find-class '8-bit-byte-disk-output-stream))

(add-stream-class :bidirectional '(unsigned-byte 8) 'disk
                  (find-class
                    '8-bit-byte-disk-bidirectional-stream))


;;;; ADDING 8-BIT-BYTE TAPE STREAMS

(add-stream-class :input '(unsigned-byte 8) 'tape
                  (find-class '8-bit-byte-tape-input-stream))

(add-stream-class :output '(unsigned-byte 8) 'tape
                  (find-class '8-bit-byte-tape-output-stream))


;;;; ADDING 32-BIT-WORD DISK STREAMS

(add-stream-class :input '(signed-byte 32) 'disk
                  (find-class '32-bit-word-disk-input-stream))

(add-stream-class :output '(signed-byte 32) 'disk
                  (find-class '32-bit-word-disk-output-stream))

(add-stream-class :bidirectional '(signed-byte 32) 'disk
                  (find-class
                    '32-bit-word-disk-bidirectional-stream))
```

```
;;;; ADDING 32-BIT-WORD TAPE STREAMS

(add-stream-class :input '(signed-byte 32) 'tape
                  (find-class '32-bit-word-tape-input-stream))

(add-stream-class :output '(signed-byte 32) 'tape
                  (find-class '32-bit-word-tape-output-stream))
```

11.11 SUMMARY OF TECHNIQUES USED IN STREAMS

We have shown an example using CLOS and object-oriented techniques to solve a complex problem. The important techniques are as follows:

- Identifying classes that represent the types of objects manipulated by the program

- Documenting an external protocol to be used by clients to create and manipulate the objects

- Maximizing the sharing of code while minimizing the duplication of both code and information (knowledge), by

  - Arranging the classes into an organization that accurately reflects the interaction among the different types of objects

  - Documenting an internal protocol to be used by the different classes to communicate with one another

- Providing a mechanism for linking the classes themselves to the external interface for creating objects

Although we have documented the external and internal stream protocols, we need to document the implementation of streams to enable other programmers to extend streams. The alternative would be to make the source code of streams available to programmers.

11.12 DOCUMENTING THE IMPLEMENTATION OF STREAMS

The task of documenting an implementation is a challenge, because it requires you to be aware of which aspects of the implementation are internal and which are external. We recommend a conservative approach, which is to document the implementation on a strict "need to know" basis. That is, document only those portions of the implementation that outside programmers must understand in order to extend the program.

(Documentation of the internals would be useful for maintainers; this is, however, a different issue from that of documenting an implementation for other programmers to extend.)

It is important to document the existence and organization of the stream classes. Programmers need to know what methods are defined for the generic functions in the internal and external protocols, which classes those methods are attached to, and what the methods do. We can, however, omit the details of how the methods work. Some methods do not need to be documented at all. For example, the method for `wait-for-disk` is purely internal to disk streams. Programmers who want to extend streams to handle other devices or element types would have no need to call `wait-for-disk`, to specialize it, or to be aware of its existence. On the other hand, if we want to enable programmers to extend disk streams, we do need to document `wait-for-disk`.

We would probably choose not to expose the slots of a class, in favor of documenting the methods that access them. For example, documenting the methods for `stream-state` and `(setf stream-state)` gives programmers sufficient information to query a stream for its state and to change that state. There is no need to expose the fact that these are reader and writer methods for a slot.

12

Highlights of CLOS

In this chapter, we discuss the original design goals for CLOS, and how they were achieved. We address three important design goals of CLOS and one nongoal:

- CLOS should be a standard language extension that includes the most useful aspects of the existing object-oriented paradigms

- The CLOS programmer interface should be powerful and flexible enough for developing most application programs

- CLOS itself should be designed as an extensible protocol, to allow for customization of its behavior and to encourage further research in object-oriented programming

- CLOS should not provide automatic support for specifying and enforcing protocols

The third goal leads to an advanced topic of CLOS—the metaobject protocol. We introduce the motivation for the metaobject protocol and discuss it briefly.

12.1 DESIGNING A STANDARD OBJECT-ORIENTED PARADIGM

When CLOS was designed (starting in 1986), a number of object-oriented paradigms had been available in various LISP implementations for several years. The goal of designing CLOS was to define a *standard* language extension to COMMON LISP. The immediate benefit of this standard would be to enable LISP programmers to write portable code in an object-oriented style.

Many of the existing object-oriented paradigms had important similarities. The CLOS Working Group wanted to gather the most useful aspects of these paradigms into a single, unified language extension. From the beginning, the Working Group agreed that a primary goal in defining a language standard was to be conservative — to include in the CLOS standard only those features and techniques that were well understood. The Working Group tried to define a consistent model based on the strengths of existing paradigms, while excluding unnecessary features.

12.2 SUMMARY OF THE PROGRAMMER INTERFACE

Here we summarize the major techniques supported by the CLOS programmer interface:

- *Defining organizations of classes.* You can conveniently define organizations of classes. A class inherits structure and behavior from its direct superclasses, which are listed in the defclass form. CLOS automatically computes a class precedence list based on the constraints specified locally in the defclass forms.

- *Creating and initializing instances.* You can create instances with make-instance. CLOS provides you with a good measure of control over how the instances are initialized. You can specify that a slot should be filled by an initarg and provide default initial values for slots and initargs. You can perform further initialization by specializing initialize-instance.

- *Defining different kinds of methods.* You can define methods for many different purposes, including:

  ○ Specializing the behavior of a reader or writer
  ○ Specializing on a COMMON LISP type
  ○ Specializing on more than one argument (multi-methods)
  ○ Specializing on an individual LISP object

- *Defining methods that work together.* The default behavior of the generic dispatch (the `standard` method combination type) allows for methods of different roles, including primary methods, before-methods, after-methods, and around-methods. This is an extremely flexible framework that—together with the class inheritance mechanism—enables you to define code in modules. Each module comes into play when it is appropriate, according to the arguments to the generic function and the method's role.

- *Using a different framework for generic dispatch.* You can easily use one of the built-in method combination types or define a new one based on a LISP function, macro, or special form. The freedom to use other method combination types allows you to control how the methods are called and what is done with their values.

- *Redefining elements dynamically.* You can redefine generic functions, methods, and classes on the fly. You can redefine a class even after instances of the class exist. CLOS ensures that everything that is affected by the redefinition is automatically updated, including instances, subclasses, and instances of subclasses. When instances are updated, the default method adds or deletes slots according to the new definition, and preserves the values of slots that have not changed. You can perform further action during the redefinition by specializing `update-instance-structure`.

These features add up to a great deal of expressive power. However, the goal of "satisfying most applications" has a tradeoff. To satisfy most applications, the programmer interface is very flexible. The disadvantage of this flexibility is that CLOS users might be overwhelmed by the wide assortment of techniques and features to be learned. Also, CLOS often supports more than one way of doing a single thing, and there is not always a clear guideline as to which way is preferable.

Certainly, it is not necessary to understand all these techniques to write a good-sized application program. Any single program will require only a subset of these techniques. We encourage new users to concentrate on learning the central themes of how CLOS works, especially the generic dispatch. If you understand what happens when a generic function is called, you are well on your way. The next step is to start writing CLOS programs. In the course of development, you might find problems that cannot be conveniently solved with the most basic CLOS features (such as primary methods, before-methods, and after-methods), and you can then investigate the more advanced features (such as around-methods, or other types of method combination).

12.3 EXPLORING ALTERNATIVE PARADIGMS

With all the expressive power mentioned so far, what more is needed? The CLOS programmer interface supports one model of object-oriented programming, but there are alternative paradigms.

For example, in CLOS, a class inherits nearly every aspect of its superclasses: slots, some slot and class options, and methods. We can call this "open sharing"; a class inherits nearly everything by default, but can choose to override some of the inherited behavior or characteristics, if desired. An alternative paradigm might support "closed sharing," where a class inherits nothing from its superclasses by default, but can explicitly specify which aspects of its superclasses it wants to inherit.

Two other key aspects of any object-oriented paradigm are how the organization of classes is specified, and how the precedence among those classes is controlled. In CLOS, the programmer specifies an organization of classes in the defclass forms; each class has a list of superclasses. The order of these superclasses sets up local constraints on the precedence of the classes. CLOS uses an algorithm to compute a class precedence list for each class, which is always consistent with the set of local constraints. This is just one of many possible ways to control inheritance.

When CLOS was being defined, most developers who had experience with one or more of the existing paradigms agreed that object-oriented programming was essential for designing and implementing large systems. However, even the phrase "object-oriented programming" had different meanings for different people. Each individual paradigm invented not just its own syntax, but also its own semantics.

The Working Group had to make certain decisions and choices, in order to define CLOS as a consistent model. The Working Group also believed that it was important to encourage ongoing experimentation with alternative paradigms. The solution was to define and document CLOS itself as an extensible protocol, which is called the Metaobject Protocol. We discuss this in "The CLOS Metaobject Protocol," page 219.

12.4 A NONGOAL: AUTOMATIC PROTOCOL SUPPORT

Some object-oriented paradigms actively assist the programmer in specifying protocols. The definition of a class can describe more of the semantics of the class. For example, a class definition can state that the class is intended to be a building block only, and that no instances of it should be made. The requirements of a class can be stated explicitly in the class definition. For example, a mixin class such as ordered-lock-mixin has some implicit requirements: It is intended to be used as a building block along with another lock class (such as `simple-lock` or `null-lock`), and that lock class must provide the methods for the lock protocol. Some object-oriented languages provide a means for stating those requirements explicitly, and for enforcing them.

CLOS does not provide automatic support for protocols. This is an area that the Working Group deemed experimental and not yet ready for standardization.

In this book, we have focused on the theme of protocols as a valuable means of designing programs. Although CLOS does not actively support protocols, it is nevertheless a language conducive for defining them. The aspect of CLOS that makes protocol definition convenient is the fact that generic functions are not called by a special syntax. To the caller, there is no discernible difference between ordinary and generic functions. In other object-oriented paradigms, the caller must know whether a function is ordinary or generic in order to choose the appropriate calling syntax. The difference in calling syntax obscures the essential distinction between interface and implementation.

Currently, the vehicle for defining protocols is documentation. We recommend documenting the external protocol and advertising it to the clients. For a large application, it is also useful to document the internal protocol and advertise it to the developers and maintainers of the program. Sometimes, an internal protocol is implicitly defined as the set of operators that are not advertised in the external protocol.

Although CLOS itself does not support protocols, the Working Group believes that protocols are valuable and important. CLOS itself is documented as an extensible protocol. The foundation of the CLOS programmer interface lies in the metaobject protocol, which is documented to allow researchers and developers to experiment with other object-oriented paradigms.

12.5 THE CLOS METAOBJECT PROTOCOL

This section gives a brief overview of the metaobject protocol—just enough to give you an idea of how it is related to the CLOS programmer interface.

The Classes of CLOS Elements

An important aspect of CLOS is that every LISP object is an instance of a class. This means that a class object itself has a class, as do method objects and generic function objects. CLOS uses the term *metaclass* to denote a class that is the class of a class. Here are three predefined metaclasses:

standard-class
> The default class of class objects defined by defclass.

built-in-class
> The class of class objects that are implemented in a special way (not by defclass). Most class objects corresponding to COMMON LISP type specifiers are implemented as instances of built-in-class, although others might be implemented as instances of standard-class.

structure-class
> The class of class objects defined by defstruct, when the :type option is not given.

We have used the informal term "user-defined class" when describing a class whose metaclass is standard-class. Similarly, the term "built-in class" denotes a class whose metaclass is built-in-class. The metaclass is important to users, because it determines the behavior of the classes. For example, standard-class supports make-instance, but built-in-class does not. In other words, CLOS provides a method for make-instance attached to the class standard-class, but there is no method for make-instance attached to built-in-class.

CLOS extends defstruct to enable you to write methods for defstruct structures. If you use defstruct without giving the :type option, the defstruct structure is implemented as a class whose metaclass is structure-class. The advantage of this is that you can write methods for that class. If you want to write methods, however, using defclass is probably better than using defstruct. For one thing, using defclass frees you from the limitation of single inheritance. Also, the flexibility of redefining classes is supported by standard-class, but not by structure-class or built-in-class.

CLOS uses the term *metaobject* for objects that represent CLOS elements, such as class objects, method objects, and generic function objects. Here are two predefined classes of metaobjects:

standard-method
> The default class of method objects defined by defmethod

standard-generic-function
> The default class of generic function objects defined by defgeneric

The basic CLOS elements are themselves implemented as CLOS elements, so we see that classes, generic functions, and methods follow the CLOS model. The structure and behavior of a class (or generic function, or method) is defined by its class. The predefined metaobject classes have methods that support the default behavior of CLOS.

For most CLOS application programs, the default behavior of CLOS is sufficiently powerful and flexible that there is no need to know or care that classes, methods, and generic functions are themselves instances of classes. Programmers interested in other object-oriented paradigms can use CLOS as a basis for experimentation. Programmers can define new metaclasses (usually built on the standard metaclasses) that support new and different behavior for classes. Programmers can also define new metaobject classes to be the classes of generic functions or methods. This is an additional level of CLOS, called the *metaobject level*. It is the foundation of the functional level, which in turn is the foundation of the macro level.

In addition to fostering research and experimentation, the metaobject level makes it possible to develop tools for browsing or analyzing CLOS programs. The metaobject protocol describes how to obtain information about user-defined CLOS elements: A class object can be queried for its class precedence list, slots, and `defclass` options; a generic function object can be queried for its set of methods. Information is available; browsers and environmental tools can devise ways to present it usefully to CLOS programmers.

CLOS Level	Deals with	Context of Use
Macro	names	most CLOS applications
Functional	objects	programs using anonymous objects
Metaobject	metaobjects	tools, research, experimentation

Classes, Superclasses, and Metaclasses

Discussing metaclasses adds a degree of complexity to the CLOS model. Even the terminology is confusing. Here we make some statements that should help clarify the meanings of classes, superclasses, and metaclasses. The following concepts are used in CLOS application programming:

- Every LISP object is an instance of a class. You can use (class-of *object*) to find out the class of an object.

- The class of an object determines its structure and behavior. All instances of a given class have the same set of slots. Any method that specializes on a given class is applicable to all instances of that class.

- A class has a set of superclasses. The class inherits structure and be-havior from its superclasses. In other words, methods attached to a class are applicable to instances of subclasses of that class.

The following are concepts of CLOS metaobject programming. Notice that each of these concepts is a natural extension of a concept used in application programming.

- Since every LISP object is an instance of a class, a class object itself is an instance of a class. You can use (class-of *class-object*) to find out the class of a class object. The term for the class of class objects is *metaclass*. In other words, the instances of a metaclass are class ob-jects.

- The class of a class object (which is a metaclass) determines the structure and behavior of that class object. All classes of a given metaclass have the same set of slots. Methods that specialize on a given metaclass are applicable to all class objects of that metaclass.

- A class has a set of superclasses. The class inherits structure and be-havior from its superclasses. Because a metaclass is a class, it can al-so have superclasses from which it inherits structure and behavior. In other words, methods attached to a metaclass are applicable to in-stances of subclasses of that metaclass.

Metaobject Programming

The CLOS specification documents a set of predefined metaobjects and the protocol they follow. Developers can use these metaobjects as a point of departure. To support classes with entirely different behavior, you can define a new metaclass. You can modify the default behavior only slightly by defining a class built on standard-class; in this way, you can override some aspects of behavior while inheriting other aspects.

We have already stated that CLOS application programs are portable. The portability benefit applies to metaobject programs as well. A devel-oper can invent a new paradigm and applications based on it, and can run them on other CLOS implementations. New paradigms can be shared freely, which facilitates further research. Applications using al-ternative paradigms are portable, so end users can also benefit from the metaobject protocol.

Appendix A
Glossary of CLOS Terminology

Accessor

A generic function for reading or writing the value of a slot. The term "accessor" includes both readers and writers. The `:accessor` slot option to `defclass` causes methods for a reader and a writer for that slot to be generated automatically.

After-method

A method whose role is to be called after the primary method, usually to do some sort of cleanup work. The standard method combination recognizes an after-method by the method qualifier `:after` in the `defmethod` form.

Aggregate class

A descriptive term for a class composed of several building block classes. An aggregate class usually derives all its structure and behavior from its superclasses and does not provide further customizations.

Applicable method

A method whose required parameters are all satisfied by the corresponding arguments to the generic function. When a generic function is called, CLOS locates the set of applicable methods.

Argument
> An object given as input to a function.

Around-method
> A method whose role is to surround all other kinds of methods. An around-method usually performs some computation and uses call-next-method to invoke the before-methods, primary method, and after-methods. An around-method can set up an environment to be in effect during the execution of the other methods, such as setting up a catch, binding a special variable, or owning a lock. The standard method combination recognizes an around-method by the method qualifier :around in the defmethod form.

Basic class
> A descriptive term for a class that is the root, or foundation, of a set of classes. A basic class provides characteristics that all its subclasses have in common, such as their type (for example, all locks are of type lock), and default methods.

Before-method
> A method whose role is to be called before the primary method, usually to do some sort of set-up work in advance of the primary method. The standard method combination recognizes a before-method by the method qualifier :before in the defmethod form.

Built-in class
> A predefined class that is implemented in a special system-dependent way; in other words, it is not implemented as a user-defined class. Many of the classes corresponding to COMMON LISP types (such as array, list, number, and t) are implemented as built-in classes.

Built-in method combination type
> A predefined method combination type provided by CLOS. The default method combination type is called standard. The others are operator method combination types, including: +, and, append, list, max, min, nconc, or, and progn.

Class A COMMON LISP type that defines the structure and behavior of a set of objects, which are called instances of the class. The structure of the class lies in its slots. The behavior is implemented by methods. Classes can be "built on" other classes, to inherit structure and behavior from them.

Class precedence list

A list of classes containing the class itself and all its superclasses, ordered from most to least specific. CLOS computes a class precedence list for each class, based on the `defclass` forms of the class and all of its superclasses. The class precedence list governs how methods, slots, and other characteristics are inherited. When one class is more specific than another, it has precedence (or dominance) over the other class. Thus, if the two classes offer competing traits, the more specific class takes precedence over the less specific class.

Client A LISP program that uses a CLOS program; the client calls generic functions defined by the CLOS program.

CLOS implementation

A body of code that supports CLOS as defined by the CLOS specification and runs on a particular operating system. This term is useful for discussing portability issues (issues of writing programs with the intention of running them on different operating systems).

Constructor

A function used to create new instances. Constructors are ordinary LISP functions that call `make-instance`. Constructors provide a more abstract interface than does `make-instance`, and they can use the full power of LISP argument processing.

Default method

A descriptive term for a method whose purpose is to be inherited by a family of classes. CLOS provides several default methods, which we call "system-supplied default methods" to distinguish them from methods that users define.

Direct subclass

A direct subclass is the inverse of a direct superclass. If the class `shape` is a direct superclass of the class `triangle`, then `triangle` is a direct subclass of `shape`.

Direct superclass

A class that is included in the `defclass` form of another class. The relationship between a class and its direct superclass is like that between a child and its parent, in that there is no intervening ancestor. A class inherits structure and behavior from its direct superclasses. Class inheritance is transitive, so a class inherits from each of its direct superclasses, their direct superclasses, and so on.

Effective method

> The LISP code that comprises the implementation of a generic function for a given set of arguments. An effective method combines the applicable methods according to the method combination type.

Generic dispatch

> The CLOS mechanism that occurs when a generic function is called. The generic dispatch chooses the implementation appropriate for the arguments. This entails selecting the set of applicable methods, ranking the applicable methods in precedence order, combining the applicable methods into an effective method, calling the effective method, and returning the values of the effective method.

Generic function

> A LISP function whose implementation is distributed across one or more methods. To the caller, a generic function looks like an ordinary LISP function. It accepts arguments, performs some operation, and returns values. Invisibly to the caller, an internal and automatic procedure (the generic dispatch) occurs when a generic function is called; this entails choosing the method or methods appropriate to the arguments.

Implementation

> The inner workings of a program or function. This information is usually known to the developer of the program but is concealed from callers. The implementation of an ordinary function consists of the body of the defun, whereas the implementation of a generic function is distributed across a set of methods. See also "CLOS implementation" in this glossary.

Individual method

> A method that specializes one of its parameters on an individual LISP object. The lambda-list of an individual method contains a parameter specializer name such as (eql *form*). This method is applicable if the corresponding argument is eql to the object that is the value of *form* (and if all other specialized parameters are satisfied).

Inheritance

> The sharing of characteristics or behavior among related classes. CLOS supports inheriting methods, slots, most slot options, and one class option.

Initarg

An argument given to `make-instance` to control the initialization of instances. An initarg can be used to fill a slot with a value, or by an initialization method, or both. Initargs can be used in related initialization tasks, such as updating an instance when a class is redefined, changing the class of an instance, and reinitializing an instance. Initarg is shorthand for "initialization argument."

Initform

A default value for a slot. The `:initform` slot option to `defclass` is used to provide a default value for a slot.

Instance

A LISP object. With the advent of CLOS, every LISP object is an instance of a class. Objects of the COMMON LISP types, such as numbers, arrays, and lists, are instances of classes whose name is the same as the name of the type specifier. Other objects are instances of user-defined classes. All instances of a given class have the same type, the same structure, and the same behavior. (Note that individual methods can be used to cause one particular instance to behave differently from the other instances of its class.)

Interface

The information about a function (whether it is ordinary or generic) that callers need to know, including: its expected arguments, the job it does, and its returned values.

Lambda-list

A list that specifies the names of parameters of a function. Methods and generic functions have lambda-lists, as do ordinary LISP functions.

Local slot

A slot that stores information about the state of an instance. A local slot is defined when the `:allocation` `:instance` slot option to `defclass` is provided, or when the `:allocation` slot option is omitted.

Metaobject

An object that represents a CLOS element, such as a class object, method object, or generic function object.

Metaclass

A class whose instances are class objects, such as `standard-class`, `built-in-class`, and `structure-class`.

Method

> LISP code that implements a portion of (or the entire) implementation of a generic function for a set of arguments. Like functions, methods take arguments, perform some computation, possibly produce side effects, and return values. Unlike functions, methods are never called directly; they are called by the generic dispatch procedure. Each method has a role, which states its purpose in the generic function and controls how it interacts with other methods.

Method combination type

> A mechanism that specifies, for a generic function, what method roles are allowed, how the applicable methods are combined into an effective method, and how the values of the generic function are computed. A method combination type is a LISP object named by a symbol.

Method qualifier

> A symbol appearing in the `defmethod` form that indicates the method's role. The symbols `:after`, `:before`, and `:around` are three examples. A method whose qualifier is `:after` is an after-method.

Method role

> The way this method interacts with the other applicable methods. The method combination type uses the method's role when combining it with the other methods into the effective method.

Mixin class

> A descriptive term for a class intended to be a building block for other classes. It usually supports some aspect of behavior orthogonal to the behavior supported by other classes in the program; typically, this customization is supported in before- and after-methods. A mixin class is not intended to interfere with other behavior, so it usually does not override primary methods supplied by other classes.

Multi-method

> A method that specializes more than one parameter. The technique of using multi-methods is intended for operations whose implementation truly depends on the type of more than one argument.

Multiple inheritance

> A system in which a class can share the characteristics and behavior of more than one direct superclass. CLOS supports multi-

ple inheritance, in that a class can have any number of direct superclasses. This flexibility makes all sorts of class organizations possible, whereas single inheritance is limited to strictly hierarchical organizations. CLOS controls the multiple inheritance by using a class precedence list, which unambiguously states the precedence of each class with respect to the others.

Operator method combination types

A method combination type that defines a framework that combines all applicable primary methods inside a LISP function, macro, or special form. CLOS offers a set of built-in operator method combination types, and you can define new ones with the short from of `define-method-combination`.

Parameter

A specification of the expected input of a function, generic function, method, or other kind of LISP operator. Each parameter specifies a variable name, which is bound to the corresponding argument when the function is called. Methods can have specialized parameters, which indicate the method's applicability, as well as variable names.

Parameter specializer

The object indicated by a parameter specializer name. If a parameter specializer name is a class name, the parameter specializer is the class object named by that name. If a parameter specializer name is a list (eql *form*), the parameter specializer is the list (eql *object*), where *object* is the result of evaluating *form* at the time the method is defined.

Parameter specializer name

The portion of a specialized parameter appearing in a method's lambda-list that indicates the applicability of the method. A parameter specializer name can be a class name or a list (eql *form*).

Primary method

A method whose role is to perform the bulk of the work of a generic function. In the standard method combination, only the most specific applicable primary method is called; however, a primary method can use `call-next-method` to cause the next most specific applicable primary method to be called. The standard method combination recognizes a primary method by the absence of any method qualifier in the `defmethod` form.

Procedural definition

> A technique in which a high-level task is broken down into separate generic functions, each of which is responsible for a clearly defined portion of the task. Usually there is a default behavior for the generic functions. Programmers use these generic functions as entry points; they can control portions of the task by specializing one or more of the generic functions.

Protocol

> A definition of the behavior of a set of objects. Some protocols are intended for programmers who are developing client programs, whereas other protocols are intended for programmers who wish to extend a program.

Reader

> A generic function for reading the value of a slot. Reader methods can be generated automatically, through use of the :accessor or :reader slot options to defclass.

Shared slot

> A slot that stores information about the state of a class (or of all instances of the class). A shared slot is defined when the :allocation :class slot option to defclass is provided.

Single inheritance

> A system in which a class can be built on no more than one other class, which in turn can be built on no more than one other class, and so on. Single inheritance results in a strictly hierarchical organization. COMMON LISP defstruct supports single inheritance.

Slot A place where state information is stored. A slot has a name and a value. The :allocation slot option to defclass controls whether a slot is local or shared. A local slot stores information about the state of an instance, and a shared slot stores information about the state of a class (or of all instances of the class). The value of a slot can be read and written by accessors.

Specialized parameter

> A parameter expressed as a list whose first element is a variable, and whose second element is a parameter specializer name. Any required parameter in a method's lambda-list may be specialized.

standard-object

> A class that is implicitly included in the class precedence list of every user-defined class. Several default methods are attached to

the class `standard-object`.

standard method combination type

The default method combination type: It supports around-methods, before-methods, primary methods, and after-methods.

Subclass

The inverse of superclass. If the class `t` is a superclass of the class `triangle`, then `triangle` is a subclass of `t`.

Superclass

A class from which another class inherits. The superclasses of a class include all of its direct superclasses, all of their direct superclasses, and so on.

Unbound slot

A slot that has no value. A slot that was neither initialized nor written to is unbound. CLOS signals an error if an attempt is made to read the value of an unbound slot.

Writer

A generic function for writing the value of a slot. Writer methods can be generated automatically, through use of the `:accessor` or `:writer` slot options to `defclass`. Usually, the name of a writer is a list such as `(setf reader)`; such a writer is called with the `setf` syntax, which is `(setf (reader object) new-value)`.

Appendix B
Syntax of CLOS
Operators

This appendix is intended to be used as a reference. It briefly describes the purpose, syntax, and return values of the operators covered by this book, and refers to the sections in the book where the operator is presented in context. The operators are listed alphabetically.

The descriptions of the CLOS operators are adapted from the "Common Lisp Object System Specification" with permission from the authors. This book does not cover every operator in the CLOS programmer interface, and the descriptions given here are not complete reference documentation. Refer to the "Common Lisp Object System Specification" for the complete definition of CLOS.

In Appendix C, we list the operators in the programmer interface that are not covered by this book.

call-next-method &rest *arguments*   *Function*

> Used within a method to call the "next method," which is defined by the method combination type in use by the generic function. `call-next-method` returns the values of the next method. If there is no next method, an error is signaled. (The default behavior of signaling an error is supported by the `no-next-method` generic function, which is called whenever this error is detected.) You can use `next-method-p` in the body of a method to test whether there is a next method.

233

The `standard` method combination type supports `call-next-method` in around-methods and primary methods. The operator method combination types support `call-next-method` in around-methods only.

arguments   Arguments to be passed to the next method.

Usually, you call `call-next-method` with no arguments, and the original arguments given to the generic function are passed to the next method. However, you can pass different arguments to the next method as long as the new arguments would cause the same set of applicable methods to be selected, as did the original arguments.

For related information, see

"Around-Methods," page 102
"Calling a Shadowed Primary Method," page 105
"Summary of the Standard Method Combination Type," page 113
"Controlling the Generic Dispatch," page 101

change-class *instance new-class*   *Generic Function*

Changes the class of an instance to a new class and calls the generic function `update-instance-for-different-class`. The `change-class` function returns the instance.

instance   An object.

new-class   A class object or the name of a class.

CLOS guarantees that `change-class` is supported when both the original class of the instance and the new class are of the metaclass `standard-class`. An individual CLOS implementation might support `change-class` in other circumstances as well.

For related information, see

"Changing the Class of an Instance," page 151
"A Procedural Definition: Initialization," page 165

class-name *class*   *Generic Function*

Returns the name of the class object.

class   A class object.

You can use setf with class-name to change the name of the class object.

For related information, see

"Mapping Between Names and Objects," page 134

class-of *object*   *Function*

Returns the class of the *object*. Note that every object is of some class. class-of returns a class object.

object   Any object.

defclass *name* ({*superclass*}*)   *Macro*
           ({*slot-spec*}*) {*class-option*}*

Defines a new class or redefines an existing one. The name of the class and the class object are made valid type specifiers. defclass returns the class object that represents the new class.

name   A symbol naming this class.

superclass   A symbol naming a direct superclass of this class.

slot-spec   Defines a slot of the new class. Can be given as a symbol (the name of the slot), or as a list containing the name of the slot followed by one or more slot-options pertaining to the slot:

> *slot-name*
> (*slot-name slot-options...*)

The *slot-options* are as follows:

:accessor *reader-name*
                        Defines methods for a reader and a writer generic function. You can then use the reader named *reader-name* to read the value of this slot, and use the writer named (setf *reader-name*) to write the value of this slot.

:reader *reader-name*
                        Defines a method for the reader generic func-

tion named *reader-name* for reading the value of this slot.

:writer *function-spec*

Defines a method for the writer generic function named *function-spec* for writing the value of this slot. If *function-spec* is a symbol, you call the writer with the normal LISP syntax: (*symbol new-value instance*). If *function-spec* is a list such as (setf *symbol*), you call the writer with the setf syntax, which is (setf (*symbol instance*) *new-value*).

:documentation *string*

Specifies documentation for the slot.

:allocation *allocation-type*

States whether this is a shared or local slot. The default *allocation-type* is :instance, which indicates a local slot; :class indicates a shared slot.

:initform *form*

Gives a default initial value form for the slot. *form* is evaluated each time it is used, in the lexical environment in which the defclass was evaluated.

:initarg *name*

Specifies an initarg for the slot. You can then initialize the value of the slot when making an instance, by providing this initarg name and a value in the call to make-instance.

:type *type-specifier*

States that the value of this slot is expected to be of the type named by *type-specifier*. This can result in compiler optimizations, but CLOS does not guarantee error checking when the value is stored in the slot.

class-option

An option pertaining to the class as a whole. The *class-options* are as follows:

(:documentation *string*)

Specifies documentation for the class.

(:default-initargs {*initarg-name form*}*)

Specifies default values for initargs. Each *form* is treated as a default initial value form for the initarg of *initarg-name*. The :default-initargs class option is the only class option inherited by subclasses; see "Initialization Arguments," page 160.

(:metaclass *class-name*)

States the class of the newly defined class; this is known as the metaclass. The default metaclass is standard-class.

For related information, see

"Defining the Kinds of Objects—Classes," page 19
"Implementation Choices: Methods versus Slots," page 66
"Class Inheritance," page 117
"Redefining Classes," page 140
"Creating and Initializing Instances," page 155

defgeneric *name lambda-list* {*option*}*   *Macro*

Defines a new generic function or redefines an existing one. Enables you to specify aspects of the generic function, such as the lambda-list, documentation, method combination type, argument precedence order, and declarations. You can also define methods within the defgeneric form. defgeneric returns the generic function object.

name   Names the generic function; it is either a symbol or a list such as (setf *symbol*).

lambda-list   Describes the parameters of this generic function. It cannot contain any &aux variables. Optional and keyword arguments may not have default initial value forms or use supplied-p parameters. No parameter in this lambda-list may be specialized.

options   The options are as follows:

(:argument-precedence-order {*parameter-name*}+)

> This affects the ranking of methods by precedence order. Instead of the default left-to-right order, the arguments are considered in the order of the parameter names given here. Each required parameter must appear in this list. For more information, see "Summary of Method Inheritance," page 98.

(declare {*declaration*}+)

> Specifies declarations for the generic function. optimize can be given to specify whether the generic dispatch procedure should be optimized for speed or space. The following declarations are not allowed: special, ftype, function, inline, notline, and declaration.

(:documentation *string*)

> Specifies documentation for the generic function.

(:method-combination *symbol* {*arg*}*)

> Specifies that this generic function uses the method combination type whose name is *symbol*. *args* are any arguments used by the method combination type. For example, all method combination types defined by the short form of define-method-combination accept an optional *order* argument, which can be :most-specific-last to reverse the order of the primary methods. :most-specific-first is the default. For more information, see "Defining a New Method Combination Type," page 109.

(:method {*qualifier*}* *specialized-lambda-list* {*decl* | *doc*}* {*form*}*)

> Defines a method for this generic function. The method's qualifier, specialized lambda-list, declarations, documentation, and forms are the same as for defmethod.

(:generic-function-class *class-name*)

> Specifies the class of the generic function object; the default is standard-generic-function.

(:method-class *class-name*)
> Specifies the class of the methods for this generic function; the default is standard-method.

defgeneric is used to define a named generic function. You can use generic-function to define an anonymous generic function. generic-function has the same syntax as defgeneric, except the *name* argument is omitted.

For related information, see

"Defining the Interface—Generic Functions," page 27
"Congruent Lambda-Lists," page 132
"Redefining Methods and Generic Functions," page 143
"Removing Generic Functions and Methods," page 136

define-method-combination *name* {*option*}*   *Macro*

Defines a new method combination type. Provides a convenient short-form syntax, which defines an operator method combination type. The syntax given here is for the short form.

name
> A symbol naming this method combination type.

option
> These are the options for the short form:

:documentation *string*
> Specifies documentation for the method combination type.

:identity-with-one-argument *boolean*
> Requests the compiler to optimize for cases when there is only one method; this indicates that the value of that method should be returned as the value of the generic function, rather than the operator being called. This makes sense for operators such as progn, and, +, and max.

:operator *operator*
> Specifies the operator that receives the values of the methods.

The alternate long form provides a more flexible syntax that allows for defining more complex method combination types. This book does not cover the syntax of the long form.

For related information, see

"Defining a New Method Combination Type," page 109

defmethod *name {qualifier}* specialized-lambda-list*   *Macro*
          {decl | doc }* {form}*

Defines a new method for a generic function or redefines an existing one. defmethod returns the method object.

name	The name of the generic function that this method is implementing. This is either a symbol or a list such as (setf *symbol*).
qualifier	A non-null atom used to identify the role of this method, according to the method combination type of the generic function. When standard method combination type is used, the lack of any *qualifier* indicates a primary method. The standard method combination also recognizes the method qualifiers :before, :after, and :around.

specialized-lambda-list
          An ordinary function lambda-list except that the name of any of the required parameters can be replaced by a specialized parameter. That is, a required parameter is either *var* or (*var parameter-specializer-name*). The optional parameters have exactly the same syntax as they do in an ordinary lambda-lists, and they may not be specialized.

parameter-specializer-name
          Can be a list such as (eql *form*) or a symbol naming a class. The class can be a user-defined class, a built-in class, or a structure defined by defstruct if the :type option was not used.

decl   A declaration pertaining to this method.

doc	A documentation string for this method.
form	The body of this method. This is LISP code to be executed when the generic dispatch calls this method.

For related information, see

"Methods for Null Locks," page 32
"Methods for Simple Locks," page 35
"Programming with Methods," page 65
"Summary of Method Inheritance," page 98
"Congruent Lambda-Lists," page 132
"Redefining Methods and Generic Functions," page 143
"Removing Generic Functions and Methods," page 136

describe *object*   *Generic Function*

Prints a description of an object on the standard output stream. This is a generic function for which you can write methods, to specialize its behavior for a given class. describe returns no values.

object	Any LISP object.

CLOS provides a default primary method for describe. describe uses the standard method combination type.

For related information, see

"Specializing describe for Locks," page 39
"An After-Method for Describing Simple Locks," page 40
"Specializing describe for Ordered Locks," page 49
"Specializing describe for Print-Request Queues," page 56

find-class *symbol* &optional (*errorp* t) *environment*   *Function*

If the symbol is the name of a class, find-class returns the class object.

symbol	The name of a class.
errorp	States what to do if there is no class by this name: If *errorp* is true, an error is signaled;

otherwise, `nil` is returned.

You can use `setf` with `find-class` to change the class associated with this symbol.

For related information, see

"Mapping Between Names and Objects," page 134

find-method *generic-function qualifiers*   *Generic Function*
         specializers &optional *errorp*
Returns the method object identified by the generic function it implements, the method's qualifiers, and the parameter specializers.

generic-function   A generic function object, which can be obtained by using `symbol-function`.

qualifiers   A list of the method's qualifiers.

parameter-specializers
                       A list of the method's parameter specializer objects. This list must contain one element corresponding to each required parameter. For any unspecialized parameters, the class named t should be given.

errorp   If *errorp* is `t`, CLOS signals an error if there is no such method. If *errorp* is `nil`, CLOS returns `nil` if there is no such method. The default is `t`.

For related information, see

"Mapping Between Names and Objects," page 134
"Removing Generic Functions and Methods," page 136

initialize-instance *instance* &rest *initargs*   *Generic Function*

Invoked automatically by the system when `make-instance` is called; `initialize-instance` should not be called by users. You can specialize `initialize-instance` to control how new instances are initialized. This generic function returns the instance.

instance   The newly created instance.

initargs   Alternating initarg names and values. The valid
                                initarg names include the slot-filling initarg
                                names for the class (defined by the :initarg op-
                                tion to defclass) and the names of keyword pa-
                                rameters specified in methods for initialize-
                                instance or shared-initialize.

A system-supplied default primary method performs slot initialization by calling shared-initialize with the instance, t (indicating
that all slots should be filled with the values of their initforms), and
the initargs. In most cases, you should supply after-methods to allow the default primary method to run. This generic function uses
the standard method combination type.

For related information, see

   "Creating and Initializing Instances," page 155
   "Controlling Initialization with Methods," page 159
   "A Procedural Definition: Initialization," page 165

make-instance *class* &rest *initargs*   *Generic Function*

Creates a new instance of the specified class and initializes the slots
of the new instance by calling the generic function initialize-
instance with the newly created instance and initargs. make-instance
returns the initialized instance.

class   The name of a class or a class object.

initargs   Alternating initarg names and values. The valid
                                initarg names include the slot-filling initarg
                                names for the class (defined by the :initarg op-
                                tion to defclass) and the names of keyword pa-
                                rameters   specified   in   methods   for
                                make-instance, initialize-instance, and shared-
                                initialize.

For related information, see

   "Creating and Initializing Instances," page 155
   "Summary of What make-instance Does," page 156
   "Controlling Initialization with defclass Options," page 157
   "Controlling Initialization with Methods," page 159

next-method-p   *Function*

Can be called within a method to find out whether there is a "next method." This function is useful in methods where you expect to use call-next-method, and you want to ensure that there is a next method to call. This function takes no arguments. It returns true if there is a next method, and nil if there is not.

The method combination type defines what the "next method" is. The standard method combination type defines the next method as follows:

- In an around-method, the "next method" is the next most specific around-method if there is one. Otherwise, the "next method" consists of the before-methods, the most specific primary method, and the after-methods.

- In a primary method, the "next method" is the next most specific primary method.

For related information, see

print-object *object stream*   *Generic Function*

Writes the printed representation of an object to a stream. The purpose of print-object is to allow you to control the printing behavior of objects of a given class, by writing methods that specialize print-object. CLOS provides a default primary method for print-object. print-object uses the standard method combination type.

print-object is called by the print system and should not be called by users. All COMMON LISP printing functions call print-object, including write, prin1, format ~A and ~S, and others.

print-object returns the object, its first argument.

object   Any object.

stream   This must be a real stream, and cannot be t or
                                  nil.

The generic function print-object has a protocol that all methods
should follow. Methods should obey the print control special variables described in Steele's *Common LISP: The Language*. For more
details on print-object, see the CLOS specification.

For related information, see

"Controlling How Locks Print," page 37
"Specializing print-object for Locks," page 38

reinitialize-instance *instance* &rest *initargs*   *Generic Function*

Reinitializes an instance according to the initargs. You can specialize
reinitialize-instance to control how instances are reinitialized.
This generic function is rarely used in application programs, but is
used within the implementation of CLOS itself, in the metaobject
protocol. This generic function returns the instance.

instance   The instance to reinitialize.

initargs   Alternating initarg names and values. The valid
                        initarg names include the slot-filling initarg
                        names for the class (defined by the :initarg op-
                        tion to defclass) and the names of keyword pa-
                        rameters specified in methods for reinitialize-
                        instance or shared-initialize.

A system-supplied default primary method performs slot initialization by calling shared-initialize with the instance, nil (indicating
that no slots should be filled with the values of their initforms), and
the initargs. In most cases, you should supply after-methods to allow the default primary method to run. This generic function uses
the standard method combination type.

For related information, see

"A Procedural Definition: Initialization," page 165

remove-method *generic-function method*   *Generic Function*

Removes a method from a generic function and returns the modified generic function object.

generic-function   A generic function object.

method   A method object.

CLOS signals an error if the method is not one of the methods for the generic function.

For related information, see

"Removing Generic Functions and Methods," page 136

shared-initialize *instance slots-for-initform*   *Generic Function*
        `&rest` *initargs*

Called in four contexts to initialize an instance: to initialize a new instance (`initialize-instance`), to reinitialize an instance (`reinitialize-instance`), to update an instance to a new class redefinition (`update-instance-for-redefined-class`), and to update an instance to a different class (`update-instance-for-different-class`). The `shared-initialize` generic function should not be called by users. You can specialize `shared-initialize` to control how instances are initialized in these four contexts. This generic function returns the instance.

instance   The instance to initialize.

slots-for-initform Indicates which slots should be filled with the values of their initforms (if they are still unbound). Either a list of slot names, or `t` to indicate all slots, or `nil` to indicate no slots.

initargs   Alternating initarg names and values. The valid initarg names include the slot-filling initarg names for the class (defined by the `:initarg` option to `defclass`) and the names of keyword parameters specified in methods for `shared-initialize`.

A system-supplied default primary method first initializes all slots for which a slot-filling initarg is given. Then, for any slots indicated by the *slots-for-initform* argument that are still unbound, the method fills those slots with the values of their initforms. In most cases, you should supply after-methods for `shared-initialize`, to allow the default primary method to run. This generic function uses the `standard` method combination type.

For related information, see

"A Procedural Definition: Initialization," page 165
"Creating and Initializing Instances," page 155

slot-boundp *instance slot-name*   *Function*

Returns true if the indicated slot of the instance is bound; otherwise, returns false.

instance   An instance.

slot-name   A symbol naming a slot of the instance.

This generic function is useful in methods for `print-object` or `describe`, if you want to ensure that the methods do not signal errors if slots are unbound. It can also be useful in methods that initialize instances.

For related information, see

"Specializing print-object for Locks," page 38

slot-value *object slot-name*   *Function*

Returns the value of the specified slot of the object. If there is no slot of that name, an error is signaled. You can use `setf` with `slot-value` to write a new value into the slot. `slot-value` is the primitive used to implement accessor methods.

object   A form evaluating to an object that has slots.
                    Usually this is an instance of a user-defined
                    class, since the structure of these classes is in
                    the form of slots.

slot-name   A symbol naming a slot.

For related information, see

"Programming with Accessors," page 70

update-instance-for-different-class   *Generic Function*
    previous new &rest *initargs*

Invoked automatically by the system when `change-class` is called; `update-instance-for-different-class` should not be called by users. You can specialize `update-instance-for-different-class` to control how instances are updated to the target class. Any value returned is ignored by the caller, `change-class`.

previous   A copy of the previous version of the instance.

new   The new version of the instance.

initargs   Alternating initarg names and values. The valid
                        initarg names include the slot-filling initarg
                        names for the class (defined by the `:initarg` op-
                        tion to `defclass`) and the names of keyword pa-
                        rameters specified in methods for `update-`
                        `instance-for-different-class`   or   `shared-`
                        `initialize`.

A system-supplied default primary method performs slot initializa-tion by calling `shared-initialize` with the instance, a list of the names of the added local slots (indicating that they should be filled with the values of their initforms), and the initargs. In most cases, you should supply after-methods to allow the default primary method to run. This generic function uses the `standard` method combination type.

The caller of `change-class` arranges the arguments such that a copy of the previous version is accessible, as well as the new version of the instance. This allows methods to access information stored in the previous version and to use that information to update the new version of the instance. Any value returned is ignored by its caller.

For related information, see

  "Changing the Class of an Instance," page 151
  "A Procedural Definition: Initialization," page 165

update-instance-for-redefined-class *instance*   *Generic Function*
        added-slots discarded-slots plist
        &rest *initargs*

Invoked automatically by the system when a class is redefined; update-instance-for-redefined-class should not be called by users. You can specialize update-instance-for-redefined-class to control how instances are updated to the new version. Any value returned is ignored by the caller.

The caller of update-instance-for-redefined-class provides the arguments *added-slots*, *discarded-slots*, and *plist* to be used by methods. These arguments allow methods for update-instance-for-redefined-class to access information stored in the previous version and to use that information to update the new version of the instance.

instance	The instance after its structure has been updated.
added-slots	A list of slots that were added to the instance.
discarded-slots	A list of slots whose values are being discarded. This includes any slots specified in the old class definition but not in the new one, and any slots specified as local in the old definition and shared in the new one.
plist	A list of alternating slot names and values. Each discarded slot with a value appears in the *plist*. No unbound slots appear in the *plist*.
initargs	Alternating initarg names and values. The valid initarg names include the slot-filling initarg names for the class (defined by the :initarg option to defclass) and the names of keyword parameters specified in methods for update-instance-for-redefined-class or shared-initialize.

A system-supplied default primary method performs slot initialization by calling shared-initialize with the instance, *added-slots* (indicating that all added local slots should be filled with the values of their initforms), and the initargs. In most cases, you should supply after-methods to allow the default primary method to run. This generic function uses the standard method combination type.

For related information, see

"Redefining Classes," page 140
"Example of Redefining CLOS Elements," page 144
"A Procedural Definition: Initialization," page 165

---

with-accessors ({*accessor-entry*}*) *instance-form* &body *body*   *Macro*

Creates a lexical context for referring to accessors by variables. This is a convenient shorthand for calling reader or writer generic functions. with-accessors returns the values of the last form in the body.

instance-form   A form that evaluates to an instance.

accessor-entry   A   list   of   the   form   (*variable-name accessor-name*).

Within the body of with-accessors you can use setf or setq with the variable to call the writer generic function.

For related information, see

"Programming with Accessors," page 70
"Using with-accessors and with-slots," page 73

---

with-slots ({*slot-entry*}*) *instance-form* &body *body*   *Macro*

Creates a lexical context for referring to slots by variables. This is a convenient shorthand for calling slot-value. with-slots returns the values of the last form in the body.

instance-form   A form that evaluates to an instance.

slot-entry   Either a slot name alone or a list (*variable-name slot-name*). If the slot name is given alone, you can access the slot by a variable with the same name as the slot. The alternate syntax allows you to specify a different variable name for accessing the slot.

Within the body of `with-slots` you can use `setf` or `setq` with the variable to write a value into the slot.

For related information, see

"Programming with Accessors," page 70
"Using with-accessors and with-slots," page 73

Appendix C
CLOS Operators
Not Documented in
This Book

This appendix briefly mentions the CLOS operators that are not covered in this book.

Generic Functions with Local Names or No Names

CLOS enables you to define generic functions whose names are local in much the same way that COMMON LISP enables you to define ordinary functions whose names are local. You can also define a generic function with no name; this is analogous to defining an ordinary LISP function with no name.

generic-flet special form
> Defines new generic functions and methods; the scoping is like flet.

generic-labels special form
> Defines new generic functions and methods; the scoping is like labels.

with-added-methods special form
> Defines new generic functions and methods; the names are

scoped within the lexical context of the body. This is an extension to `generic-labels`.

`generic-function` macro
> Defines an anonymous generic function and methods for it.

Generic Functions Called in Error Situations

These generic functions are not intended to be called by users; they are called when errors are encountered. These generic functions are exception handlers. The default method signals an error, but you can specialize the generic function to do something different.

`slot-unbound` generic function
> Called when an attempt is made to read an unbound slot.

`slot-missing` generic function
> Called when an attempt is made to access a slot of an instance, but there is no slot by that name accessible to the instance.

`no-applicable-method` generic function
> Called when a generic function is called and there is no applicable method for it.

`no-next-method` generic function
> Called when `call-next-method` is used and there is no "next method."

Tools for Defining Method Combination Types

The long form of `define-method-combination` offers a rich syntax for defining new method combination types. The other operators mentioned here are used within the body of `define-method-combination`.

`define-method-combination` macro
> Defines a new method combination type.

`call-method` macro
> In the framework of a method combination type, indicates that a method should be called.

`method-qualifiers` generic function
> Returns a list of the qualifiers of a method.

`method-combination-error` function
>   Signals an error encountered in the method combination process.

`invalid-method-error` function
>   Signals an error when an applicable method has method qualifiers that are not recognized by the method combination type.

Miscellaneous Operators

`add-method` generic function
>   Adds a method object to a generic function; this function level operator implements `defmethod` and other macros that create methods for generic functions.

`documentation` generic function
>   Retrieves the documentation string of various kinds of LISP objects.

`ensure-generic-function` function
>   Defines a generic function object; this function level operator implements `defgeneric` and other macros that create generic functions.

`function-keywords`
>   Returns the keyword parameters of a given method.

`make-instances-obsolete` generic function
>   Called by the system when a class is redefined to trigger the updating process. Users can call `make-instances-obsolete` to cause the `update-instance-for-redefined-class` generic function to be called for instances of a given class (and for instances of subclasses).

`slot-makunbound` function
>   Makes a slot of an instance unbound.

`slot-exists-p` function
>   Tests whether an instance has a slot of a given name.

`symbol-macrolet` macro
>   Associates forms with variables within its body; using such a variable causes the form to be executed. This macro implements the `with-accessors` and `with-slots` macros.

Bibliography

The most important reference is the specification of the COMMON LISP Object System (CLOS). The specification is a complete definition of the behavior of CLOS, and should be considered the primary source of information on CLOS.

Bobrow, Daniel G., Linda G. DeMichiel, Richard P. Gabriel, Sonya E. Keene, Gregor Kiczales, David A. Moon. *Common Lisp Object System Specification*, X3J13 Document 88-002R, June 1988.

We used the following reference as our definition of COMMON LISP:

Steele, Guy L. Jr. *Common LISP: The Language.* Digital Press, 1984.

The following references are related to object-oriented programming in LISP:

Bobrow, Daniel G., Gregor Kiczales. "The Common Lisp Object System Metaobject Kernel: A Status Report." *Proceedings of the International Workshop on LISP Evolution and Standardization*, February, 1988. Also available in *Proceedings of the ACM Conference on Lisp and Functional Programming*, September 1988.

Bobrow, Daniel G., Kenneth Kahn, Gregor Kiczales, Larry Masinter, Mark Stefik, Frank Zdybel. "CommonLoops: Merging Lisp and Object-Oriented Programming." *Proceedings of the ACM Conference on Object-Oriented Systems, Languages, and Applications* (OOPSLA), September/October, 1986.

Cannon, Howard I. "Flavors: A non-hierarchical approach to object-oriented programming," Symbolics, Inc., 1982.

DeMichiel, Linda G., Richard P. Gabriel. "The Common Lisp Object System: An Overview." *Proceedings of the European Conference on Object-Oriented Programming*, Paris, 1987.

Kempf, James, Warren Harris, Roy D'Souza, Alan Snyder. "Experience with CommonLoops." *Proceedings of the ACM Conference on Object-Oriented Systems, Languages, and Applications* (OOPSLA), October, 1987.

Moon, David A. "Object-Oriented Programming with Flavors." *Proceedings of the ACM Conference on Object-Oriented Systems, Languages, and Applications* (OOPSLA), September-October, 1986.

Moon, David A. The Common Lisp Object-Oriented Programming Language Standard. *Object-Oriented Concepts, Applications, and Databases*, eds. W. Kim and F. Lochovsky, Addison-Wesley (in press).

Snyder, Alan. *Object-Oriented Programming for Common Lisp.* Report ATC-85-1, Software Technology Laboratory, Hewlett-Packard Laboratories, 1985.

Stefik, Mark and Daniel G. Bobrow, Object-oriented Programming: Themes and Variations. *AI Magazine* 6:(4), Winter 1986.

Index